Balance of the Heart

Balance of the Heart

*Desert Spirituality for
Twenty-First-Century Christians*

LOIS M. FARAG

CASCADE *Books* · Eugene, Oregon

BALANCE OF THE HEART
Desert Spirituality for Twenty-First-Century Christians

Cascade Books
An Imprint of Wipf and Stock Publishers
199 W. 8th Ave., Suite 3
Eugene, OR 97401

www.wipfandstock.com

ISBN 13: 978-1-55635-977-4

Cataloguing-in-Publication data:

Farag, Lois M.

Balance of the heart : desert spirituality for twenty-first-century Christians /
Lois M. Farag.

xiv + 268 pp. ; 23 cm. Includes bibliographical references and indexes.

ISBN 13: 978-1-55635-977-4

1. Spirituality—History—Early church, ca. 30–600. 2. Apophthegmata
Patrum. 3. Desert Fathers. 4. Christian literature, Early. 5. Monasticism and
religious orders—Egypt—History—Early church, ca. 30–600. 6. Theology,
Doctrinal—History—Early church, ca. 30–600. I. Title.

BX2465 F15 2012

Manufactured in the U.S.A.

To

St. Athanasius the great theologian

and

St. Anthony the spiritual exemplar

*whose spiritual vision has formed
many Christian generations*

Contents

Contents

Figures[1]

1. All photographs by author. All rights reserved.

Figures

Acknowledgments

I WOULD LIKE TO thank the Lilly Endowment and the Association of Theological Schools for supporting this project through the Theological Scholars Grant and the Faculty Fellowship Grant. I am grateful the Lilly Endowment supports scholarship valuable to both the academy and church. I would like to thank: Victoria Smith the faculty secretary and the librarians at Luther Seminary who helped overcome many obstacles to complete this work; my students who participated in various offerings of the Desert Discipleship course and expressed their profound appreciation of the monastic wisdom literature; the pastors and lay leaders who participated in Kairos and Continuous Learning classes, assuring me of the importance of this work to pastors and laity. I would also like to thank the churches that invited me to speak about desert spirituality. They all challenged and encouraged me, and helped me articulate my ideas; they also confirmed the need for this book. I am obliged to all those who helped this work to come to light.

Abbreviations

AParadise *Bustān al-ruhbān* (Paradise of the Monks), 3rd ed.
(Egypt, Diocese of Beni Suef, 1977) (my translation)

ASWard Benedicta Ward, trans., *The Sayings of the Desert Fathers: The Alphabetical Collection*, rev. ed., Cistercian Studies 59 (Kalamazoo, MI: Cistercian, 1984)

gent. Saint Athanasius, *Against the Gentiles*

inc. Saint Athanasius, *On the Incarnation*

Is. Scetis Saint Isaiah of Scete, *Abba Isaiah of Scetis Ascetic Discourses*, trans. John Chryssavgis and Pachomios Penkett, Cistercian Studies 150 (Kalamazoo, MI: Cistercian, 2002)

LQ E. C. Tappert, "Desert Wisdom: The Sayings of the Anchorites," *Lutheran Quarterly* 9 (1957) 157–72

SABudge E. A. Wallis Budge, ed. and trans., *The Paradise of the Fathers: Being Histories of the Anchorites, Recluses, Monks, Coenobites and Ascetic Fathers of the Deserts of Egypt between A.D. CCL and A.D. CCCC Circiter*, vol. 2 (Seattle: St. Nectarios, 1984)

SAChaîne Marius Chaîne, ed., *Le manuscrit de la version Copte en dialecte sahidique des "Apophthegmata Patrum"*, Bibliothèque d'études coptes 6 (Le Caire: L'institut Français d'Archéologie Orientale, 1960)

SAGuy Guy, Jean-Claude. *Les apophthegmes des Pères: Collection systématique*, 3 vols., Sources chrétiennes 387, 474, 498 (Paris: Éditions du Cerf, 1993)

SAHartley John E. Hartley, "Studies in the Sahidic Version of the *Apophthegmata Patrum*," PhD diss., Brandeis University, 1969

SSWard Benedicta Ward, trans., *The Desert Fathers: Sayings of the Early Christian Monks* (New York: Penguin, 2003)

Sync. Elizabeth Castelli, "Pseudo-Athanasius: The Life and Activity of the Holy and Blessed Teacher Syncletica," in *Ascetic Behavior in Greco-Roman Antiquity: A Sourcebook*, ed. Vincent L. Wimbush, 265–311 (Minneapolis: Fortress, 1990)

v. Anton. Saint Athanasius, *The Life of Antony*

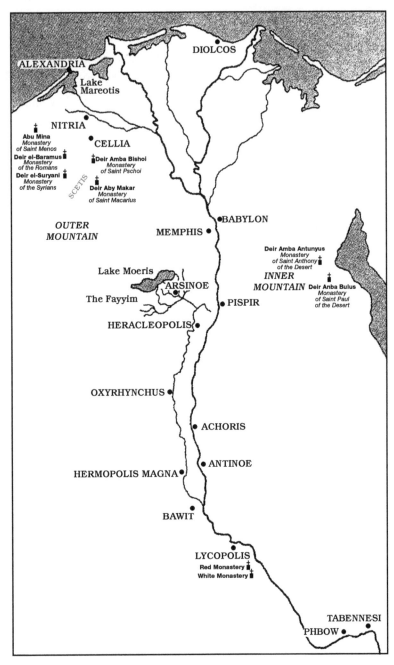

Monastic Centers in Egypt

Part One

INTRODUCTION

T HIS BOOK IS AN introduction to the wisdom literature of the early
Egyptian monastics found in the work known to scholars as the
Apophthegmata Patrum, usually translated as "The Sayings of the Desert
Fathers," and also in some of the lives and letters of these desert dwellers.
It is not only twentieth- and twenty-first-century scholars who have been
enamored of these monastics, in the fourth-century world, too, people
came to know about them and were attracted to their lifestyle. Many
visitors traveled across seas and deserts to listen to their wisdom. Among
these visitors and guests were John Cassian, Palladius, and Evagrius Ponticus, all of whom wrote down their experience among the Egyptian monastics in different forms. The ancient literature of and about Egyptian
monasticism is vast and each text can have a study of its own. This book
will not discuss every text lest the focus shift from an introduction to a
survey. A few texts have been selected as representative of the essence of
the wisdom and spirituality of the Egyptian (also called Coptic) monastic
tradition. It is hoped that the reader will continue reading through the
rest of the literary corpus and beyond. This book is an introduction and a
companion text to the desert sayings. It is not intended to be comprehen-
sive or to replace reading the sayings as written in the primary texts. It is
a guide that will enable you to enjoy the words of the fathers and mothers
themselves.

Coptic monasticism inspired and was the foundation of other monastic communities beyond the Egyptian borders. Basil of Caesarea (c.
330–79) founded a communal monastic system based on what he saw in
the Egyptian desert as well as in Syria. His rules became the foundation
of Byzantine monasticism. Benedict of Nursia (c. 480–c. 550) based his
monastic ideal on the writings of Basil and the Copt Pachomius, founder
of communal monasticism in Upper Egypt, as well as those of Cassian.
The Benedictine order was the starting point of all Western monasticism

and religious orders. Anthony and his disciples in their isolated desert had a far reaching impact on the universal church.

Though both Byzantine and Latin monastic communities were based on Coptic monastic ideals, they did not develop the genre of monastic wisdom literature and sayings. One of the reasons might be that Coptic monasticism was founded on and flourished through the anchoritic and semi-anchoritic models, where the notion of discipleship to a great Abba was the underlying principle. A person would be inspired by a certain Abba and wish to follow his life style. He settled beside the Abba in the desert and tried to emulate his spiritual practice. When the disciple faced difficulties in his spiritual journey he sought guidance from his Abba. Sometimes he approached his spiritual father with a specific question related to a personal problem. On other occasions he merely sought general advice with the request: "Abba, tell me a word to live by." On both occasions, this would be a moment of instruction and divulging of personal spiritual experience through a saying, though the father usually tried to avoid any personal association to the saying out of humility. Byzantine and Latin monasticism emphasized the communal aspect of monasticism and thus a father-disciple model was not adopted. The cultural, geographical, historical, and communal settings of the Byzantine and Western orders did not allow a similar wisdom literature to flourish. The monastic wisdom literature presented here stems from and represents the cultural, social, and religious temperament of the Egyptian population.

This unique literary genre had its precursors in ancient Egypt. The genre took three forms in the Egyptian context, one of which was a didactic speech or teaching of a father to his son. This type of wisdom literature, didactic literature or literature belonging to the genre of *Instruction*, originated in Egypt during the Old Kingdom (c. 2650–2135 BC) and gradually developed through the Middle Kingdom (c. 2040–1650 BC), the Eighteenth Dynasty (c. 1550–1305 BC) and the Late Period that ended with the Greek conquest of Egypt by Alexander the Great in 332 BC. During the Nineteenth and Twentieth Dynasties (c. 1305–1080 BC), also known as the Ramesside Period, we find the culmination of the *Instruction* genre in the long work of *The Instruction of Amenemope*. The genre reflects on problems of life and death. It developed the new ideal man as one "content with a humble position and a minimal amount of material possessions. His chief characteristic is modesty. He is self-controlled, quiet, and kind toward people, and he is humble before God."[1] The ideal man's worth lies in his inner quality.[2]

This type of literature, sometimes called "Wisdom literature," "contributed significantly to the subsequent flowering of the genre among the Hebrews."[3] It was during the Ramesside Period that the Hebrews' "knowledge of things Egyptian is reflected in the Bible." Biblical scholars have agreed that Proverbs 22:20-2—"Have I not written for you thirty sayings of admonition and knowledge, to show you what is right and true, so that you may give a true answer to those who sent you?"—refers to the "thirty" chapters of instruction of Amenemope.[4] A few examples will demonstrate the influence of the *The Instruction of Amenemope* on Proverbs. Chapter 23 of the *Instructions* gives the following advice:

> Do not eat in the presence of the official
>
> And then set your mouth before <him>;
>
> If you are sated pretend to chew,
>
> Content yourself with your saliva.[5]

This compares with Proverbs 23:1-2:"When you sit down to eat with a ruler, observe carefully what is before you, and put a knife to your throat if you have a big appetite." Another example from the *Instructions*:

> Do not move the markers on the borders of fields,
>
> Nor shift the position of the measuring-cord.
>
> Do not be greedy for a cubit of land,
>
> Nor encroach on the boundaries of a widow.[6]

Compare Proverbs 22:28: "Do not remove the ancient landmark that your ancestors set up," and Proverbs 23:10, "Do not remove an ancient landmark or encroach on the fields of orphans."

---

1. Miriam Lichtheim, *Ancient Egyptian Literature: A Book of Readings*, vol. 2, CAL 382 (Berkeley, CA: University of California Press, 1976) 146.

2. Ibid.,

3. Ibid., 134.

4. Ibid., 147.

5. Ibid., 160.

6. Ibid., 151.

The *Instructions* is also attentive to moral teachings, such as "Guard your tongue from harmful speech," found in Instruction 8.[7] Again:

> Keep firm your heart, steady your heart,
>
> Do not steer with your tongue;
>
> If a man's tongue is the boat's rudder,
>
> The Lord of All is yet its pilot.[8]

The ideas and vocabulary are familiar from James 3:4–5:"Or look at ships: though they are so large that it takes strong winds to drive them, yet they are guided by a very small rudder wherever the will of the pilot directs. So also the tongue is a small member, yet it boasts of great exploits."

Stories are another ancient Egyptian literary genre. The stories of Setne Khamwas revolved around Khamwas, the fourth son of King Ramses II (1290–1224 BC). Si-Osire, the son of Khamwas, goes to the netherworld with his father. During their visit they witness the suffering of those who sinned and the blessedness of those who have done good deeds. They see a rich man undergoing torture and a poor man being honored, which conveys the message of the parable of Lazarus and the rich man of Luke 16:19–31. Ancient Egyptian literature and culture had deep concern with the life after death.[9] From its earliest recorded literature during the Old Kingdom (ca. 2650–2135 BC) Egyptian civilization has reflected on life and how to lead a moral life that would ensure a healthy and comfortable afterlife.

When Christianity came to Egypt with Mark the Evangelist in AD 42 the religious climate was receptive to many of the Christian teachings, included belief in one God, contemplation on the essence of life and death, moral behavior, seeking the wisdom of the elders, and seeking the heavenly kingdom. With the gradual Christianization of the society, the biblical message of renunciation for the sake of the kingdom appealed to early Christians, especially in Egypt. Following Christ meant full dedication to the Christian message, which meant renouncing everything. Monasticism responded to a culture that was deeply rooted in thinking about moral issues and living a moral and righteous life here for the sake of the kingdom to come. A similar trend can be observed in the Mesopotamian culture that was also receptive to the monastic ideal.

7. Ibid., 153.
8. Ibid., 158.
9. Lichtheim, *Ancient Egyptian Literature*, vol. 3, 125–26.

Renunciation gradually led to a more ascetic society and eventually to the rise of monasticism. There was an accompanying development of wisdom literature, which took the Christian form of the *Apophthegmata Patrum*, or the *Sayings of the Fathers*, together with their lives and letters. The *Apophthegmata* are a collection of pithy statements that reflect the wisdom of fathers and mothers "instructing" or handing down their spiritual and life experience to their spiritual children, sometimes called "disciples." These sayings are going to be the main focus of our work as they represent the classic wisdom literature of desert spirituality.

The *Apophthegmata* are preserved in two main forms: a systematic collection that follows the sayings topically and an alphabetical collection that follows the sayings of certain monastic figures. Each collection has its merits. The systematic collection gives the reader a quick introduction to topics such as progress in perfection, non-judgment, unceasing prayer, hospitality, and other similar topics. If the reader wants to know the sayings of a specific desert father or mother, then he or she can refer to the alphabetical collection. The latter form enables the reader to know the father or mother, his or her temperament, character and teachings, more intimately. The reader will discover that he or she is more comfortable with the spiritual approach of one father or mother over another. Developing a special spiritual bond with one of the fathers or mothers of the desert is more difficult to achieve by reading the systematic collection. This book will approach topics systematically. It will also select sayings or stories from the lives of many of the desert dwellers such as Abba Anthony of Egypt, Abbas Macarius the Great and Macarius of Alexandria, Abba Daniel of Scetis, Abba John the Little, Amma Syncletica, Ammas Theodora and Sarah, and Abba Isaiah of Scetis, just to mention a few.

The monastic texts have captured the interest of modern scholars and excellent scholarly research has shed light on many aspects of monasticism in the early church. This book will focus on the spiritual aspects of these texts without delving into many details about the scholarly debates. For example there are discussions about Athanasius' agenda in writing the *Life of Anthony*, or how much editing was involved, or how accurately the historical person is rendered in the *Life*. Though all these are legitimate and worthy questions and should be considered seriously, there is another aspect of the text: its historical effect on popular spirituality and church life. When Augustine of Hippo, the great philosopher, thinker, and theologian, read the *Life of Anthony* it was a major catalyst in his conversion to the Christian faith. It is this transforming power of the text and its message that is of interest to us. The agenda of the author or the exact historicity of the life were never a hindrance to its ability to effect change in the lives of its readers. The *Life of Anthony* has set the monastic model for the universal Christian church, and it is this spiritual model that is of concern to this study. The same approach applies to the *Apophthegmata Patrum* and the other texts discussed in this book.

Scripture is at the center and the soul of desert spirituality. Desert spirituality is an attempt to live the Bible faithfully, to live according to the word of God. It is not a literal but a practical interpretation of Scripture. It is an attempt to live the Bible in every minute of one's life. In a nut shell, it is to ". . . love the Lord your God with all your heart, and with all your soul, and with all your strength, and with all your mind . . ." (Luke 10:27). The desert monastics memorized parts of Scripture to preserve it in memory so it would be accessible for their daily discernment and prayers. Thus they memorized the book of Psalms to be able to pray and contemplate at any time of the day. After sunset, the memorized psalms would be the substance of their prayer and contemplation without the need to burn the oil of their lamps. While traveling, while moving from one place to another, or while working or while engaged in some other activity, they could recite some of the psalms as prayer or object of contemplation. Memorizing psalms was a means for achieving unceasing prayer; a means to be in the constant presence of God and having one's thought contemplating God. They also memorized one or two Gospels and some of the New Testament epistles and an Old Testament text for the same purpose: to meditate on the word of God. Early Christians and monastics viewed the Bible as the "word of God" and took it very seriously. Scripture was the means by which God spoke to them and they spoke to God. Scripture was a personal message to each one of them. Biblical verses were transformed into prayers. The findings of modern biblical studies, e.g., that there are Pauline epistles and pseudo-Pauline epistles, would have been totally alien to the early church. The notion that the Johannine Epistles were written by the Johannine community rather than John himself would have been unfathomable. Thus the texts under discussion consider the "Pauline Epistles" to be written by Paul and the Pentateuch by Moses, and we will follow the ancient textual pattern. That is not to be dismissive of modern scholarship. But it is not sound methodology to apply modern scholarly concepts to ancient texts; it is anachronistic.

The book is divided into two main parts. Part One gives the necessary historical and theological background for desert spirituality. Some readers might be tempted to skip Part One assuming that history and theology have little to do with spirituality; but as people of the twenty-first century, we are far removed from the biblical and monastic setting of the desert. The aim of Part One is to anchor the reader in the world of the first Christians and how they lived their faith. There the life of renunciation and simplicity was the message for all Christians, whether married and caring for their families or single. Monasticism and life in the desert were a natural outcome of such a worldview. Part One will also go in some detail into the theology of the incarnation and the understanding of salvation in the Egyptian church. In this view of salvation we were created in the image and likeness of God, but lost this image because of the fall. The incarnation, crucifixion, and resurrection granted us a renewal of life that renewed the image of God within us. It is within this theological setting that monasticism and desert spirituality flourished. This theological vision guided the desert fathers and mothers in the desert and shaped their behavior and worldview. They wanted to preserve without blemish God's image and the renewed life granted by the resurrection. The way to do that was to avoid all the downfalls that our first parents did not. The desert monastics examined their thoughts and hearts very carefully lest any thought impede them from being in God's presence. Within this framework, we understand Anthony and the *Life of Anthony*. Anthony became the example or guide on how to be in God's presence at all times. This was enough for many to follow in his footsteps.

Part Two is about the experience of all those who followed Anthony and the theological vision he embraced. It goes into great detail into the inner thoughts of their hearts. The *Apophthegmata* will be approached thematically. In separate chapters we will discuss Scripture, thoughts and the works of the mind, prayer, renunciation, discernment, love, transgressions of the tongue, and humility. In the interests of space a few topics, such as spiritual goals, fear of God, hope, patience, hospitality and others, will be summed up in one chapter. Each chapter is followed by a short reader for further independent contemplation. Those interested in more study of the desert fathers should consult the "Suggested Titles for Further Reading" at the end of the book.

Two topics that will not be discussed are sexuality and demonic temptations. Among the topics the desert fathers discussed most are fornication, adultery, and lust. It is no surprise that sex occupied a major portion of the monks' conversation as it still occupies the conversation of twenty-first-century people. But discussions of this topic in the *Apophthegmata* are geared towards preserving chastity within celibacy in the total seclusion of the desert. Adapting these sayings to our modern context would require a separate study. Some of the desert fathers, like Anthony himself, would not discuss such topics. Others thought they were more beneficially discussed on a personal level rather than in general terms or publically.[10] The topic of demonic temptations is unavoidable and will be touched on briefly in connection with other topics. But the desert fathers always recommended that the person tempted by the devil seek spiritual guidance and take their spiritual practices to a very advanced level. Since this is an introductory book and many readers might not have spiritual guidance, this topic will not be discussed at great length.

Through this presentation of the inner spiritual experience of the desert fathers and mothers the reader will discover that they are closer to us than we think. Their spiritual experience transcends time. One of the main challenges of desert spirituality to the modern reader may be the idea of renunciation for the sake of a heavenly kingdom. The ancient Egyptian and early Christian cultures out of which desert spirituality emerged both acknowledged the necessity of renunciation for the sake of a spiritual and better eternal life. Modern culture emphasizes the now and making the most of present worldly pleasures. Our modern culture emphasizes the present world, the *now* as the ultimate goal in life, as if there is nothing beyond it. Thus we have the right to the best schools for the sake of landing the best—meaning the highest paying—job, to the best and largest house, the most luxurious clothes, the tastiest, most sensually satisfying and exotic foods, the biggest and latest car model, and to be engaged in a life of leisure and constant entertainment and so on. We are constantly striving to acquire the goods that the media has convinced us to purchase because the media has assured us that these commodities will make us happy, safe, comfortable, and respected in society. We all believed and bought into this message and the whole society plunged into debt to achieve these assurances.

By contrast, desert spirituality focuses on God and the heavenly kingdom and not on this world and what we achieve in this world. Desert spirituality is countercultural, against consumerism, against indulging oneself in pleasure, against entertainment offered by our modern civilization. The aim is to acquire riches not in this world but in the heavenly kingdom. Be assured, it is not a life of misery, poverty, and deprivation. Desert spirituality is a life of careful reasoning about how much we

10. *v. Anton* 19.5.

can consume and indulge in the world without impacting our spiritual progress, how much accumulated wealth is not detrimental to our spiritual growth and does not make us dependent, consumed, and addicted to wealth. It is the art of reaching the balance where the demands of the body and its necessities and desires do not overwhelm the soul. It is the art of living according to the Christian message. The desert fathers and mothers examined their hearts carefully for thoughts that blemished the image of God within them. In fact, the western Egyptian desert, where most of the sayings take place, was called the Desert of the Balance of the Heart. In ancient Egyptian culture the heart is the seat of the mind and the soul. The daily examination of the heart characterized the desert dwellers as they scrutinized their inner thoughts, the movement of their hearts, and their inner desires, and balanced them on the scale of biblical teachings. It is the attentiveness to the inner person and the purification of the heart that made desert spirituality the spirituality of the heart and the desert, the place of the balance of the heart.

The reader should be prepared to embrace a different mindset, a mindset that will liberate the soul from the clutches of all the enticements of modernity. The reader has to experience and to reason within him/herself what is really necessary and important in life. This requires deep thinking and honest examination of the heart and the soul. Facing oneself is the most difficult thing that we can do in our lives, which is why most people avoid it, dread it, and do not know how to do it. Indulging in shopping, eating, working, or other forms of self-indulgence from which we all suffer is a way to avoid examining our hearts. Desert spirituality is the deep examination of the heart in God's presence and in the light of Scripture. Self-examination requires purifying our environment of all clutter, not only material but spiritual as well. This process requires spiritual and emotional strength and is unattainable if God is not involved. If the Spirit does not come to our aid when the road is difficult, if we are not armored with the strength of the Spirit, we will lose hope and not reach our goal. It is a journey that many Christians and especially desert monastics have taken before us. They have left us a wealth of information. They left us their lives to emulate and learn from; they left us their sayings, their letters, and their experience to learn from and to build on. The spiritual experience of the desert fathers and mothers is deeply rooted in theology and Scripture. The sayings might look simple and to some even naïve, but in reality if we miss the cultural, biblical, and theological roots of this spirituality we are missing the depth of these sayings. If we read them without considering this background we will still benefit a lot. But when we immerse ourselves in the roots of this spirituality we will discover the fullness of its wealth and wisdom. We will discover a wisdom that transcends the fourth-century setting and can benefit twenty-first-century Christians.

1

Follow Me

The Beginning of Monasticism

Sell all that you own and distribute the money to the poor,
and you will have treasure in heaven; then come, follow me.

LUKE 18:22

THE SOCIAL AND RELIGIOUS climate within which desert spirituality emerged was rooted in the biblical narrative and reflects how the early Christians, from the time of the apostles, interpreted the gospel message in their lives. Christ asked his disciples to "follow me." Desert spirituality is a response to the call to follow Christ. How this call was interpreted in the early church and how it developed is the subject of this chapter.

"Follow me.... Immediately they left their nets and followed him": Responding to the Christian Call

The Samaritan woman went to fetch water as she did every day. But it was not like every day. She met the Messiah. The meeting was transformative and life changing. She "left her water jar and went back to the city" and proclaimed to the people that she had found the Messiah (John 4). Knowing Christ and accepting his call is always transformative. The response to this transformation varies in form and intensity. Sometimes the transformation is deep, inward, and quiet; other times it is active and energetic. Hardly any two calls are the same. This makes each call unique and special, but also puzzling. Calls follow certain patterns, which helps those who are called recognize the authenticity of the message. But calls are also unique to each person and require a special gift and spiritual guidance to navigate.

Calls, when accepted, are transformative, life changing, and require courage. Some of the women who followed Christ, like Mary Magdalene, Joanna, and Susanna, were healed of their infirmities (Luke 8). These women followed Christ not just for the benefits and perks; they followed him even when everyone else forsook him. These women, who "followed him from Galilee" (Luke 23:49, 55), i.e., from the beginning, were very loyal disciples, and their discipleship was tested during and after the crucifixion. Everyone else abandoned him. Mary Magdalene, Joanna, and Mary the mother of James among others disregarded the threats against their lives; their love for the Crucified One overcame their fear. They were close to the cross and after his death they followed him to the tomb. This is an extreme test of discipleship that requires not only faith but also courage.

Calls, when accepted, demand sacrifices, which usually include self-renunciation. Levi, the tax collector, was called to follow Christ, "and he left everything, and rose and followed him" (Luke 5:27, 28). Matthew gives a detailed description of the call of the two fishermen brothers, Andrew and Peter. When Christ saw them he said to them, "'Follow me, and I will make you fish for people.' Immediately they left their nets and followed him" (Matt 4:19, 20). Levi, Andrew, and Peter left their businesses and what defined them. They renounced their old lives and embraced a new one. The call gave their lives a new definition. They were not to be known by their profession but rather as disciples and followers of Christ.

After the resurrection and Pentecost the message was just as powerful: "All who believed were together and had all things in common; they would sell their possessions and goods and distribute the proceeds to all, as any had need" (Acts 2:44, 45). All those who accepted to follow Christ, were expected to live this life of full renunciation and sell all their possessions. Ananias and his wife Sapphira (Acts 5) are notable exceptions. Following Christ and self-renunciation went hand in hand in the early years of the church.

"But whoever denies me before others" (Matt 10:33): Following and Witnessing in Society

With the spread of Christianity, the connection between following and renunciation weakened. We begin hearing about Christians following Christ but at the same time keeping their jobs, their families, and their daily routine, though this was accompanied by a strong witness to their faith. The demand for renunciation also took another form: renouncing one's life, literally, to the point of martyrdom for the sake of not renouncing one's faith. For the first four centuries, up until the time of the reign of Emperor Constantine in 312, some Christians witnessed to their faith by sacrificing their lives. Those who gave the strongest testimony of their faith and died for keeping their faith were called martyrs, which literary means "to bear witness."

Not all Christians were faced with this difficult decision of witnessing to the faith to the extent of martyrdom. The remaining Christians were to witness to their faith in the society in other forms. They were to give witness to the society and proclaim their faith through their conduct. Christian conduct was a form of witness, for "whoever denies me and does not witness to me before others, I also will deny before my Father in heaven" (Matt 10:33). Christians began avoiding public boisterous events such as public games in the arena where violence against animals and sometimes humans was a common sight. They began avoiding social events that pitted their loyalty to the emperor against their loyalty to God. Their appearance and dress began to be more modest, their conduct more restrained and selective, and their demeanor distinct from the rest of the society. Their non-Christian neighbors noticed the gradual transformation the Christian message had on the new converts. Living the Christian faith was not an inner and private decision, but rather a decision that transformed the essence of the person. This transformation was manifested in witness to one's faith through one's conduct. Christians wanted to "live" their faith. But how? Clement of Alexandria responded to this question.

Clement of Alexandria (c. 150–c. 215)

Clement studied philosophy in several places and came to Alexandria to be a student of Pantaenus (d. 190) a famous teacher and head of the Theological School in Alexandria, Egypt. As a writer, Clement's treatises expressed his philosophical training but also his dedication to live according to the gospel. He wrote the *Paedagogus* ("educator" or "teacher"), in which Christ the Logos is the teacher instructing the faithful how to live a virtuous and moral life. It includes a guideline of social conduct and sometimes even etiquette.

The second and third book of *Christ, the Educator* (*Paedagogus*) give extraordinary details—sometimes too many details—about how to live as a Christian in society. This text is very interesting and an extraordinary window on the daily life of early Christians. Topics covered include eating and drinking, laughter, marriage and sexual relationships, sleep, clothing (including shoes), jewelry, makeup and hairstyles, bathing and ointments, and amusements, just to mention a few. Most of the discussions reflect the living conditions in second- and third-century Alexandria. For example, Clement is not very enthusiastic about bathing. Up until recently, before the wonderful innovation of home plumbing, the bathing options available to people were bathing beside a source of water, such as a river, or public baths. One of Clement's concerns was that this public, communal activity required public nudity that did not conform to Christian modesty. We are going to examine two topics: eating and dressing. Clement's discussion reflects second-century social habits, but it also shows the existential significance of eating and dressing. These two issues were as relevant to Christians in the second century as they are to us now. The way we view and interact with food and clothing is related to our self-understanding and spirituality.

Clement is concerned with the Christian's conduct towards the body as the window of the soul and the sanctity of the spirit. To sanctify the flesh is to sanctify the eye of the soul, which leads to the knowledge of God.[1] The relevance of all the topics Clement discusses in the second book of *Christ the Educator* is that they are means of guiding the soul to its spiritual potential and the spirit to the knowledge of God. The interconnection between the spirit and the body is a pivotal theme in desert and Egyptian spirituality in general. Personal conduct, habits of living, and managing the body are integral to the conversation about spirituality.

Clement opposes the notion that humans were created to eat. For Clement food is for the nourishment of the health and strength of the body. Any food that does not meet these two criteria should be eliminated from the menu. Luxurious and elaborate culinary dishes are to be avoided

---

1. Simon P. Wood, trans., Clement of Alexandria, *Christ, the Educator*, Fathers of the Church 23 (Washington, DC: Catholic University of America Press, 1954) 93; *Paedagogus* (hereafter *Pedag.*) 2.1.

because, in his opinion, they cause stomach disorders. He considers elaborately cooked dishes unhealthy because in the process of sophisticated cooking the primary nourishing elements of the food are spoiled. Clement thinks eating countless different types of meat and unusual foods from all over the world (and he has a long list of food from exotic places from which second- and third-century people sought their food) only caters to gluttony. God provided humans with food and drink for sustenance not for pleasure. Clement argues that those who eat prudently are stronger, healthier, and philosophically wiser than the rich, who are heavier in weight and whose mind is clouded and buried beneath food.[2] Habits of indulgence in eating do not make us rulers over food, but rather let food rule us. Clement assures his readers that he seeks moderation and is not demanding his readers to abstain from eating varieties of food. Some food tempts one to eat when one is not hungry. The ancients recognized that snacks and tempting food make people crave food and eat beyond their fill. Thus Clement's counsel is to limit varieties of food and stick to the basic, simple, nourishing food essential for sustenance.

Clement anticipates an objection: what about hospitality, suppers, and *agape* meals? One cannot invite people to eat basic food; it has to be elaborate as a sign of hospitality.[3] Clement argues that the love behind the invitation and the discussions around the table are more important than the food offered. "For the kingdom of God is not food and drink but righteousness and peace and joy in the Holy Spirit" (Rom 14:17). If the supper is offered without the presence of the Holy Spirit accompanied by righteousness, peace, and joy then it is a meal not worthy of a Christian. "One does not live by bread alone, but by every word that comes from the mouth of God" (Matt 4:4; Deut 8:3). Clement reminds his readers that those who enjoyed their festivity by "killing oxen and slaughtering sheep, eating meat and drinking wine," who followed the motto "Let us eat and drink, for tomorrow we die," were not pleasing to God: "The LORD of hosts has revealed himself in my ears: Surely this iniquity will not be forgiven you until you die, says the Lord GOD of hosts" (Isa 22:13–14). Clement was not short of biblical verses to support his argument that "food will not bring us close to God": "We are no worse off if we do not eat, and no better off if we do" (1 Cor 8:8); "those who eat, eat in honor of the Lord, since they give thanks to God; while those who abstain, abstain in honor of the Lord and give thanks to God" (Rom 14:6).

2. Ibid., 98; *Pedag.* 2.7.

3. Ibid., 95ff.; *Pedag.* 2.4.

Clement used not only biblical verses to convince his readers, but also biblical narratives. How did God nourish the people of Israel? The Exodus narrative and the book of Leviticus are full of prohibitions against food with instructions not to eat certain types of animals and other types of food. In spite of the lengthy list of food prohibitions, the Israelites did not die of insufficient food. When Christ appeared to his disciples after the resurrection he ate bread and fish (John 21:13). In all these biblical examples, the food mentioned was not elaborate, but simple, nourishing food. This is how God fed his people in the wilderness, this is the way Christ himself ate, and this is the way Christians should eat. Clement does not believe that food is for pleasure but primarily for nourishment, for "pleasure generally gives rise to some sense of loss and of regret; overeating begets in the soul only pain and lethargy and shallow mindedness."[4]

Clement provided a lengthy and elaborate argument against consuming food for pleasure. Indulgence affects not only our physical health, but also our mental judgment; it weakens our spirituality. Clement is conveying the ethics of simplicity, non-indulgence in pleasures, in addition to common-sense health advice. The focus of the Christian should be on heavenly food and the heavenly kingdom. Scripture has modeled for us such behavior. Not being overly occupied with bodily pleasures will enable the mind to contemplate heavenly matters and know God. These guidelines were given to all Christians. Clement presents this model for the Christian family, not for ascetics living in the desert. The ethos of the early church is simple living. The food practices that Clement discusses could be the same whether we think of the third- or twenty-first-century family. The eating habits that he advocates can be found in a modern wellness magazine: eat with moderation and eat simple, non-processed food. Wellness magazines, however, do not go on to discuss the impact of food on the spirit. Clement informs us that food indulgence clouds the mind, weakens the spirit, and prevents us from contemplating and comprehending God.

Clement's ideas about clothing are similar to those on food. One should not seek expensive clothes in the same way that one should not seek elaborate dishes.[5] For Clement, the Gospel is clear: "Therefore I tell you, do not worry about your life, what you will eat, or about your body, what you will wear. For life is more than food, and the body more than

---

4. Ibid., 109; *Pedag.* 2.18.
5. Ibid., 178; *Pedag.* 2.102.

clothing" (Luke 12:22–23). Clement introduces his thought about clothing with the following comment:

> Now, if Christ forbids solicitude once and for all about clothing and food and luxuries, as things that are unnecessary, do we need to ask Him about finery and dyed wools and multicolored robes, about exotic ornaments of jewels and artistic handiwork of gold, about wigs and artificial locks of hair and of curls, and about eye-shadowings and hair-plucking and rouges and powders and hair dyes and . . . ?[6]

When Clement opposes hair-plucking and hair dyes, he is addressing not only women but also men. He devotes a full section of his treatise against men dying and plucking their hair and trimming or shaving their beards.[7] The key issue for Clement is that these are "things that are unnecessary." He informs his readers that clothes are for "bodily covering, as a protection against excessive cold or intense heat, so that the inclemency of the weather may not harm him in any way."[8] He even advocates that both men and women wear exactly the same clothes because its utility is the same for both sexes. He also thinks dying cloths is unnecessary since white and plain garments fulfill the purpose of covering and protection from harsh weather. Clement explains to his reader that the attentiveness to colored cloth, ornaments, and other luxuries are not for bodily protection but rather for appearance and showing off. Clement is against the social statement that these luxury items convey and the spiritual implications of vanity; excessive attentiveness to one's appearance, vanity, will obstruct our contemplation of God.

Clement's opinion with respect to food and clothing is that they are to be used frugally. In general, his approach towards all material things is that what is not necessary should not be considered or allowed. The aim of the Christian is to live a simple life without any constraints or clutter clouding our relationship with God. Indulgence in elaborate dishes and luxurious clothing will not only affect our health and budget, it will also affect our spirituality. According to Clement, excess food will physically sicken us and will cloud our mental abilities. Our mind will be consumed with acquiring luxurious food and clothes and will not be attentive to the heavenly kingdom. Clement lists many biblical figures who lived a simple and frugal life: Elijah, Isaiah, Jeremiah, and of course John the Baptist. The

6. Ibid., 180; *Pedag.* 2.104.
7. Ibid., 211–20; *Pedag.* 3.15–25.
8. Ibid., 181; *Pedag.* 2.105.

latter ate honey and locusts and wore camel hair as an example of how to prepare for the coming of the Lord. "He fled from the false pretence of the city and led a peaceful life in the desert with God."[9]

Clement's exhortations are not addressed to monastics. There was no organized monasticism in the second and third centuries. He is advising lay Christians how to live a Christian life in society. Clement's description of the social behaviors of Christians in second- and third-century Alexandria—indulging in exotic food and elaborate dishes, and being attentive to luxurious dress as a sign of social status—does not seem to be different than ours in the twenty-first century. Our accumulation of material possessions, living a lifestyle beyond our means, and indulging in pleasures are what Clement addressed in second-century terms. His message of simplicity, moderation, and renunciation is relevant to the life of excessiveness and indulgence regardless of the time period. In the Christian ethos of the second and third centuries, living a simple, frugal life was consistent with biblical teachings, the life of Christ himself, and the life of renunciation that the church was leading at the time of the apostles. In Clement's time families did not renounce all their possessions and give all to the church, but they were advised to live a life of renunciation while still living in the world. To live the life of renunciation that the Gospels and the book of Acts presented was attained by living the life of simplicity and frugality. We only addressed food and clothing, but these two areas exemplify the general approach to living a Christian life: live simply; what is not necessary is not needed; renounce the world and all its luxuries so that your mind will be unhindered to contemplate spiritual and heavenly matters. These teachings were clearly demonstrated by another early Christian scholar, Origen, who exemplified the life of biblical renunciation and spirituality of third-century Christians of Egypt.

Origen (c. 185–c. 254)

Origen was raised in Alexandria, Egypt. We have no information that indicates that Origen and Clement were acquainted, though both lived in the same city. Origen had a good education and Eusebius, the church historian, informs us that he was eager to read Scripture from a very early age. Eventually he became the most renowned biblical scholar of the early church. His education in Greek literature enabled him to teach at a young

9. Ibid., 186; *Pedag.* 2.112.

age and support his family after the martyrdom of his father.[10] His fame as a scholar did not hinder him from living an austere life. Philosophers were expected to live by the principles they taught their students. Pagan philosophers did not consider philosophy an intellectual exercise, but rather a way of life. Thus Origen, like the early Christian monastics, was called a "true philosopher" because he lived the life preached in the gospel. Christianity is not a subject of intellectual speculations or debates but rather a way of life. Origen became a true philosopher because he taught his students the elements of Christian philosophy and at the same time was an example to his students by implementing the Christian philosophy as a way of life. He slept very little at night and spent his time studying and meditating on Scripture. He lived a very ascetic life. He fasted for long periods of time and when he ate, Eusebius informs us, he ate only the food necessary for sustenance. The notion that food is for sustenance and not for pleasure is a theme shared by Clement and Origen and reflects the general attitude toward the consumption of food among second- and third-century Egyptian Christians. Origen did not sleep in his bed, did not have shoes, had one coat, did not drink wine, and did not worry about the future.[11] He practiced what he preached and taught his students that biblical precepts must be followed. His life was a witness to the faith. His ascetic life and conduct was so inspiring that many of those who came to listen to him lecture renounced everything; some became his students, others became martyrs.[12]

Asceticism is not an end in itself, but rather a vehicle for a life of reflective prayer and contemplation on Scripture. Origen the biblical scholar advises his readers to read Scripture in a state of "utmost purity and sobriety."[13] They are to spend the night in prayer and reading Scripture so that they might uncover the deep meaning of the Spirit hidden in the ordinary narrative of the text. This prayerful reading of Scripture might enable the reader to "become a sharer of the Spirit's knowledge and a partaker of his divine counsel."[14] Prayer combined with an ascetic life enables a person to delve into the inner meaning of the biblical message; it

10. Eusebius, *Hist. eccl.* 6.3.

11. Ibid.

12. Ibid.

13. G. W. Butterworth, trans., Origen and Paul Koetschau, *On First Principles; Being Koetschau's Text of the De Principiis* (New York: Harper & Row, 1966) 283; *Peri archon* 4.2.

14. Ibid.

becomes fertile soil for the work of the Spirit to guide the reader through the deeper meaning of Scripture. For the early church fathers, reading Scripture was not an intellectual exercise or an obligation, but rather an inner spiritual exercise that immerged from the depth of the life of prayer. Reading Scripture nourishes prayer and prayer prepares the soul for the work of the Spirit to understand Scripture.

Among the many inspired by Origen's exemplary life and the depth of his philosophical and theological teachings was Gregory Thaumaturgus (the "Wonder Worker"). Gregory lost his father at the age of fourteen but the family wealth enabled him to continue his studies in Latin language and Roman law. He wanted to study law in Berytus (present-day Beirut, Lebanon) but first had to accompany his sister as she went to join her husband in Palestine. It is there that he met Origen. He became so captivated with Origen's teachings and character that he abandoned his plan to study law at Berytus and remained with his teacher. In an *Address of Thanksgiving* in honor of his teacher Origen, Gregory writes about his mentor's scholarly knowledge and "the divine virtues concerning how to act, which brings the soul's impulses to a calm and steady condition."[15] Gregory also writes about Origen: "This man did not explain to us about virtues in that fashion, in words, but rather exhorted us to deeds, and he exhorted us even more by deeds than by what he said."[16] This is an early description of spiritual Christian discipleship. It is not planned or organized, but rather an unstructured and unpremeditated process that emerges from a teacher who is just acting as himself as he makes an honest attempt to live according to biblical teachings. Gregory gives this further description:

> This man too at first used words to exhort me to philosophize, while preceding the verbal exhortation with his deeds. He did not just recite memorized formulas; on the contrary, he did not even think it worthwhile to speak if he could not do so with a pure intention and striving to put his words into action. He tried to offer himself an example of the person trying to live a good life whom he described in words, and presented a paradigm, I would like to say, of the sage.[17]

15. Michael Slusser, trans., *St. Gregory Thaumaturgus: Life and Works*, The Fathers of the Church 98 (Washington, DC: Catholic University of America Press, 1998) 110; *Address of Thanksgiving* 9.115.

16. Ibid., 112; *Address of Thanksgiving* 9.126.

17. Ibid., 113; *Address of Thanksgiving* 11.135.

Origen's way of life also induced his students to "put aside career anxiety and the hurly-burly of public life, inciting us to look carefully at ourselves and to do what was really our responsibility."[18]

Origen exemplifies the power of witness to the gospel message. He presented to all who knew him the paradigm of the sage. It was a paradigm not only of philosophical or scholarly wisdom, but also of Christian wisdom. It was a paradigm beyond words that surpassed the Greek philosophical wisdom that many of Origen's students sought, though they ended by attaining the paradigm of Christian wisdom. Origen's impact and power over his students was more by his deeds than by his words. Origen was a Christian teacher and scholar who went about doing his job as a teacher. But what is special about Origen is that his teachings were not divorced from his personal spirituality. His behavior reflected the inner spirituality he practiced. His spirituality impressed all who came to hear him to the extent they renounced their old way of life and followed him. His life of renunciation and asceticism, fasting, and Scripture reading through the night accompanied by prayer was reflected in his person, his teaching, and above all his deeds. Origen was not a monk, since monasticism was not yet organized at that time, but a person living in the society, doing his job, attempting to live loyal to the biblical precepts. Gregory comments in his address: "I think that everything has no other goal than to come to God, having been conformed to him in purity of mind, and to remain in him."[19]

"You are the salt of the earth . . . you are the light of the world . . . let your life shine before others" (Matt 5:13, 14, 16): Following and Witnessing in the Desert

Origen was not the only one living a pious ascetic style of life while attending to his work within society. There are many examples of men and women who decided to renounce the world and live according to scriptural precepts. Most of them did not leave detailed information about their way of life, but archeological sites and papyri give us some sense of their way of living.

The possibilities differed for men and women. Men had more liberty and could live on their own by doing manual work suitable for their spiritual pursuit. Many of these men either lived in their family homes or,

18. Ibid., 114; *Address of Thanksgiving* 11.138.
19. Ibid., 116; *Address of Thanksgiving* 12.149.

if the extended family was occupying the family house, moved out and rented lodgings. There is enough documentation in papyri of complaints, from either landlords or tenants, that indicates that the tenant was an ascetic. Men also had the opportunity simply to live on the outskirts of their hometowns, as Anthony, Macarius, and others did. Some ascetics, both men and women, were sponsored by rich families who supported their monastic lifestyle. These various living settings were all attempts to find a way beyond the family structure to devote time to spiritual life.

Women were constrained by the financial resources available to them and social perceptions. Women were divided into three categories based on their marital status: widows, married, or celibate. Widows who had fulfilled their obligations towards their children were able to attend to their spiritual life and to church service as described in 1 Timothy 5:3–16.[20] Married women were expected to attend to their families first and foremost. Married women with means were able to attend to their spiritual life since most of their families' immediate needs were taken care of.[21] Celibate women who wanted to pursue a life devoted to God either lived in their family homes in seclusion, depending on their family for financial support, or lived alone or with other women to share living expenses. The model of women living an ascetic life in their own residence seems to be a rather lasting model that persisted even after the formation and regulation of monastic communities.[22] Bishops were supportive of individual or small groups of women living an ascetic life. The earliest historical confirmation of such groups comes in reference to Pope Alexander of Alexandria (312–328) who used to receive these women monastics regularly in his episcopal residence for Bible study.

There was another model in which celibate women lived with celibate men; the men provided some financial support and shelter and the women provided domestic services. This model was frowned upon and

---

20. There are indications that the early church followed the precepts in 1 Tim 5:3–16 to some extent. See Susanna Elm, *Virgins of God: The Making of Asceticism in Late Antiquity* (Oxford: Clarendon, 1996) 166–70.

21. Elizabeth Clark, "Authority and Humility: A Conflict of Values in Fourth-Century Female Monasticism," in idem, *Ascetic Piety and Women's Faith: Essays on Late Ancient Christianity* (Lewiston, NY: Mellen, 1986) 209–28.

22. See the eighth-century letter from Maria the nun to Kyriakos the anchorite, in Roger Bagnall and Raffaella Cribiore, *Women's Letters from Ancient Egypt 300 BC–AD 800* (Ann Arbor: University of Michigan Press, 2006) 200; and see Lois Farag, "Beyond Their Gender: Contemporary Coptic Female Monasticism," *Journal of World Christianity* 2 (2009) 111–44.

later condemned because it was a fertile ground for rumors and sometimes led to inappropriate conduct.[23]

Early Christians who wanted to live a life devoted to God lived primarily in urban areas, in a variety of settings based primarily on their
personal and social conditions and economic resources. They were inven-
tive in finding ways to live their spirituality at a time when an organized
monastic system was not yet in place. On the other hand, the society welcomed such styles of living.

Living a simple, frugal life accompanied by prayer and reading Scripture was very much the norm of Christian living during the early centuries
of Christianity, regardless of one's social status. The best example would be
Emperor Theodosius II. As an emperor he kept the Wednesday and Friday fasts. Socrates the historian informs us that he transformed the palace
into a kind of monastery. He would rise early in the morning, along with
his two sister princesses; together they read Scripture, said psalms and
hymns, memorized Scripture passages, and had spiritual and exegetical
discussions with the bishops invited to the palace. He also collected a large
library of religious books in the palace, which became a good resource to
the royal family.[24]

In short, we can say that there were many monastics before the rise of
organized monasticism. They lived in their houses and followed scriptural
injunctions about prayer, fasting, and following the example of Christ.
They were individuals forming their spiritual life based on their personal
social and economic status. Such a pious, austere, spiritual style of living
was normative and welcomed in the society until a certain Anthony, who
in his attempt to follow this exact same life, changed the course of Christian spirituality.

Saint Anthony the Great (251–356)

Anthony the Great, also known as Anthony of Egypt, is called the "founder
of monasticism." Most of our information about Anthony is derived from
Athanasius' presentation of Anthony in the *Life of Anthony*. Some scholars
criticize the idealized life presented. But it is precisely this portrayal that
has impacted the lives of Christians throughout history. St. Athanasius

23. Elizabeth Clark, "John Chrysostom and the Subintroductae," in idem, *Ascetic
Piety and Women's Faith: Essays on Late Ancient Christianity* (Lewiston, NY: Mellen,
1986) 265–90. Also see Canon 3 of the First Council of Nicaea (325).

24. Socrates Scholasticus, *Hist. eccl.* 7.22.

wrote the biography of St. Anthony to provide an example to be emulated. For centuries people have read the *Life of Anthony* and been transformed by his example. The most famous is St. Augustine, who credits his conversion to Anthony's biography. Anthony has inspired the imagination of many artists and their paintings are exhibited in many museums. Scholarly criticism of some aspects of the text should not negate the spiritual benefit that this life has brought for centuries and that will transform many for centuries to come. It is this spiritual impact that is our concern here.

Anthony was born from Egyptian Christian parents in the modern-day village of Qimn al-'Arws, situated in the middle of Egypt. He was brought up as a Christian and from an early age "he listened attentively to the reading from Scripture."[25] Scripture was central to Anthony and guided him throughout his life. Though he came from a wealthy family, "as a child, he did not pester his parents for all sorts of expensive foods, nor did he look for the pleasures associated with them. He was satisfied solely with what he had and never looked for more."[26] Anthony was typical for his times; he lived the life of renunciation while living in his family's home. His family's wealth did not affect his ascetic lifestyle. That was the way Christians lived the gospel message; they lived among their families in cities or villages and were not attached to their worldly possessions or lured by the life of luxury and pleasure that the world had to offer.

Anthony's parents passed away when he was eighteen or twenty and he was confronted with the responsibility of managing an estate and taking care of a younger sister. He entered church one Sunday, reflecting on the life of the apostles and the early Christians. The gospel reading was from Matthew 19:21: "If you wish to be perfect, go, sell your possessions, and give the money to the poor, and you will have treasure in heaven; then come, follow me." Anthony considered this to be a message from God and he immediately left church and sold his possessions. He distributed the money to the poor, but kept some money for his sister. When he visited the church again he heard the gospel message from Matthew 6:34: "So do not worry about tomorrow, for tomorrow will bring worries of its own." He left the church and distributed the rest of his possessions and entrusted his sister to a group of women living the life of prayer and contemplation. Athanasius does not call this women's residence a monastery, though it functioned as one, since monasticism was not yet an organized system.

---

25. Tim Vivian, trans., Athanasius, *The Life of Antony: The Coptic Life and the Greek Life*, Cistercian Studies 202 (Kalamazoo, MI: Cistercian, 2003) 57; *v. Anton* 1.1.

26. Ibid.; *v. Anton* 1.1.

Anthony at first lived in front of his house and then moved to the outskirts of his village. There was another ascetic man there who lived the life of solitude and renunciation. Anthony emulated this man's style of life.[27] This is the beginning of Anthony's spiritual journey. We will continue to follow Anthony's journey in chapter 3.

As mentioned, Anthony will eventually acquire the label "founder of monasticism," though there were many monastics before him. After Anthony's death, a monastery was founded close to his cell in the eastern desert near the Red Sea. The monastery still exists to the present day and is active with monks following the Antonian monastic tradition. Another monastic community sprouted up near the grave of Paul the Hermit, whom Anthony had befriended and later buried. The Monastery of St. Paul the Hermit has been closely connected to the Monastery of St. Anthony, which is about thirty kilometers northwest of it. Two of Anthony's disciples, St. Macarius and St. Amoun, were founders of monastic communities in the western desert of Egypt.

Figure 1: General view of the Monastery of St. Anthony with the mountain where the cave of Anthony is located. (Photo by author)

27. Ibid., 60; *v. Anton* 3.1.

Figure 2: View of the gate and wall of the Monastery of St. Anthony with the mountain where the cave of Anthony is located in the background. (Photo by author)

Figure 3: Interior view of the Monastery of St. Anthony. (Photo by author)

Figure 4: General view of the Monastery of St. Paul. (Photo by author)

Figure 5: Another general view the Monastery of St. Paul, the ancient monastery with gate and a modern extension at the top of the mountain. (Photo by author)

Figure 6: Interior view of the Monastery of St. Paul, ancient wall and cells. (Photo by author)

Figure 7: Interior view of the Monastery of St. Paul. (Photo by author)

Abba Macarius (c. 300–c. 390)

Also known as Macarius the Great, Macarius of Egypt, and Macarius the Spiritbearer, Abba Macarius was born to a wealthy Christian family. His father was a priest. They lost their first-born daughter, and then their possessions.[28] Abraham, the first patriarch, appeared to Macarius's father and informed him that he was to leave his town and move to Jijber, in the Egyptian Delta, and there he would have a son.[29] Macarius was born after another vision. He grew up helping his father in farming, by which the family's wealth increased. His parents taught him to give daily alms.

The town clergy, observing Macarius's conduct and constant meditation on Scripture, ordained him a reader, a position reserved for literate and articulate men knowledgeable in Scripture to read Scripture during services or other readings during gatherings. He was forced to marry and was later promoted to the diaconate.[30] To avoid consummating his marriage he decided to work as a camel driver so that his long trips to gather natron (sodium carbonate) or simple salt from Scetis in the northwestern desert of Egypt would take him away from home. In Scetis, he saw a vision in which he was told that he would be a father of many monks in the Scetis area. This was Macarius's first vision and everyone accompanying him on the trip noticed he was "thunderstruck."[31] On his return from the trip his wife fell sick and passed away; soon afterward his parents passed away. Macarius found it an opportune time to follow his spiritual dreams.

What is interesting at this point is that Macarius lived a spiritual life among his family and took care of them until they all passed away. The spirit of renunciation was inward and he was living his spiritual life within the society. It was because he demonstrated pious conduct that he was chosen to become a reader, then a deacon, with the anticipation that he would be ordained to the priesthood. Thus, the necessity of his forced marriage, since church ordinances required him to get married before priestly ordination.

Macarius was troubled by many thoughts and decided to take council from an anchorite living on the outskirts of his town. Monasticism was not yet organized and, as mentioned above, each person had to discover the way to satisfy his or her own spiritual longings. Many men left their

28. Tim Vivian, trans., *Saint Macarius, the Spiritbearer: Coptic Texts relating to Saint Macarius the Great* (Crestwood, NY: St. Vladimir Seminary Press, 2004) 153.

29. Ibid., 154.

30. Ibid., 156.

31. Ibid., 157–59.

homes and lived on the outskirts of the city. The anchorite saw Macarius' future but did not inform him lest he become vain. He advised Macarius to live as an anchorite at the outskirts of his village. Macarius immediately distributed all his possessions and lived on the outskirts of another village. When the people of the village saw his piety they ordained him a priest.[32]

The life of Macarius informs us of a major test that confronted him. A young woman falsely accused Macarius of being the father of her unborn child. The people of the village believed the young woman's accusation. They tortured, humiliated, and beat Macarius. All that Macarius said was, "What an injustice! I do not acknowledge this charge brought against me."[33] The woman's father demanded that Macarius provide for his daughter and the child. Macarius agreed to do this. He worked very hard to provide for the new family and began sending all his earnings to the mother-to-be. At the time of delivery the woman had a hard time and could not deliver until she confessed the true father of her child. The truth became known.

A good number of the lives of the early desert fathers and mothers include stories of testing. In most cases the stories are of some sort of false accusation. The aim of these stories is to portray the saint's reaction in times of trouble and show how his faith and total submission to God sustain him during the time of trial. In this case, Macarius was humble, took responsibility to support the mother-to-be, and accepted shame and slander against himself in silence. He did not attempt to exonerate himself by slandering the woman, but rather accepted the blame to save her from more shame. He showed concern for the welfare of his accuser. He imitated Christ, who did not seek vengeance against those who crucified him. He had faith in God's words that "the LORD will fight for you, and you have only to keep still" (Exod 14:14). We do not know how long the slander lasted, but it must have been a few months until the woman was in delivery. Other saints have been falsely accused and their innocence not revealed for many years.

In a modern culture driven by litigation in all aspects of life, it is hard to comprehend the notion of silently waiting for the truth to be revealed, or to wait for the culprit to confess the truth because of a tormented conscience. Sometimes lawsuits and courts cannot prove innocence, nor can dependence on humans provide full justice, and this is where faith can sustain a person. This is not a statement against the law or court justice;

32. Ibid., 164.
33. Ibid., 166.

it is rather a statement against personal vengeance and retribution. It is against the hatred within the heart that disturbs the tranquility of the soul and mind. When the mind is held captive by thoughts of anger, all possibility for the mind to contemplate God is ended because the senses have been taken over by anger. St. Athanasius describes this as the mind contemplating evil rather than good, which is the image of what God is.[34]

After this episode, an angel appeared to Macarius to strengthen him and guide him through the second phase of his life.[35] Again this is a common theme in desert spirituality: after a person triumphs in a test, God always sends divine consolation. When Christ triumphed over the devil's temptation, the Gospel of Mathew tells us, "then the devil left him, and suddenly angels came and waited on him" (4:11). The angel guided Macarius to Scetis where he founded a monastic community. This is considered another call for Macarius. Since with a call comes renunciation, the life of Macarius informs us that Macarius left everything in his cell and followed the angel, or the power of God, to Scetis.[36] He arrived at Scetis and dug two caves, one for his use and the other for a chapel. He spent his days in prayer and work. He plaited baskets and sold them, and with the money he bought his necessities and wheat to celebrate the Eucharist.[37] Work is vital in desert spirituality. All monastics have to sustain themselves from their own labor.

Staying alone in the desert, Macarius fell victim to many thoughts he did not know how to handle. He decided to visit St. Anthony to seek his guidance and advice. This is another theme in desert spirituality: discipleship. Desert spirituality started with solitary monastics like Anthony and Macarius, not within a community; thus spiritual direction was crucial in guiding the novices as well as the more spiritually mature through the pitfalls of the spiritual life. The thoughts troubled Macarius for a second time and he visited Anthony again. During the second visit, Anthony clothed Macarius with the monastic *schema* (or habit), officially making Macarius his disciple.[38] Macarius stayed with him until Anthony died; he buried him and returned to Scetis. People began gathering around Macarius and he let them remain near him. He began instructing and guiding them in their spiritual lives and put them to work to support themselves. Macarius built

34. *gent.*, 4.
35. Vivian, *Saint Macarius*, 168–70.
36. Ibid., 170.
37. Ibid., 171.
38. Ibid., 176.

a church to serve the brothers but the brothers did not form a "monastery" since they were still living their solitary discipline.[39] As Macarius grew old, he became more famous and many of his disciples began to form their own monastic groups, still preserving the solitary lifestyle. Macarius died at the age of ninety-seven. He laid the foundation of monasticism in Scetis, which flourishes with monastics to the present day. Four active monasteries still survive in Scetis (present-day Wadī al-Naṭrūn): the Monastery of the Virgin Mary (commonly known as *al-Barāmūs*), the Monastery of the Virgin Mary (commonly known as that of the Syrians—*al-suryān*), the Monastery of Saint Bishoy, and the Monastery of Saint Macarius.

Figure 8: Monastery of the Virgin Mary (known as *al-suryān*). (Photo by author)

39. Ibid., 178.

Figure 9: Interior view of the Monastery of the Virgin Mary (known as *al-suryān*) with view of the keep at the far end. (Photo by author)

Figure 10: Interior view of the Monastery of the Virgin Mary (known as *al-barāmūs*) with view of the keep at the far end. (Photo by author)

Figure 11: Interior view of the Monastery of the Virgin Mary (known as *al-barāmūs*). (Photo by author)

Figure 12: Interior view of the Monastery of St. Macarius; view of old entrance to the monastery. (Photo by author)

Figure 13: Interior view of the Monastery of St. Macarius. (Photo by author)

Figure 14: Interior view of the Monastery of St. Macarius with new library, ancient church and modern tower that holds a water tank. (Photo by author)

Figure 15: Interior view of the Monastery of St. Macarius with view of new wall at the back and older buildings in the front. (Photo by author)

Figure 16: General view of the main church of the Monastery of St. Bishoy. (Photo by author)

Figure 17: Exterior view of the main church of the Monastery of St. Bishoy. (Photo by author)

Figure 18: Interior of the main church of the Monastery of St. Bishoy. Fourth century monastics would meet in similar churches during the weekend. (Photo by author)

Balance of the Heart

Abba Amoun (c. 280–c. 350)

The second disciple of Abba Anthony is Abba Amoun. [40] According to Palladius, an early visitor to the Egyptian desert, Amoun was an orphan and his uncle pressured him to marry at the age of twenty-two. He wanted to consecrate his life to God and he tried to convince his bride to separate; she refused but suggested they live separately in the same house. After eighteen years, his wife decided that they should separate and each live on their own. She kept the house and continued to live her ascetic life, while Amoun went to the Mountain of Nitria, where he lived for twenty-two years. Soon people began gathering around Abba Amoun and Nitrian monasticism was founded. Nitrian monasticism followed the solitary life style. The number of monks in Nitria, according to Palladius, reached five thousand. [41] Though the accuracy of the number is open to discussion, it indicates that Nitria was crowded with monks. This is when Amoun decided to establish another monastic center at Kellia (or The Cells). [42] According to the *Apophthegmata Patrum*, when Anthony visited Amoun at Nitria, Amoun consulted Anthony about the increase in the brethren's number:

> Abba Anthony once went to visit Abba Amoun in Mount Nitira and when they met, Abba Amoun said, "By your prayers, the number of the brethren increases, and some of them want to build more cells where they may live in peace. How far away from here do you think we should build the cells?" Abba Anthony said, "Let us eat at the ninth hour and then let us go out for a walk in the desert and explore the country." So they went out into the desert and they walked until sunset and then Abba Anthony said, "Let us pray and plant the cross here, so that those who wish to do so may build here. Then when those who remain there want to visit those who have come here, they can take a little food at the ninth hour and then come. If they do this, they will be able to keep in touch with each other without distraction of mind." The distance is twelve miles. [43]

40. Also spelled as Ammoun, Ammon, or Amon.

41. Socrates Scholasticus, *Hist. eccl.* 4.23; Sozomen, *Hist. eccl.* 1.14; *Historia Monachorum* 22; *v. Anton.*, 60; Robert T. Meyer, trans., *Palladius: The Lausiac History*, Ancient Christian Writers 34 (New York: Paulist, 1964) 41–43.

42. The monastic dwelling is called a "cell." It is usually a small room, and sometimes a room with an antechamber. The inner room is for the privacy of the monastic; the outer chamber is for more public activities such as receiving guests or work.

43. *v. Anton.*, 34; ASWard, 8.

According to this tradition, monasticism at Kellia was blessed by Anthony and part of the tradition of the Antonian monastic solitary lifestyle. The monastic community at Nitria and Kellia declined by the seventh century.

Amma Syncletica

Amma Syncletica is one of the very few women monastics about whom we know anything. Her life seems to follow the traditional pattern of the most famous desert fathers. She began living her ascetic life while still in her parents' house. Syncletica, meaning "heavenly assembly," was born in Alexandria of wealthy parents. Her two brothers died in their youth and she was left with a blind sister. Her parents were very eager to get her married, as she had excellent prospects of marriage and was the only child left to preserve the family line. She endured the unrelenting pressure of suitors attracted to her wealth as well as beauty. After her parents' death she renounced all her wealth and withdrew from society with her sister to the outskirts of the city of Alexandria. She fasted to an extent that affected her physical health. Then she decided to reduce her ascetic exercises. She advised others to eat twice per day for the "security of the soul," that is to protect oneself from pride.[44] "Wherefore it is fitting for the soul to be made safe from all sides, and to turn back toward the shadowy places the harshest ascetic practice inflamed by the fever of arrogance, and sometimes to prune back the extravagant things, so that the root might become more flourishing."[45] She lived a solitary life for some time until word of her ascetic practices and piety spread; eventually, women who came seeking her guidance settled with her. This is usually the way a monastic settlement and discipleship began. The sayings indicate she is addressing a female monastic community, but we do not know much about its structure. She left many sayings preserved in what seems to be a lengthy discourse, which forms the majority of the "life" that has been preserved.[46] She was surely considered one the famous desert monastics since a good number of her sayings are preserved in the collection of sayings.

The life tells us that she prepared for her eternal journey not only by renouncing her material possessions but also by the internal renunciation

44. *Sync.*, 283, #38; 287, #50.

45. *Sync.*, 289, #54.

46. *Sync.*, 265–311. See also Elizabeth Bryson Bongie, trans., Pseudo-Athanasius, *The Life & Regimen of the Blessed & Holy Syncletica*, Peregrina Translations 21, Akathist Series 3 (Toronto, ON: Peregrina, 2001).

of "anger and memory of past injuries, . . . envy and love of fame."[47] She died at the age of eighty after battling for three and a half years with what might have been lung cancer.

We know of other desert mothers, such as Theodora and Sarah, who also left us some sayings, but we know absolutely nothing about their lives. The mere fact that some sayings have been preserved indicates that these mothers lived a pious life attested to by many; they had some disciples who came to ask their advice and cared to record their sayings for posterity. The mere fact that someone cared to collect and preserve their sayings indicate they were founders of monastic communities similar to those of their male counterparts. Female founders of female cenobitic communities suffer from the same fate: we do not know much about them, sometimes not even their names, especially because they did not leave sayings.

In the early stages, all monastic clusters in the eastern and western desert of Egypt had a direct connection with Anthony and all followed the solitary monastic lifestyle. Anthony, together with Paul the Hermit, Macarius the Spiritbearer, Amoun, Ammas Syncletica, Theodora, and Sarah, lived ascetically like the men and women of the early centuries of Christianity who wanted to live a life dedicated to God. Their main focus was to live a saintly life through prayer, reading Scripture, and working both to support themselves and to give alms. These four precepts of ascetic early Christians remained the main guidelines of Egyptian monasticism.

To achieve these goals they had to live the life of renunciation and simplicity. What Anthony and his disciples did is take renunciation and dedication to God to its full, going to the desert rather than living within society or on the outskirts of their towns and villages. They started in the urban setting and then gradually began to seclude themselves until ultimately the desert became their home. At this stage they were called *monachos*, that is, "solitary" or "single," and ultimately this became the title affiliated with the monastic movement; those living this lifestyle were called "monastics" and "monks." This is what Anthony made known to the rest of the world. People followed his lifestyle and he became the founder of monasticism.

Because of the solitary bent of this lifestyle, the practices, sayings, and experience of these monks as well as the early Christians can serve as

47. *Sync.*, 271, #13.

guidelines for twenty-first-century Christians. We can follow in the footsteps of the early Christians and benefit from the experience and wisdom of the desert fathers and mothers. We can live among our families and communities, as these monastics first started, and learn from their experience and practical wisdom that they left us.

"Encourage one another and build up each other" (1 Thess 5:11); "One will lift up the other" (Eccl 4:10): Following and Witnessing in Community

Not all Christians can live in solitude. This is what St. Pachomius and St. Shenoute realized. Some might have equally strong aspirations to the spiritual life but not have the psychological or physical stamina to live the life of solitude: psychological, because not everyone can endure silence and quietness for long periods of time; physical, because the life of the desert requires excellent health to endure some of the harsh and inclement weather or lack of essential supplies. Even living within the urban setting was not possible for everyone, either for financial reasons or because of family and social pressures. Even strong spiritual leaders such as Macarius and Amoun could not withstand the social pressure and were forced into marriage. St. Pachomius and St. Shenouta understood these challenges. To overcome these obstacles they formed the monastic lifestyle of cenobiticism, or communal life. This lifestyle provides a spiritual milieu where seekers can achieve their spiritual aspiration without the anxiety of securing their social freedom. It provides spiritual support where each member of the community encourages and builds up the other. The communal system was the preferred lifestyle of St. Basil, the founder of the Byzantine monastic structure, and of St. Benedict, the founder of the Western monastic structure. Both monastic leaders based their rule on that of St. Pachomius. We will now attend to cenobiticism and its founding fathers, Pachomius and Shenoute.

Abba Pachomius (c. 292–346)

Pachomius was born of pagan parents.[48] At the age of twenty he was conscripted into the army.[49] During his service in the army he was moved by

---

48. Armand Veilleux, trans., *Pachomian Koinonia*, vol. 1, Cistercian Studies 45 (Kalamazoo, MI: Cistercian, 1980) 25; *Bohairic Life of Pachomius* (hereafter *Bo.*).

49. Ibid., 27; *Bo.* 7.

the charity of the Christians who provided food and alleviated the suffering of the military recruits. Pachomius understood from his inquiry that these were Christians and decided to become a Christian once he left the army. He was baptized and after three years he decided to become an ascetic. He became a disciple of and learned the ascetic life from Abba Palamon, an anchorite who lived on the outskirts of a village in southern Egypt.[50] One day while praying in the deserted village of Tabennesi, he heard a voice instructing him to "dwell in this place and build a monastery; for many will come to you to become monks with you, and they will profit their souls."[51] He built a monastery at Tabennesi and that was the beginning of the *Koinonia* (Greek for "common life"). His sister Mary later joined him and built a monastery for women close to that of Pachomius; there the same rule and style of living of the brothers was followed by the women.[52] Pachomius "did not want any clerics in the monastery, for fear of jealousy and vainglory."[53] He assigned some of the brothers to assist him in leadership; he also divided the monastery work among all the brothers so that the work rotated among them. He organized three meetings per week for theological, biblical, and monastic instructions, one on Saturday and two on Sunday. In addition, the house masters gave two instructions on fast days, one on Wednesday and the other on Friday.[54] In the *Koinonia* everything was common and shared among the brothers. Though many aspects of the *Koinonia* were regulated and the monks shared meals instead of eating alone, they were to eat their meals in silence and to work together in silence while praying unceasingly. The solitary aspect is still valued and visible in the rules and daily activities of the Pachomian *Koinonia*. The *Koinonia* model was successful during the lifetime of Pachomius and thousands joined his monasteries, of which there were nine for men and two for women.

Abba Shenoute the Archimandrite (348–466)

Abba Shenoute was born in a village close to present-day Akhmym in southern Egypt. He was a shepherd and at a young age he stayed with his maternal uncle, Abba Pjol, who was a monk and archimandrite of the

50. Ibid., 28–30; *Bo.* 8–10.
51. Ibid., 39; *Bo.* 17.
52. Ibid., 49; *Bo.* 27.
53. Ibid., 47; *Bo.* 25.
54. Ibid., 48–49; *Bo.* 25–26.

White Monastery. Shenoute lived a very ascetic life and soon became a monk in his uncle's monastery. At the death of Abba Pjol in 385 he succeeded his uncle and became the archimandrite of the White Monastery.[55] His saintly reputation attracted about 2,200 men and 1,800 women.[56] They formed a federation of three monasteries. This required some building projects, including a large church attended by monastics of both genders. The Shenoute federation followed the *Koinonia* model, though with a different monastic philosophy and in a more strict fashion. What is distinctive about the Shenoute federation was that it accommodated both the communal lifestyle of Pachomius and the anchoritic or desert style. Shenoute himself would retreat for long periods in the desert.

The community met for prayer twice per day, in the morning and evening. The Eucharistic liturgy was celebrated on Saturdays and Sundays. The monastics had a stricter diet than that of Pachomius; no meat, milk, eggs, or wine was permitted.[57] The Shenoute monasteries exhibited extraordinary social concern to thousands of refugees who fled tribal attacks on their villages. The federation was also a literary center with a large library. Shenoute was well versed in Greek and Coptic and wrote many treatises and canons in Coptic for the instruction of his monastics.

From the solitary model arose the communal model exemplified in the pioneering model of the Pachomian *Koinonia* and later that of Shenoute. But these communal models still anchored themselves in the experience and writings of the desert fathers and mothers. Though living in community, they were still solitary in their spiritual journey.

When Christ pronounced the words "Follow me," the fishermen immediately left their nets, the Samaritan "left her water jar," and the women followed him to the cross and then to the tomb and remained there mourning, disregarding any danger to their lives. In the following hundreds of years, thousands if not millions of Christians followed him. Each

55. David N. Bell, trans., Besa, *The Life of Shenoute*, Cistercian Studies 73 (Kalamazoo, MI: Cistercian, 1983) 41–45.

56. Emile Amélineau, *Monuments pour servir à l'histoire de l'Égypte chrétienne aux IVe, Ve, VIe, et VIIe siècles*, Memoires publiés par les membres de la Mission archéologique française au Caire 4 (Paris: E. Leroux, 1888–95) 1:289–478.

57. Bentley Layton, "Social Structure and Food Consumption in an Early Christian Monastery: The Evidence of Shenoute's Canons and the While Monastery Federation A.D. 385–465," *Le Muséon* 115 (2002) 25–55.

Christian who followed Christ understood that they had to leave a "net" or a "water jar." Renunciation and letting go of things is an integral part of following Christ. What they left has taken many forms, but each understood the price of discipleship. Hundreds of men and women in the early church understood the message clearly and lived a life of renunciation within their families, sometimes on the outskirts of their villages or towns, sometimes renting houses, separating themselves from social noise to live a quiet life of prayer and holiness. Though generally the life of previous generations was much simpler and more austere, still they strived to live a more ascetic life. Few left us their names; others left us their traces on papyri or on wall inscriptions, letting us know that in such humble abodes within the city men and women lived the Christian philosophy, that is to say, the Christian way of life. They are the nucleus of the early monastic ideal.

Clement encouraged the Christians of Alexandria to renounce the luxuries of life in a great metropolitan city, to let go of their luxurious food and dress for a simpler life attending to necessities rather than luxuries. His contemporary, Origen of Alexandria, not only wrote about it, he lived this life of austerity, thus becoming a role model not only to all his students but to following generations. He not only taught about the Christian way of life, his life became an actual demonstration of his spiritual teachings. Anthony, Macarius, Amoun, Syncletica, Pachomius, and Shenoute all started living the Christian way of life in their homes, then gradually moved to the outskirts of their towns and villages. It is within this social and religious context that the desert fathers and mothers emerged.

But it was Anthony who made the greatest move that would leave its mark on the Christian heritage forever: he moved to the desert, and then to the inner desert. Macarius and Amoun followed. Anthony lived not only external and material renunciation; through his stay in the desert he perfected inner renunciation. Anthony mastered the interconnection between God and the inner and the outer self. Anthony's inner spiritual journey in the desert is the topic of the chapter 3. First, however, we will look at the theological foundations of desert spirituality.

2

For God So Loved the World

*Theology of the Incarnation as Foundation
of Desert Monasticism*

For God so loved the world that he gave his only Son,
so that everyone who believes in him may not perish
but may have eternal life.

JOHN 3:16

GOD'S LOVE FOR HUMANITY is the gripping story of the Christian
faith. The divine love is manifested in the events of the incarnation
and crucifixion. The resurrection, the culmination of this love and its
transformative power, granted humanity renewal and the power to overcome death, that is, in essence, eternal life. John the Evangelist gives in a
single verse, cited above, this story of divine love, presenting it as a transformative event in the history of humanity. This verse is clear, succinct,
and straightforward. Its meaning and implications are what humanity
has been trying to unfold for centuries. From the earliest days, Christians
have attempted to grasp the depth of the incarnation. Some contemplated
it in their own hearts; others wrote lengthy treatises attempting to explain
it. The desert fathers and mothers sought to realize the meaning of the
incarnation in their lives. Sometimes the impression given in academic
studies of these desert monastics is that they were illiterate peasants for
whom theology had little meaning. To the contrary, the interconnection

between theology and spirituality is at the root of desert spirituality. In this chapter we will examine the theological writings that furnished the background for the theological thinking of the desert fathers and mothers. How they lived out this theology and its implication for our daily lives is the focus of Part II of this book.

At the center of theological thought in fourth-century Egypt is Athanasius of Alexandria. Athanasius was born and raised in Egypt (295–373). In his youth, Athanasius became closely acquainted with St. Anthony and in time wrote the *Life of Anthony*. At a very early age he became acquainted with Pope Alexander of Alexandria and eventually became his spiritual son, then his personal secretary and deacon, and finally his successor as pope of the church of Alexandria. While still young, Athanasius became involved in a theological controversy that rocked the church of Alexandria and in due course the rest of the universal church—the Arian controversy. Arius asserted that the Son was not equal to God and was not eternal because "there was a time when he was not." Arius teachings reduced the Son to a created being. Alexander opposed this teaching, and when the Arian controversy began threatening the peace of the Roman Empire, an ecumenical council convened in Nicaea in 325, which Athanasius attended as Alexander's deacon. The Nicene council in its creed asserted the divinity of the Son. Athanasius suffered five exiles in defense of the Nicene theology.

Many studies of Athanasius' theology emphasize the polemical debates during the Arian controversy or the influence of the Greco-Roman context on his writings. This is not what is attempted here, however. The relevance of Athanasius to desert spirituality is that his writings represent the theological as well as the spiritual tradition of the Egyptian church. As a native of Egypt, his theological and spiritual thoughts are a culmination of his own personal thought together with the indigenous theological traditions that formed and nourished his theological thinking. This is neither a study of the roots of Athanasius' thinking nor a survey of Athanasian scholarship. It is rather a survey of three works of Athanasius, namely *Against the Gentiles* and *On the Incarnation* in this chapter, followed in the next chapter by the *Life of Anthony*. It is an attempt to introduce the reader to the theological writings that furnished the background for the theological thinking of the desert fathers, to recreate the theological space desert spirituality inhabited.

Against the Gentiles and *On the Incarnation* are two parts of a single work. Athanasius' main concern is the story of human salvation. His focus in the first part is the story of fallen humanity. God created humanity through his own Word, after his own image.[1] He gave humanity the ability to understand reality through this similarity with himself. Humanity was also granted special intellectual powers and knowledge through the Word and with this knowledge humanity had the ability to contemplate God at all times. God gave humanity the knowledge of his own eternity so that humanity would never abandon God but might have fellowship and communication with God and live the life of immortality. Humans were capable of the constant contemplation of God so that the thought of God would never depart from their mind.

It is through purity of soul that we can see God (Matt 5:8).[2] Contemplating the Word, who is the image of the Father, after whose image humanity was made, is the way to preserve this purity so that we are not hindered from fellowship with God. When the human mind transcends the things of the body and the senses, it is raised high and takes pleasure in contemplating the Word and the Father and gains renewal. This is the state of our first parents in paradise. This theological concept expressed by Athanasius is at the heart of the spirituality of the desert fathers and mothers. Desert spirituality strives to be in this state of purity of thought where nothing hinders the mind and soul from constantly contemplating God.

"Then God said, 'Let us make humankind in our image, according to our likeness'" (Gen 1:26). Based on this verse in Genesis and the Pauline saying in 2 Cor 4:4 and Col 1:15 that Christ is the image of God, Athanasius says—though never so succinctly—that humanity was created in the image of the Word who is the image of the invisible God. Being created in the image of the Word, the Logos, implies that humanity was created with reason, since the Greek word *logos* means "word," "speech," or "reason." The likeness that humanity shares with the Word is reason, intellect (or *nous*, "mind"), and the ability to express itself in speech. Being created in the image of the Logos means the human soul is endowed with a *nous* that is always oriented towards the contemplation of God.[3] It means that finding God starts by searching within oneself.[4] The search starts by perceiving

---

1. Pierre Thomas Camelot trans., Athanasius, *Contre les païens*, 2nd ed., Sources chrétiennes 18 (Paris: Éditions du Cerf, 1977) 54; *gent.* 2.

2. Ibid., 52–57; *gent.* 2.

3. *gent.* 19–21.

4. Athanasius points to the following verses: "No, the word is very near to you; it is in your mouth and in your heart for you to observe" (Deut 30:14); ". . . the kingdom of God is among (or within) you" (Luke 17:21); and "The word is near you, on your lips and in your heart" (Rom 10:8).

and contemplating the Divine in the soul and the *nous* that resides within each one of us.

For Athanasius, each member of humankind has a soul, and that soul is rational.[5] To illustrate the rational nature of the soul, Athanasius points out the difference between humankind and irrational creatures. Irrational animals, according to Athanasius, act based on what their eyes see and their senses feel; humans reflect on what they see, master their impulses, and choose to act after reasoning the consequence of their actions. This is what makes humans distinct among the rest of creation. Humans judge the senses, and their *nous* or mind discerns and decides what is best. The senses hear, see, taste, smell, and touch. But what we ought to do with these senses is something beyond the senses; it is what the soul and the *nous* that resides within it discern and decide. When the body is quiet and still, the rational soul can behold what is outside itself.[6] The soul and the *nous* residing within it can behold and contemplate God.

Athanasius makes the point again using the idea of the immortality of the soul. People know their bodies are mortal, but they recognize that the soul is immortal and so are even ready to die if virtue requires it.[7] If the soul wants to follow the path of virtue that requires sacrifices that might affect the mortal body, the soul pursues virtue and leads the body. The soul aspires to what is beyond and eternal and despises what is in front of it. This aspiration leads some to choose service to church, country, family, or neighbor that includes sacrifice, and sometimes martyrdom for the sake of the faith, without any gratification of body or senses. The rational and immortal soul recognizes what is beyond the immediate senses and introduces it to the body. The soul and the *nous* residing within it preside over the body.[8] The soul recognizes immortality because it is immortal and has the capability of moving itself as well as the mortal body. The movement of the soul does not cease with the death of the body. Thoughts of immortality never desert the soul, which is why the soul has the capacity of beholding God and receives the knowledge of God from within.[9]

Athanasius starts his argument in *Against the Gentiles* with the following assertion: evil did not exist from the beginning, but it was people

5. *gent.* 30.
6. *gent.* 31.
7. *gent.* 32.
8. *gent.* 32.
9. *gent.* 33.

who began to contrive of it and imagine it in their own likeness.[10] Athanasius did not attribute to evil a real physical existence. Anything that exists is created or came to be through the Creator; nothing exists without him. If evil exists, if it has a physical dimension and is part of the created world and part of its nature, then God created evil. But God is all goodness and creates what is good; therefore, evil does not exist. The whole notion of evil started in imagination and mind of men.[11] Athanasius rejects Greek philosophic ideas that evil exists as an independent reality. He also opposes Greek and Gnostic ideas that make matter the principle of evil.[12]

Denying evil substantive reality is crucial to desert spirituality. A saying from the desert illustrates the point: Abba Arsenius used to eat of every fruit when ripe in its season. He explained that he wanted to taste each fruit every season to give thanks to God.[13] Matter, exemplified in creation and its produce, is considered a gift from God for which thanks and praise are due. Matter is not evil or the source of evil; it is rather the motivation for giving thanks and contemplating God's creation and work. In this apophthegm (saying), matter is the source of thanksgiving. When

10. The term "people" (ἄνθρωποι) here is in the plural, thus he is not referring specifically to Adam, but to humanity in the collective sense.

11. The Greek word νοῦς, *nous*, has many connotations and more than one meaning can be implied within one usage. In the linguistic sense νοῦς generally means *mind* as in perceiving and thinking. It is also used to mean "to have sense" or "be sensible," or to have one's *mind* directed to something. It might also indicate the "heart." Also, it can mean "reason," "intellect," or "thought." See Henry George Liddell and Robert Scott et al., *A Greek-English Lexicon*, (Oxford: Clarendon, 1996) s.v. νόος. Theologically, the term has developed a more spiritual meaning. When the Bible was translated into Coptic in the second century, the Greek *nous* in 1 Cor 14:14 was translated by the Coptic word *hēt*, which translates as "heart" or "mind." The Coptic word *kati* is the usual word to translate *nous*. The translator made a conscious choice of words based on the native understanding of the interconnection of the mind and heart reflected in the meaning and the use of the word *hēt*. This understanding was solidified with Christian teachings where Scripture has connected the mind, soul, and heart as defining the outcome of human behavior, thus "you shall love the Lord your God with all your heart, and with all your soul, and with all your mind, and with all your strength" (Mark 12:30; similarly Matt 22:37). See also Deut 10:12; 11:13; 11:18–20; Num 15:39; Ps 16:8–9; 26:2–3; 37:4; 64:6; 119:11; Matt 12:34; 15:18–20; Mark 7:21–23; 12:32–33; Luke 6:45.

12. The reader might notice that this understanding of evil is very distinct from the Augustinian understanding of evil as a deprivation of good. Augustine's main interlocutors in this argument were the Manicheans, who considered evil a concrete entity opposed to God. The Manichean and Platonic ideas were the main influences on Augustine's understanding of evil, thus the difference from Athanasius.

13. *ASWard*, 11, Arsenius #19.

misused, however, matter can be the source of evil—when it becomes the object of gluttony, for example. Evil is not in matter itself but rather in the relationship we have with matter and how we perceive it. There is a constant tension and fear that matter will override our senses and debilitate our reason. Matter captivates the senses.

When the soul of humans became attached to sensible things—the things that are near to their bodies and senses—they were no longer able to contemplate God. When humans were deceived by their surroundings and preferred to contemplate themselves rather than God, they forgot the power they originally had from God. Athanasius reiterates that when humans were pure they contemplated God and could see God. When they contemplated their bodies and all that belongs to the senses, they were deprived of the contemplation of divine things. It was then they knew they were naked. When humans discovered they were naked, they clung to their desires. They became comfortable in their desires; it became a habit, and they became subject to the fear of death. Because of their fear, they were not gratified with anything and they learned to commit wrong.[14]

This downward spiral of the soul and humanity is directly connected to human choice. People chose to contemplate evil rather than God and the Word. The soul has knowledge of its freedom and knows that it has the power to use the members of its body towards either good or evil. Good is what is; it has its exemplar in the God who is.[15] The divine name "I am who I am" (ἐγώ εἰμι ὁ ὤν, Exod 3:14) reveals God as "being" or reality. To contemplate God is to contemplate what is, what exists, God's name and who he is, reality itself. When one contemplates God, one contemplates goodness and what is good: "Why do you call me good? No one is good but God alone" (Mark 10:18). When one contemplates evil, one contemplates what is not, what does not exist; one contemplates the false imaginations of human thought. Athanasius explains that when the soul contemplates evil it averts its eyes from God and what is good and turns towards its lusts and what pleases it.

Athanasius gives a detailed description of how the body becomes a captive to its lusts. When they are not used in their proper way, the hands commit murder or robbery, the ears hear disobedience, "other members" are not used for procreation but for adultery, the feet shed blood, and the belly moves to drunkenness or gluttony. Though created to do good, each member of the body willfully chooses to do what is evil. The soul chooses to turn away from God and drives each member of the body to do what

14. *gent.* 3.
15. *gent.* 4.

is against its purpose of creation and against God.[16] Thus evil rests in the soul that has chosen to avert its gaze from God to satisfy its own personal pleasure, which the soul (because it is away from God) thought was good in itself. The soul, when it is away from God, and the mind, when it is not occupied with the contemplation of God, lose their ability to distinguish what is good from what is evil.

If the soul is not fortified with God's contemplation and image, it tends to gravitate toward the immediate gratification that matter offers it. One of the expressions of this immediate gratification of the senses is idolatry. The presence of evil is the work of the human mind or *nous*.[17] Athanasius explains that humanity left their imagination to its own devices until, finally, they fashioned what was in their minds and imagination in concrete form, that is, idols. People imagined idols, considering as real things that have no existence.[18] People imagined and contrived evil and invented for themselves non-existent gods and other superstitions.[19] They began deifying and giving honor to the heavens, sun, moon, and stars in addition to irrational beasts and stones.[20] They also deified their emperors and even the emperors' sons, such as the Egyptian gods Isis and Osiris, or the Roman emperors such as Antinous, who was the favorite of Emperor Hadrian.[21] Greek philosophers and Neo-Platonists crafted images of the Divine in addition to the pagan gods.[22] Though Athanasius speaks from his immediate experience within the Roman Empire, the notion of giving mortals divine status is a historical phenomenon. History tells us of rulers who gained fame by creating legends around their military bravery, political maneuvers, legendry wisdom (such as King Solomon), or other aura created either to honor the rulers or from fear of their tyranny.[23] Atha-

---

16. *gent.* 5.

17. *gent.* 7.

18. *gent.* 2.

19. *gent.* 8.

20. Deut 4:19: "And when you look up to the heavens and see the sun, the moon, and the stars, all the host of heaven, do not be led astray and bow down to them and serve them, things that the LORD your God has allotted to all the peoples everywhere under heaven."

21. *gent.* 9.

22. *gent.* 5–22.

23. Wis 14:16–18: "Then the ungodly custom, grown strong with time, was kept as a law, and at the command of monarchs carved images were worshiped. When people could not honor monarchs in their presence, since they lived at a distance, they imagined their appearance far away, and made a visible image of the king whom

nasius also criticizes family practices that deify the deceased, even to the extent of worshiping them and creating shrines in their honor.[24]

Athanasius' argument from idol worship is biblically based. Scripture is filled with stories about the people of Israel constantly straying from God and his worship to the worship of idols. The first commandment forbids the worship of idols (Exod 20:2–6), and the first violation of the commandments involved the worship of an idol—the golden calf (Exod 32). Isaiah 44 has a lengthy argument about the absurdity of idol worship: one throws half the piece of wood in fire for cooking and warmth and the other half is formed as an idol for worship. Isaiah explains that such incomprehensible behavior is because "they do not know, nor do they comprehend; for their eyes are shut, so that they cannot see, and their minds as well, so that they cannot understand" (Isa 44:18).[25] Isaiah addresses the senses—the eyes—and the mind as the two culprits in the delusion of the people of Israel. Athanasius cites another example from the Book of Wisdom, which explains that ". . . the idea of making idols was the beginning of fornication, and the invention of them was the corruption of life; for they did not exist from the beginning, nor will they last forever. For through human vanity they entered the world, and therefore their speedy end has been planned" (Wis 14:12–14). Paul makes this same argument when he writes that humans became depraved "because they exchanged the truth about God for a lie and worshiped and served the creature rather than the Creator, who is blessed forever! Amen" (Rom 1:25).[26]

The world of Athanasius was filled with idols and idol worship, whether in Scripture, in his native land of Egypt, or the Greco-Roman culture in general. As a native of Egypt, Athanasius was constantly reminded of idol worship. Pagan temples and monumental pyramids dominated

---

they honored, so that by their zeal they might flatter the absent one as though present. Then the ambition of the artisan impelled even those who did not know the king to intensify their worship."

24. *gent.* 11; and Wis 14:15: "For a father, consumed with grief at an untimely bereavement, made an image of his child, who had been suddenly taken from him; he now honored as a god what was once a dead human being, and handed on to his dependents secret rites and initiations."

25. *gent.* 14.

26. Also Wis 15:15–16: "For they thought that all their heathen idols were gods, though these have neither the use of their eyes to see with, nor nostrils with which to draw breath, nor ears with which to hear, nor fingers to feel with, and their feet are of no use for walking. For a human being made them, and one whose spirit is borrowed formed them; for none can form gods that are like themselves."

the Egyptian landscape; their ruins are still imposing to this day.[27] Pagan religions were still thriving in fourth-century Egypt, and the temples were a constant reminder to Athanasius of these biblical stories. Hellenistic culture did not fare any better than the Egyptian, where mythologies of the gods were pervasive. Athanasius explains idolatry, an evil imagination, and the invention of the mind.[28]

The desert fathers were very aware of the notion of deification of creation and created beings and opposed it vehemently. For example, when Anthony knew that his death was approaching, he gave a farewell speech to his disciples. They urged him to stay with them until the time came, but he refused, fearing his disciples would build a shrine after his death. Anthony condemned the ancient Egyptian funeral practices that glorified the body of the deceased. He also made sure that he died far away from his disciples and ordered two of his disciples to bury him and never tell anyone about his burial place.[29] He did not want his body to be glorified after his death or cause people to stray from glorifying God.

In modern times, we may not deify rulers, but the media in its various outlets substitutes the ancient rulers with figures in society that grab people's attention. Creating legends and heroes is the bread and butter of many of the media headlines. Modern media has perfected the art of speaking to the senses. Athanasius is addressing the issue where the senses are captivated by outward stimuli that override the ability of humans to use their reason for their benefit and for the glorification of God.

Athanasius says that it is through the senses that humans are able to know about the world and to comprehend the Divine. Idols, the representation in tangible form of invisible gods, respond to a human need. For Athanasius, this need was fulfilled in the incarnation, when the Word, the Son of the invisible God, became incarnate and took human form. Through the incarnation, through God being manifest, the Word revealed the Father. "All things have been handed over to me by my Father; and no one knows the Son except the Father, and no one knows the Father except the Son and anyone to whom the Son chooses to reveal him" (Matt 11:27; Luke 10:22). The fall means that humanity chose not to contemplate God. Their minds were drawn to the senses, thus they averted toward temporary and physical things as gods; but now that the Son is manifest

---

27. Athanasius mentions the Egyptian gods in *gent.* 9, 10, 24, and 25.

28. *gent.* 7.

29. Tim Vivian, trans., Athanasius, *The Life of Antony: The Coptic Life and the Greek Life*, Cistercian Studies 202 (Kalamazoo, MI: Cistercian, 2003) 248–49; *v. Anton* 90.

and has revealed the Father, humanity should not wander in all directions but center their mind, heart, and soul on the one God.[30] The incarnation was the last resort that God used to reveal himself once more to humanity. When humanity misused and misinterpreted creation as divine, and humanity worshiped creation rather than its creator, God sent revelation, the prophets, and Scripture to guide humanity to God the creator. When humanity did not comprehend God through all these means, the incarnation was the ultimate means by which the Father revealed himself through the Son.[31] Where would humanity start in its contemplation of God? How can this be achieved?

The soul has to be cleansed from all gratifications of the senses and be purified persistently until it returns to its simplicity. When the soul gravitates towards matter for immediate gratification, and its senses are captivated by matter, and its reason is debilitated, the rational soul has the ability from within, because the *nous* resides within it, to turn back and contemplate on God. But the only way to turn back is by getting rid of all matter that has affected the soul. When humanity by its own freewill chose to contemplate on matter and satisfy its senses, when the *nous* could no longer discern and chose good over evil, the image of the Word within humanity was lost, the simplicity of its creation was not found. Humanity needed the renewal of the Word's image and the likeness of God within itself; humanity needed to overcome death and corruption and to return to its simplicity. Humanity needed the incarnation.

This brings us to the second part of *On the Incarnation*. The necessity of the incarnation for human salvation, and the principle that this salvation cannot be fulfilled without the Word, who is the Son of God, are guiding themes of Athanasius' theology. Having established that humanity needs the incarnation, Athanasius raises the question: why was it the responsibility of the Word to save the world, rather than the responsibility of the Father or the Holy Spirit? Early church fathers agreed that creation of the world came through the Son, based on John epilogue: "In the beginning was the Word, and the Word was with God, and the Word was God. He was in the beginning with God. All things came into being through him, and without him not one thing came into being. What has come into being" (John 1:1–3). Creation of the world was through the Word; now that creation needed salvation and renewal, it was the Word who was to renew his creation.[32] Further, humanity was created according to God's

30. *gent.*, 23.
31. *inc.* 11, 12.
32. *inc.* 1.

image, who is the Word (Logos), and endowed with reason (*logos*) so that we might know God. The Word renewed this image within humanity so that through it humanity can once more come to know God and be in his likeness. It is only the Word who can do this.

Athanasius explains again how humanity reached the point that it needed salvation. Created in the image of the Word and endowed with reason, humans had the ability to choose between good and evil. Knowing that they could be swayed toward either side, God secured them in his garden and guarded them with a commandment: "You may freely eat of every tree of the garden; but of the tree of the knowledge of good and evil you shall not eat, for in the day that you eat of it you shall die" (Gen 2:16–17). The commandment was clear and simple: if you eat of the tree, if you transgress this simple commandment that I give you, you shall die. Humanity overstepped the commandment, chose the material over the contemplation of God, and suffered the consequence of this transgression. Humans came under the sentence of death in addition to corruption.[33] Humanity was created out of nothing; suffering death and corruption meant humanity would return to its original state of nothingness and non-existence.[34] For God alone is the "One Who Is" ("I am who I am," Exod 3:14), he is being and existence; not being with God makes us lose the essence of our existence and existence itself. In addition, humanity would not live in eternity with God.

The lovingkindness of the Word towards his creation would not accept that creation should suffer death and corruption and go to waste. But humanity kept turning to corruptible things, to matter and to the gratification of their senses, and corruption began gaining more power over them.[35] Only death can undo the corruption of humanity.[36] Only God the Word was able to recreate and renew humanity. He was the only one who could suffer and die on behalf of the humanity made in his image. But God does not die; God the Word is incorporeal, incorruptible, and immaterial.[37] He had to become incarnate to die on our behalf. We are the object of his incarnation.[38] He took a body like ours and made it his very own. When he died on the cross, we died in him. He overcame death by his

33. *inc.* 3.
34. *inc.* 4.
35. *inc.* 5.
36. *inc.* 9.
37. *inc.* 7, 8.
38. *inc.* 4.

resurrection and we rose with him. He conquered death and overturned the sentence of incorruption from which humanity suffered.[39] Death no longer has hold over humanity.

The resurrection, with the preceding events of the incarnation and crucifixion, has asserted, once and for all, that death has no power over humanity. When we speak about the incarnation we speak about the resurrection as part of the scheme of salvation, and vice versa; and we cannot speak about either without including the crucifixion. Salvation is the one theme of the incarnation, crucifixion, and resurrection.

What else did the incarnation achieve, other than overcoming death? The Word Incarnate revealed the Father to humanity. Humanity was created according to God's Image, and endowed with reason, so that we might know him. The Word renewed his image within humanity so that through him humanity can once more come to know God and be in his likeness. It is only the Word that can do this, and this could not be done without overcoming death and corruption.[40] In addition to the renewal of humanity, through the works of the incarnate Son humanity came to know and acknowledge God the creator rather than the creation they had worshiped. Through his resurrection, humanity came to worship their savior rather than heroes, the dead, or idols. The resurrection eclipsed the works of anyone else and proved that the Lord is the creator and ruler of all. The resurrection overshadowed all other deities that man had created for himself to satisfy his senses.[41]

Because Christ conquered death by the crucifixion and resurrection, destroying death through the cross, when Christians die they do not fear death, for it has no power over them anymore. Now, Christians die without fear and by conquering the fear of death become witnesses to the resurrection.[42] In the early church, when Christian men, women, and children faced martyrdom with eagerness and without fear, many of the pagan bystanders converted to Christianity, convinced that the way Christian martyrs faced death was the proof of the resurrection that Christianity preached. The resurrection is the greatest proof of victory over death, proof that Christ is alive and active in the world.[43] The resurrection of

---

39. *inc.* 8.
40. *inc.* 12–14.
41. *inc.* 15, 16.
42. *inc.* 27.
43. *inc.* 30.

Christ, the giver of life, has given life and incorruption to humanity and introduced virtue, immortality, and desire for heavenly things.[44]

For Athanasius, the incarnation and resurrection have transformed the world. Athanasius lived in an era that witnessed the Christianization of the Roman Empire and the decline of idol worship. For him this was the actualization of the incarnation. The world began to know Christ, began to know about God; and when humanity knows God they cease worshiping idols. Idol worship represents humanity's lack of the knowledge of God; humans resort to gods of their own creation to satisfy their senses. Knowing God makes us choose righteousness rather than evil. Knowing God makes us concerned with the virtue of the soul. It helps us endure temptations, persevere, be patient, despise death, and become martyrs of Christ.[45] This is what Athanasius has described in his famous quote: "He indeed, assumed humanity that we might become God."[46] This means that by the incarnation the Son restored the image of the Word and the likeness of God to humanity, which they lost by the transgression. By the incarnation he overcame corruption and death and restored immortality and granted eternal life to humanity. By the incarnation he renewed humanity and this new creation can be acquired by all through baptism. By the incarnation humanity can perceive the unseen Father and contemplate God.

Athanasius has taken us full circle in his understanding of the incarnation. His exposition of salvation started with the condition of the fallen humanity and the state of humanity before the fall. The solution to the deplorable situation to which humanity had fallen required the Word to become incarnate and save the world. His incarnation restored all that humanity had lost: the image of the Father, incorruption and victory over death, knowledge of God, and the ability to contemplate God. Humanity constantly seeks God in order to know him. Since the incarnation has restored the image of the Word, and restored reason and understanding, it has enabled humanity again to seek and know God. Being in the state of renewed creation, we have to keep purity of the soul so that the *nous* can constantly seek God.

Athanasius concludes his two part theological treatise thus:

> But for the searching and right understanding of the Scriptures there is need of a good life and a pure soul, and for Christian virtue to guide the mind to grasp, so far as human nature can, the

44. *inc.* 31.

45. *inc.* 48, 50–53.

46. *inc.* 54.

truth concerning God the Word. One cannot possibly understand the teaching of the saints unless one has a pure mind and
is trying to imitate their life. . . . Similarly, anyone who wishes
to understand the mind of the sacred writers must first cleanse
his own life, and approach the saints by copying their deeds.[47]

This concluding statement makes it clear that this theological vision is not
an abstract theological speculation but is very much part of our spiritual
journey. It starts with reading Scripture, which cannot be fully grasped, no
matter how scholarly or competent a person is, unless it is accompanied by
a "good life and a pure soul." The good life is not a life of leisure and wealth,
but rather a life of "Christian virtue" that "guide[s] the mind to grasp, so
far as human nature can, the truth concerning God the Word." He again
emphasizes the importance of a "pure mind," which guides the Christian
to a saintly life. A mind that understands not simply scriptures, but the
"mind" of Scripture, the true essence of God's words, cannot be attained
without a pure life, a life that is "cleansed." This is a practical and spiritual
theology. It speaks to the essence of our spiritual journey on earth.

The desert fathers and mothers knew Athanasius' theology and constantly read his writings. In a saying related to Abba Sisoes, an ascetic in
Scetis who moved to Abba Anthony's mountain after the latter's death, it
is written that when some Arians came to visit Sisoes, instead of arguing
with them he called on his disciple to "bring the book of Saint Athanasius
and read it." The title of the book is not given; whether it was the famous
Contra Arianos or *On the Incarnation*, it would have conveyed the message
to the Arians about the fallacy of their ideology.[48] We know of Alexandra,
a hermit and ascetic woman, who spent her time reading the Scriptures
and the "holy fathers."[49] A certain monk by the name of Daniel memorized "some of the treatises of the bishops."[50] These stories show us that
the writings of Athanasius and other theological writings were available
in the desert and were read by the desert dwellers and to their visitors. As
Scripture was read and memorized in the desert, so were the writings of
Athanasius and other theological writings circulating among the monks

47. Athanasius, *On the Incarnation: The Treatise De Incarnatione Verbi Dei*, trans.
and ed. by a religious of CSMV, rev. ed., Popular Patristics 3 (Crestwood, NY: St. Vladimir's Seminary Press, 1998) 96.

48. *ASWard*, 217, Sisoes #25.

49. *SABudge*, 96.

50. *SAChaîne*, 77, #250; *SAHartley*, 161, #250.

so that they were theologically astute. As they discussed and meditated on Scripture, they also discussed theology.

Athanasius' writings were informed by and informed the theology of the desert monastics. They understood that we were created in God's image and we lost this image by our fall. In the process, our senses overrode our minds and thinking and clouded our ability to think clearly about God and contemplate him. The incarnation and resurrection renewed God's image within us and our ability to know and contemplate God. This knowledge of God must be accompanied by a pure life issuing from pure thoughts, lest our reasoning be clouded and our senses drag us down again. The spiritual journey is the continuous struggle between the mind (*nous*), which is able to comprehend and contemplate God, and the senses, which want to be satisfied with earthly pleasures. Immersion in the pleasures of the world and the senses results in fear of death. The purer our life is, the purer our thoughts will be, and the more the senses will find pleasure in God rather than earthly pleasures. The holy life is a life in which the senses have their fullest pleasure by being in the presence of God. The desert fathers and mothers understood the depth of the theology of the incarnation. Their lives became the actualization of the incarnation and resurrection. They actualized the image of the Word, who is the Image of God, within them so as not to lose God's image within them and again fall into the state humanity was in before the incarnation. They fully embraced the power of renewal the incarnation had granted humanity. They lived to fulfill this vision within themselves. They worked tirelessly towards purity of thought and directed the senses to live in the constant presence of God. They lived heaven on earth.

As if Athanasius anticipated the skepticism of the human mind towards the spiritual and the objection that such purity of thought and the gratification of the senses with the Divine were unattainable, he wrote the *Life of Anthony* as a demonstration of the power of the incarnation and the resurrection to grant humanity renewal. It is to this text that we now turn.

3

Be Imitators of Me, as I Am of Christ

The Life of Anthony

I am not writing this to make you ashamed, but to admonish you as my beloved
children. For though you might have ten thousand guardians in Christ, you do
not have many fathers. Indeed, in Christ Jesus I became your father through the
gospel. I appeal to you, then, be imitators of me.

1 COR 4:14–16

Let no one despise your youth, but set the believers an example
in speech and conduct, in love, in faith, in purity.

1 TIM 4:12

Be imitators of me, as I am of Christ.

1 COR 11:1

SAINT ATHANASIUS WROTE THE *Life of Anthony* so that readers would
"emulate his character, for Antony's life provides an excellent model
for monks as they practice their ascetic discipline."[1] Athanasius goes on

---

1. Tim Vivian, trans., Athanasius, *The Life of Antony: The Coptic Life and the Greek
Life*, Cistercian Studies 202 (Kalamazoo, MI: Cistercian, 2003) 52 (C). *v. Anton.* preface. "C" refers to the Coptic *Life*, "G" to the Greek *Life*. "The word 'monk' in the *Life*
usually indicates a solitary. . . . It never indicates a person living in a cenobium or large

to warn the reader, "Do not, therefore, be skeptical about what you have heard concerning Antony from those who have spoken to you."[2] The modern reader should also take this advice to heart. Anthony and his biographer have set the bar too high, for this is exactly what a model life is supposed to portray. We are all called to imitate Christ (1 Cor 1:11), knowing very well that none of us will achieve the sanctity of or be equal to the Son of God. But that has not deterred anyone from looking to Christ and emulating him. The power of Anthony's model is that he is a normal human being who attempted to follow the biblical call to imitate Christ and follow the teachings of Scripture. We can think of Anthony's life like a book with the title *Practical Interpretation of Scripture*. It is the story of an ancient Christian who asked the same questions that modern Christians ask: How do I imitate Christ? How do I live a life of holiness? Anthony's life is an answer to these questions and portrays the struggle, downfalls, and victories of a Christian in his journey toward God. Anthony took his journey very seriously and with a dedicated mind. His journey is biblically and theologically based. We are going to follow his journey in this chapter.

"Set the believers an example" (1 Tim 4:12): Anthony's Life Journey

Anthony Described

The *Life of Anthony* gives us only a hint about Anthony's physiognomy. He was of average stature and there was nothing outstanding or distinguished about his physical appearance. Later, when his fame spread, the people who came to visit would recognize him among the crowd of other monks. Athanasius explains that people would come to him "as though drawn by

---

monastery. The life does suggest, however, that monks lived in semi-anchorite communities . . . and that Antony was their spiritual father. Also in the *Life*, *monastêrion* usually indicates a monastic dwelling, a 'hermitage', and not a cenobium or large monastery in the Pachomian or modern sense of the word . . ." (53 n. 4). As mentioned in chapter 1, solitary monasticism is the model that has endured in Coptic/Egyptian monasticism. Even cenobiticism preserved some of the solitary aspects within its model. The Pachomian monks worked and ate in complete silence and the Shenoute model preserved the anchoritic model parallel to the communal model within their monasteries.

2. Ibid., 52 (C); *v. Anton.* preface.

his eyes" or his face.[3] Athanasius explains that his outward appearance reflected the state of his inner soul, which was due to "the makeup of his character and in the purity of his soul" and how he was different in his "character and conduct."[4] "Because his soul was tranquil," Athanasius elaborates, "it produced for [him] imperturbable outer senses so that because of his joyful soul his face was filled with joy and from the movements of his body others perceived and understood the stability or quality of soul as it were, as it is written: 'A glad heart makes a cheerful countenance but it is sorrowful when there is sadness.'"[5] Athanasius provides his readers with biblical examples to show how the soul betrays the inner self: This is how Jacob figured out that Laban was scheming against him, and how Samuel recognized David from the sparkle in his eyes. We do not need biblical proof, for we have all experienced the ability to know and understand people from their eyes and body language.

Anthony was also patient and "humble in soul." He revered and respected everyone who visited him. If any of his visitors said something edifying, he would acknowledge it. All his visitors came to learn from Anthony, but he took it as an opportunity to learn from them. Athanasius concludes his description by saying that "his soul was calm" and "his thoughts were joyous" and he "was never sad because his heart rejoiced always."[6] The inner tranquility and joy manifested outwardly indicates Anthony's spiritual journey was on the right track. It was the outcome of his continuous self-examination, which led to a pure soul and a calm state of mind. He reached the inner harmony of our first parents in paradise. The inner calm and joy that characterized Anthony was the result of a long journey that started with his response to God's call.

Anthony Responds to the Call

As was mentioned in chapter 1, Saint Anthony was born in Egypt from Christian parents.[7] The biography tells us that when his parents died he was "thinking" and "reflecting" on how the apostles followed the Savior and how the early Christians sold all their possessions when they received

3. Ibid., 200 (C) and 201(G); v. Anton. 67.4.
4. Ibid., 200 (C) and 201 (G); v. Anton. 67.5.
5. Prov 15:13; Vivian, *Life of Antony*, 200 (C); v. Anton. 67.
6. Vivian, *Life of Antony*, 200, 202 (C) and 201, 203 (G); v. Anton. 67.8.
7. Please refer to chapter 1 under the heading "Saint Antony the Great (251–356)."

the call (see Acts 4:34–35).[8] At this point of his life he might have relished the idea of enjoying his newly acquired wealth and indulging in all the pleasures he could afford. But Anthony was thoughtful and reflective on what to do with his life.

When he entered the church he heard the Gospel message from Matthew 19:21 and 6:34 calling for perfection in the Christian calling and explaining that the means to obtain this was to renounce one's possessions and follow Christ for the sake of the heavenly treasure. The *Life* says that Anthony "listened attentively to the readings from Scripture."[9] Scripture was the means by which Anthony heard God's voice speaking to him, and he took the message very seriously—so seriously that he immediately responded when he received the call to renounce everything and follow Christ. From the very start of Anthony's quest we notice the centrality of Scripture in his life. Anthony's call was biblically based and also in answer to his personal quest. The message of renunciation to follow Christ is difficult and demanding; he could have easily ignored it, just as many of us have ignored or been inattentive to many of God's messages. But he understood that if he ignored the message he would be silencing the work of the Spirit within him. This is one of the important aspects of desert spirituality: being attentive to the work of the Spirit within us. Responding to the work of the Spirit is an acknowledgment by a person that he or she accepts God's work within him- or herself. It is an invitation for God to dwell within us. Silencing the work and word of the God within us causes many regrets.

The Spirit led Anthony in his spiritual journey. The reader accompanies Anthony in his gradual discovery of the way. It is uncharted territory. Before this time, Christians who wanted to live the life of renunciation beyond their hometowns usually lived a solitary life on the outskirts of their village. Anthony's first step was that he "devoted himself to ascetic discipline in front of his home."[10] Athanasius does not provide any insight into this move. Was it caution? Was it hesitancy? Or was it wise to take things slowly until he discovered himself? The second step is a sign of progress: he moved to the outskirts of his village close to a hermit already living there. The third step was toward discipleship and taking advice from the hermit.

8. Vivian, *Life of Antony*, 59; *v. Anton.* 2.1.

9. Ibid., 57 (G); *v. Anton.* 1.1.

10. Ibid., 61(G); *v. Anton.* 3.1.

Anthony's Spiritual Formation

Anthony did not limit his spiritual quest to the experiences of this one hermit. The *Life* informs us that "if he heard about someone who was serious about following good practices, he would go and search out that person like the wise honeybee and would not return to his own place until he had seen that person."[11] This was active discipleship in which one goes and seeks advice of a person more experienced in the spiritual life. Anthony also observed carefully every person he came to know. He carefully "observed the excellence of each person's zeal and ascetic discipline: he observed the graciousness of one and the intense prayer of another; he meditated on one's lack of anger and another's love for humanity; he came to understand how one passed the night in prayerful vigil and another studied the Bible. He marveled at one's patient endurance and another's fasting and sleeping on the ground; he carefully observed one's gentleness and the patience of another. He kept in his thought the devotion to Christ and the love for one another that they all shared."[12] These two excerpts describe two different types of discipleship that were formative in the life of Anthony. The first type is more active; Anthony intentionally visited a seasoned Christian ascetic or a person "following good practices" and inquired specifically about their inner way of life. He probably also inquired about advice regarding his inner struggles or his own spiritual growth. The second type of discipleship is more observant and requires humility and love. Anthony would observe the virtues and practices of all with whom he came in contact and learned from them. When everyone came to ask and learn from him, he took the opportunity to learn from everyone. This speaks also to Anthony's humility. If a person thinks himself better than anyone else, the attitude will be that of criticism rather than learning.

If someone cannot find a spiritual director, we can grow spiritually through "observant" and "contemplative" discipleship. There is no excuse in not finding spiritual examples; they surround us all our lives. This type of discipleship is a cornerstone of desert spirituality. It is more internal and contemplative in contrast to the first type, in which one seeks someone out to engage in conversation about one's spiritual struggle. The more contemplative discipleship seeks virtue in everyone one meets. No matter who that person is, there is always a virtue from which one can learn. This can be a type of meditation, in which one contemplates on the virtue of a

11. Ibid., 60 (C); *v. Anton.* 3.
12. Ibid., 63, 65 (G); *v. Anton.* 4.1.

colleague, a neighbor, a store teller, a member of the church congregation, a Good Samaritan on the road, or a family member in order to learn how they acquired their distinctive virtue. This spiritual exercise is not only beneficial for our spiritual growth; it also makes us observe Christ and the image of Christ in each person we interact with. It is a free school for learning how to acquire virtue. It helps one develop an attitude in one's life of seeking what is good in people rather than criticizing them. It is an exercise in acquiring the virtue of love. This type of discipleship is available to every person, wherever you are and wherever you go.

A practical example of this type of discipleship and its implications is found in the story of Abba Macarius the Egyptian and a pagan priest. Abba Macarius was walking with his disciple and asked his disciple to go ahead of him. The disciple met a pagan priest and spoke with him in harsh words. The pagan priest gave the disciple a beating and left him half dead. When Abba Macarius met the same priest later, Macarius greeted him with kind words and complimented him on his hard work. The priest replied, "What good do you see in me that you honor me by speaking to me? . . . Your greeting made me think and I realized that you have a great god on your side. But when another monk, a wicked one, met me he cursed me. I beat him within an inch of his life."[13] The kind words of Macarius were a turning point for the priest. He asked to remain with Macarius and later was baptized and became a monk. Abba Macarius comments on the story by saying, "One evil word causes other good words to be bad, just as one good word causes other evil words to become pleasing."[14]

Abba Macarius' spiritual training in finding the good in every person is reflected in this episode. We have to think inwardly about the virtues of our neighbor because "what comes out of the mouth proceeds from the heart" (Matt 15:18). He commended the priest's hard work. The disciple's response, on the other hand, also reflects the way he was thinking; he could not see any good in the pagan priest. In this story, the same priest was met by two people: one saw the bad in him and was beaten, while the other saw the good in him and was able to change the priest's life. It is a powerful spiritual exercise that changes not only the life of the person practicing it, but also the life of the person witnessing it. It is a powerful witness to the Christian faith.

13. Tim Vivian, trans., *Saint Macarius, the Spiritbearer: Coptic Texts Relating to Saint Macarius the Great*, St. Vladimir's Popular Patristics (Crestwood, NY: St. Vladimir's Seminary Press, 2004) 60.

14. Ibid.

Temptations, Purity of Thought, and the Incarnation

The second phase of Anthony's life was one of temptations. As Christ was tempted by the devil before starting his ministry (Matt 4:1–11), so also was Anthony tempted by the devil. His faith and the truth of his response to the calling were tested. This is the description of Anthony's temptation:

> First, he [the Devil] attempted to lead him away from his ascetic discipline, filling him with memories of his possessions, his guardianship of his sister, the intimacy of his family, love of money, love of honor, the pleasure that comes from eating various kinds of food, and the other indulgences of life, and finally the difficulty of living virtuously and the great suffering that that entails. He demonstrated for Antony the body's weakness and the long life ahead of him. In short, he raised up in Antony's mind a great dust cloud of thoughts, wanting to separate him from his ability to make correct choices.[15]

The quote reveals that the essence of this temptation was a targeting of the thoughts to cloud the mind from making the correct decision. This is very much connected with Athanasius' understanding of our humanity and the cause of our fall. The same strategy was used against our first parents in paradise, against Christ on the mountain of temptation, against Anthony at the beginning of his spiritual journey, and is still used against every human being attempting to live a life in imitation of Christ. It all starts with the thoughts and the clouding of the thoughts. As humans we have common weaknesses, yet each is more vulnerable at specific points related to our character, which shapes the weakness of the individual. For Anthony it was possessions and money, thoughts about his sister, honor, and pleasures of the senses regarding food and life indulgences. All these were targeted to make him lose hope in his ability to live a virtuous life so as to turn him away from his ascetic discipline. An attack on the specific weakness of a person is in reality an attack on the larger goal the person wants to attain. Thus every thought has to be analyzed with regard to the small picture and then with regard to what it means in the larger picture of what makes us who we are.

Anthony's temptation was focused not only on his renunciation of his possessions, but also the "memories" of his possessions. Renouncing one's possessions is not enough to grant liberty of thought; one has also to renounce the memories of these possessions. If one cannot renounce the memories, renunciation is worthless and has not fulfilled its aim. The

15. Vivian, *Life of Antony*, 65–67 (G); *v. Anton.* 5.1–3.

thought of possessions and money was considered a temptation to Anthony because he was committed to complete renunciation. Renunciation is an act of strong faith and trust that God will provide.

Possessions and money are temptations even to those who are not aiming for an ascetic life. At the time of the writing of this book the world economy is suffering because people have spent beyond their means. Families are suffering from a debt crisis. It is natural to own, but it is not natural to hoard. Anthony's temptations are more relevant to our society than ever before. When the thought of possessions is obsessive, it is a temptation that clouds the thoughts and makes a person make wrong decisions. Many people were tempted and their thoughts totally overridden by the thought of accumulating possessions and by lusting for pleasures beyond their means. The decision-making of every single person in the society led to a world economic crisis. Athanasius' theology and the desert spirituality that recognized the power of thoughts and the virtue of renunciation are doubtlessly relevant to our daily lives today.

Though Anthony's temptations were specific to him, we still share some aspects of them. In Anthony's case, thoughts about his sister were directly related to his life story. He had placed his sister in a house with other women who wanted to live a life according to the Scriptures and this caused some worry since he was her guardian after his parents' death. Such thoughts might be considered natural. But if they become obsessive, then they move from the natural to the category of temptation since they start to cloud the mind. Abba Amoun lived in Nitria for twenty-two years after separating from his wife. But while most of the desert fathers did not see their family members, as in the case of Anthony, Amoun used to see his wife twice per year. Thus the issue is not in the family but in the distraction that the thought of family can cause. We all know hundreds of people we meet throughout our lifetime. Most of them are part of our spiritual journey and each one of them can be a means to bring us closer to God. Only a few cause us spiritual turmoil. It is these few that this discussion is addressing. In most of the narratives and sayings, the desert fathers and mothers examine a thought to discern whether it is "natural" or whether, because of its frequency, it threatens their spiritual balance and tranquility.

Anthony struggled with the "love of honor." "Pride," "vainglory," and "arrogance" are words we will encounter many times; they express a constant struggle of the desert fathers. The difficulty with thoughts of pride is keeping the balance between too much self-confidence and destructive self-deprecation. Humility is a major spiritual struggle that is mentioned in various forms in the sayings of the desert dwellers.

Anthony struggled with the temptation of indulging in life's pleasures, including food. The church fathers clearly understood the relationship between the body and the spirit. In the Sermon on the Mount, Christ speaks about fasting immediately after he teaches the people how to pray to "Our Father in heaven" (see Matt 6:15–16). This is no coincidence. As we previously discussed, Clement wrote to his fellow Christians of the second and third centuries advising them to use food frugally and consume it primarily for sustenance. Fasting has always been a main component of Christian spirituality. Again, Anthony was aiming at a very high ascetic practice of fasting and renunciation, but his struggle with temptations is relevant to each one of us when we sit to have a meal. The question to be asked is: Is our thought about food obsessive? Is it clouding our decision-making, urging us to take wrong choices? If so, then we are struggling with temptations very similar to Anthony's.

The narrative of Christ's temptation in Matthew 4 is central to desert spirituality. After Christ prayed in the solitude of the desert while fasting for forty days and forty nights, the "tempter," who is also the "enemy," or Satan, came to test him. Since Christ is the model that Christians follow, when Christians start their spiritual path with prayer and fasting and other ascetic and spiritual exercises they should expect the adversary to come and test them. Christ was tempted, Anthony was tempted, and every one of us who takes the spiritual life seriously will be tempted.

The temptations in Matthew 4 represent what hinders us from loving God. In the passage quoted above there is a list of what might undermine Anthony's love for his creator and separate him from God: possessions, family ties, indulgence in worldly pleasures, and losing hope of living a life of virtue because of the difficulty of following the commandments. Athanasius analyzes Anthony's list of temptations as a war of thoughts that can prevent Anthony from making correct choices. Managing thoughts is a major struggle for the desert fathers and mothers. And not only for the desert monks: it has also been the concern of major spiritual writers and is relevant to our spiritual well-being regardless of our life status. Understanding the source of one's thoughts and managing them are of vital importance to desert dwellers, and to us too.

The theological dimension of the work of the mind and the generation of thoughts is addressed in St. Athanasius' treatises discussed in chapter 2 of this book. According to Athanasius' *Against the Gentiles*, humans were created with reason, intellect, and knowledge, which enabled them to know and contemplate God. The constant contemplation of the Word, who is the image of the Father, after whose image humanity was made, is the means for humans to preserve purity. Purity of thought is not an intellectual exercise that affects only the mind; it also affects the physical purity of humans and vice versa. Whatever hinders the constant contemplation of God is a temptation; if we do not overcome it, it will separate us from God. The preoccupation of the mind with what does not promote our knowledge of God, with the senses and their pleasures, with possessions or worldly concerns, is a distraction that affects the purity of the body, soul, mind, and thoughts. Anthony closely examined the thoughts that detracted him from being in the constant presence of God. The desert fathers and mothers followed his example to regain the purity of thought. Purity of mind cannot be attained without the incarnation, crucifixion, and resurrection. The resurrection overcame death and granted humanity renewal to a state even more elevated than that of Adam. Without the incarnation and the resurrection and its power of renewal, desert spirituality cannot attain its spiritual goal of purity of thought.

Overcoming Temptations

The "Enemy" saw Anthony's weakness and assailed his thoughts all the more. Athanasius many times calls the devil or Satan the "Enemy," envisioning a "contest" or a "combat" between the desert dwellers and the devil, the Enemy whom we want to overcome as Christ has overcome death and its sting (see 1 Cor 15:55). The Letter to the Ephesians makes this image very clear: "Put on the whole armor of God, so that you may be able to stand against the wiles of the devil. For our struggle is not against enemies of blood and flesh, but against the rulers, against the authorities, against the cosmic powers of this present darkness, against the spiritual forces of evil in the heavenly places" (6:11–12).

The language of "Satan," the "devil," and "evil" might not be popular language and modern readers tend to dismiss it, but it is abundant in desert and monastic literature and is also the language of Scripture. Though modern readers usually gloss over verses that mention the "devil" or "Satan," it is a fact that in the New Testament "Satan" is mentioned thirty-six times, "evil" is mentioned seventy-eight times, and the "devil" is mentioned thirty-four times.[16] Satan is identified as the snake who deceived Adam and Eve, "that ancient serpent, who is called the devil and Satan, the deceiver of the whole world" (Rev 12:9; see Gen 3:1–15).[17] Satan

16. Horst Balz and Gerhard Schneider, eds., *Exegetical Dictionary of the New Testament*, 3 vols. (Grand Rapids: Eerdmans, 1990) 3:134, 234.

17. Ibid., 3:234.

is called the prince of demons who reigns over an empire that opposes the divine power (Matt 12:26–28). But Christ became incarnate and destroyed the work of the devil (1 John 3:8) and gained victory over the demons (Matt 12:28). When Christ exorcised people possessed with demons it was a sign that the kingdom of God had come and kingdom of Satan had been ended (Matt 12:28).[18] Christ called Peter "Satan" when he acted as a stumbling block (Mark 8:33). Following Christ's example, in the literature of the desert fathers when someone acts as a stumbling block he or she is often called "Satan."

"Satan" in desert literature also personifies the vices. So, for example, we read about the "demon" of fornication or of anger. Let's suggest an example that translates the personification of vices in modern terms. When you drive during rush hour and are delayed for any reason, you might well lose your patience, become angry, and even experience "road rage." Almost everyone has experienced the stress of rush hour traffic. If the desert fathers had driven their cars during rush hour and experienced road rage, they might have labeled the cause of their anger the "rush hour demon." The difference is that we do not use this language anymore and we do not address the cause of our anger, we just call it "road rage." The desert fathers and mothers used language shaped by Scripture and it shaped their worldview. Because their spiritual practice included memorization of large portions of Scripture, its language became the language they used in their everyday life.

In the *Life of Anthony*, the Enemy is constantly bombarding Anthony with thoughts. Anthony counterattacks with prayer and Scripture. It is a spiritual warfare at the level of thoughts, one thought confronting another. The Enemy sends a thought that distracts Anthony, and Anthony fights back with a thought focusing on God and contemplating the Divine; that is, with prayer. The inner struggle of thoughts within a person shows the need for praying without ceasing. The exhortation to pray without ceasing (1 Thess 5:17) is addressed to all Christians. Its import is that it purifies the mind and the heart by the constant contemplation of God. The more the mind and heart are preoccupied with the matters of God, the less there is the possibility for distraction by other, destructive thoughts. This is the essence of spiritual renunciation. This is what it means to go to the inner desert seeking tranquility and peace, the essence of withdrawing from distraction; it is the attempt to purify the mind and heart with the contemplation of God. Contemplation renews the spirit through continued purification.

18. Ibid.

Anthony modeled his struggle against the devil after Christ's temptation in the wilderness in Matthew 4. Often the thoughts he uses to coun-
terattack the Enemy are biblical verses modeling Christ's response to Satan
in the wilderness. In one of the struggles with demons, Anthony responds,
"Even if you do worse things to me nothing will separate me from the
love of Christ Jesus my Lord. For it is written in the Psalms: 'Though war
should rise up against me, my heart will not be afraid.'"[19] Scripture is central in desert spirituality; it is the source of contemplation and prayer and
an arsenal for contesting unwanted thoughts. As Christ's temptation in the
wilderness ended with Christ's triumph over Satan, in the final episode
Anthony cries to God, "'Where are you? Why did you not appear at the
beginning so you could stop my sufferings?' And a voice came to him:
'Anthony, I was here, but I waited to see you struggle. And now, since you
persevered and were not defeated, I will be a helper to you always.'"[20] Anthony overcomes his temptations through Christ, which he acknowledges
by standing in prayer, thanking God for his help.

On another occasion, Anthony gave the following advice to his
disciples: have faith in the Lord and love him, have pure thoughts, pray
without ceasing, say the Psalms before going to sleep and when you wake
up "to learn by heart all the precepts of Scriptures," and contemplate on
the works of the saints as encouragement to follow their path.[21] This succinct advice summarizes Anthony's method of conquering temptations
and preserving his thoughts in God. Most of this advice is practical and
helps keep the thoughts pure. When the heart is constantly contemplating on the words of the Psalms whether one is going to sleep or rising
up, when the first thing one calls to mind are the words of the Psalms,
then the heart is trained to constantly contemplate God. The exercise of
memorizing Scripture preserves the thoughts because this exercise makes
the mind constantly contemplate God. Memorizing Scripture also instills
in one's heart the divine precepts and leads a person to make decisions
accordingly.

Anthony also spoke about the importance of daily self-examination.
He interprets the command "Do not let the sun go down on your anger"
(Eph 4:26) as follows:

---

19. Vivian, *Life of Antony*, 80 (C); *v. Anton.* 9. The two verses Anthony refers to are
Rom 8:35 and Ps 27:3.

20. Ibid., 85 (G); *v. Anton.* 10. 2–3.

21. Ibid., 175–77 (G); *v. Anton.* 55.2, 3.

This saying, he told them, applied to every commandment so that the sun should not go down not only on anger but on every sin that we have committed, "For it is good and profitable," [he said,] "for the sun not to pass judgment on us for a daytime evil, nor the moon find fault with us for a nighttime sin, or even for an evil thought. In order for this practice to save us, then, it is good for us to listen to the Apostle, for he says, 'Examine yourselves, and test yourselves daily.'"[22]

Anthony suggests that daily self-examination will make the sinner stop sinning out of embarrassment. The one who has not found much to be embarrassed by will not boast, not be negligent, and not condemn his neighbor. Anthony encourages people to write down their sins to contemplate "the movements of his soul."[23] This exercise confronts a person with his own actions and sins, and his deeds and sins will condemn him and cause personal embarrassment. This personal embarrassment will make the person not repeat his actions again because it is like reporting the sin to another person. Once the sin is written down, the mind stops thinking about it; hopefully, this will help the person not repeat the sin again. Anthony concludes: "So let this practice of writing things down take the place of our fellow ascetics' eyes so that, being as embarrassed to have our sins written down as seen, we will not think in our hearts about anything evil at all."[24]

The careful examination of the self is a guiding spiritual principle and a very important aspect of desert spirituality. It is a means of knowing oneself, understanding the movement of the soul, and analyzing the *nous*, that is, one's thoughts. It is the means of examining and guarding the soul's and heart's thoughts to see if they are conforming to God. It is the means of not letting one's thoughts stray from God, which according to Athanasius' *Against the Gentiles* is the cause of Adam's fall. The fall tarnished God's image in humanity. Self-examination is the means of preserving the image of God renewed in the person by the incarnation and resurrection.

Athanasius concludes the description of Anthony's struggle with a reference to the incarnation: "For working with Anthony was the Lord, who for us bore flesh and gave the body victory over the Devil so that each of those who struggle like Anthony can say 'It is not I but the grace of God that is in me.'"[25] It is through the incarnation that the body gained

22. Ibid., 176 (C); *v. Anton.* 55.
23. Ibid., 177 (G); *v. Anton.* 55.9.
24. Ibid., 179 (G); *v. Anton.* 55.12.
25. Ibid., 69 (G); *v. Anton.* 5.6.

victory over death and the devil, and it is through God's grace that we are able to conquer. Every aspect of desert spirituality embodies the renewal granted to humanity by the incarnation. The incarnation is the renewal of creation, the renewal of humanity, and the renewal of the image of God within humanity.

Anthony's Asceticism

Ascetic living was part of the Christian ethos of the early church, as we learned from the writings of Clement and Origen. Living an ascetic, simple life was part of renunciation that was expected of all those who followed Christ, regardless of their station in life. The monastics took asceticism to a higher level. Monastics want to minimize all distraction to their spiritual and prayer life and it is not unusual for ascetics, whether Christian or non-Christian, to minimize and control the needs of the body to the greatest extent.[26] Ascetics understand the direct correlation between the spirit and the body. Christian asceticism balances the soul and the body to reach the state of perfect harmony. If the body indulges in excessive pleasures the soul is suffocated and the body may be weakened to the extent it affects the health and the function of the whole person. Asceticism is the art of reaching a spiritual and healthy balance between the soul and the body.

The basis for Christian asceticism is biblical. Athanasius explains that we are to "walk not according to the flesh but according to the Spirit" (see Rom 8:4).[27] Walking according to the Spirit requires diligence, which meant that Anthony had to be constantly practicing asceticism. For Anthony, asceticism was for the sake of combating the thoughts of the Enemy. Anthony usually slept on the ground. He did not sleep the entire night but spent most of it in prayer. He ate bread and salt once per day, after sunset, since Scripture says that to be strong in the spirit one must be weak in the flesh (2 Cor 12:10).[28]

Based on his spiritual experience, Anthony says, "The mind of the soul is strong when the pleasures of the body are weak."[29] "The mind (*nous*) of the soul" is the intellectual aspect, the rational dimension of the soul that turns towards God in contemplation. As Athanasius explains in *Against the Gentiles*, it is when humanity by its own free will chose to

26. Richard Finn, *Asceticism in the Greco-Roman World* (Cambridge University Press, 2009) 9–33.

27. Vivian, *Life of Antony*, 73 (G); *v. Anton.* 7.1.

28. Ibid., 75, 77 (G); *v. Anton.* 7.

29. Ibid., 74 (C); *v. Anton.* 7.

contemplate matter and the senses rather than God that the *nous* could no longer discern and chose good over evil. Thus the *nous*, "the mind of the soul," must not be diverted by the pleasures of the body lest it be distracted from contemplating God. Humanity lost the simplicity of its creation when the attraction to the senses overrode the faculties of the *nous*. The incarnation renewed the Word's Image and the likeness of God within us, enabling us again to contemplate God, "seeing that you have stripped off the old self with its practices and have clothed yourselves with the new self, which is being renewed in knowledge according to the image of its creator" (Col 3:9, 10). The newness of life bestowed on humanity by the resurrection distinguishes Christian ascetic practices from other philosophical approaches to asceticism.

The *Life* describes Anthony's first ascetic practices as follows: "This was Antony's first contest against the devil; or, rather, through Antony it was the triumph of the Saviour, who 'condemned sin in the flesh.'"[30] Christian ascetic practices are "the triumph of the Saviour." Christian asceticism is neither a cause for boasting nor to prove heroic self-endurance. Nor is it for the torture of the body. It is a manifestation of the power of the incarnation within ascetic lives, the power of the new creation within us by the power of the resurrection. The spiritual journey is to live the newness of life, which is strengthened and preserved by balancing, through asceticism, the mind of the soul with the body's tendencies toward pleasure.

A New Beginning Every Day

The *Life* speaks about another spiritual principle that Anthony followed: "He did not wish to measure the path to virtuous thought by time or by withdrawal from the world for its own sake, but by love and intention. So he did not count time that had passed, but each day, as though beginning his ascetic discipline anew made great progress, meditating continually on what the Apostle says: 'We are forgetting what lies behind and straining forward to what lies ahead'" (see Phil 3:13).[31] Anthony did not measure his progress by time but rather by the quality of time. He would not boast about how many years he spent in the desert but rather about how he spent every moment of those years. An example of one moment well spent is that of one of the criminals hanging on the cross, who with one statement of repentance secured a place in paradise (see Luke 23:42–43).

30. Ibid., 73 (G); *v. Anton.* 7.1.
31. Ibid., 4, 76 (C); *v. Anton.* 7.

Going to the desert and withdrawing from the world is not an aim in itself but rather a way to purity of heart for the contemplation of God, which is driven by love for God. Love for God, rather than boasting, should be the true intention for withdrawing since living in the desert is not a virtue. What you do in the desert is what defines the life of virtue.

Another principle is that every day is a new beginning. The implications of this principle are far reaching. Living with this principle is the best remedy against despair. Anthony mentions that the Enemy tested him with thoughts of despair concerning "the difficulty of living virtuously," the difficulty of the way, and "the great suffering that that entails." Anthony warns the monks not to grow "faint-hearted in their labors nor say, 'We have spent a long time in ascetic discipline.' Instead, as though we were beginning anew each day, let each of us increase in fervor."[32] The spiritual journey lasts a lifetime and it is easy to lose focus, get frustrated, and fall into despair during the long journey. But the thought that every day is a new beginning provides hope of overcoming the blunders of the previous day and previous sins that debilitate the faithful. This idea is strengthened by the theology of the incarnation, by which we have gained newness of life. Each day reminds us of the resurrection. Each day is a new beginning because with the resurrection there is new life, new beginning, and a new creation. "Abbâ Moses asked Abbâ Sylvanus, saying, 'Is it possible for a man to make a beginning each day?' And he said unto him, 'If he be a man who is a worker it is possible for him to make a beginning every day.'"[33] Hope in desert spirituality will be discussed in the last chapter.

Spiritual Maturity

Anthony went to the "inner mountain," Mount Pispir, east of the River Nile. At Mount Pispir he was in seclusion and his struggle with the demons intensified. He remained twenty years at Mount Pispir before he claimed he was able to conquer demons.[34] Anthony started his monastic lifestyle in his early twenties and it was not until the age of thirty-five that the serious struggle with demons started. Thus Anthony reached spiritual maturity around his mid-fifties. The *Life of Anthony*, as well as the lives of other saints, informs us that spirituality takes a long time and requires patience and perseverance. Spiritual maturity also requires time of seclusion.

32. Ibid., 7 (G); *v. Anton.* 16.3.
33. *SABudge*, 204, #240.
34. Vivian, *Life of Antony*, 84 and 90 (C); *v. Anton.* 10 and 14.

Moses remained in the wilderness of Midian for "many days," meaning a long time, before he received the call from the burning bush that he was to "bring the people, the Israelites, out of Egypt" (Exod 2:23 and 3:10). It took forty years for the people of Israel to see the fulfillment of the promise; they could not enter the promised land until the next generation was ready to face the enemy. John the Baptist remained in the wilderness until at least the age of twenty-seven before he was ready to proclaim his message of repentance. God prepares a person for years for the mission or calling that he or she is to fulfill. Spiritual maturity requires a lot of patience and waiting. It takes a person twelve years of school and four years of college to be qualified to get a job. Spiritual maturity requires an equal if not greater amount of time for training. Twenty-first-century people have become accustomed to quick movement, instant decision-making, being constantly connected, and expecting immediate gratification. Spirituality does not follow the rules of modernity. Spirituality is not a quick fix; it gives no instant gratification, but requires perseverance and patience. Modernity and spirituality collide. Each has its rules; spirituality does not comply with the rules of modernity. This might be one of the greatest challenges the modern temperament faces; spirituality requires patience and does not yield quick results, which frustrates the modern person.

Fig 19: The cave of Anthony. (Photo by author)

Fig 19a: General view of the mountain where the cave of Anthony is located with the view of St. Anthony's Monastery at the foot of the mountain. (Photo by author)

Fig 20: The water spring that was the source of water for Anthony, and for the monastery until the 1990s. (Photo by author)

First Monastic Dwellings

People who heard about Anthony were astonished that he remained in complete seclusion for twenty years; other ascetics at the outskirt of their towns were often seen and people spoke to them frequently. His seclusion pricked their conscience and most probably their curiosity as well. Anthony's withdrawal to the desert was a silent and powerful witness. Eventually people knocked down his door and he was forced to come out to meet and speak with them. Athanasius describes Anthony as having a healthy appearance that was not affected by rigorous fasting or lack of exercise. Those who knocked at his door and saw him when he first appeared from his seclusion "found him just as they had known him before he withdrew. They saw that the thought of his soul was pure, and he was not sorrowful and suffering. He had neither been disturbed by pleasures nor had laughter or sadness ruled over him. Moreover, when he saw the crowd, he was not disturbed, nor was he delighted when they greeted him. Rather, he maintained complete equilibrium because reason was guiding him."[35]

Athanasius connects physical equilibrium with the mental one. He, a confined person with no exercise who was exhausted by fasting and fighting demons, was remarkably composed and not disturbed even by people smashing down his door. The source of his equilibrium was that "reason" was guiding him, which is also connected with the "thoughts of his soul." This points to his inner state of mind: his thoughts were pure and his mind was guiding his senses and his desires. Athanasius insinuates that this "reason" that leads us to goodness is Christ himself, or the Logos (a Greek word meaning "reason" or "thought").[36] This is the paradisal state of our first parents before the fall. The downfall occurred when people let their imagination and work of the mind be controlled by their senses rather than reason, for then the mind contrives evil. In short, Athanasius describes Anthony emerging from his twenty-year seclusion as a person who reached the ultimate goal of humanity and attained the power of the

35. Ibid., 92 (C); *v. Anton.* 14.

36. G. J. M. Bartelink, trans., Athanasius, *Vie d'Antoine*, Sources chrétiennes 400 (Paris: Editions du Cerf, 1994) 175 n. 1. As the Logos guided Anthony in the wilderness and no aspect of his physical appearance suffered deterioration or change, so the people of Israel were guided by God in the wilderness for forty years and "the clothes on your back did not wear out and your feet did not swell these forty years. Know then in your heart that as a parent disciplines a child so the LORD your God disciplines you" (Deut 8:3, 4).

resurrection, where the *nous*/mind does not contrive evil (his soul was pure) and nothing separates the thought from the unceasing contemplation of God. It is the state of the first creation when humanity was granted the gift of living according to the Word, the image of God. Anthony exemplified the renewed image of God within us through the renewal of the resurrection.

The people who knocked down Anthony's door were treated with great compassion. There was no anger from Anthony's side because they disturbed his twenty-year seclusion. On the contrary, many of them were sick and "the Lord healed them through Antony because the Lord gave grace to Antony by means of the words Antony spoke."[37] The equilibrium between the mind and soul is reflected in the harmony of man with nature and the world. This harmony is manifested in the saint's ability to heal, to befriend wild animals, and have control over nature. These aspects of harmony remind the reader of the harmony our first parents had with nature and the wild animals before the fall. The ability of Anthony to heal is the sign that God is working through him and has given him this grace. God has also given him the grace of words. Anthony consoled mourners and was a peacemaker for those who had enmity between each other. He spoke about God's love, which is more important than everything in the world. "He taught each person about the good things to come and about God's love for humankind which has come to us because God did not spare his own Son, but gave him for all of us."[38] All the gifts granted to Anthony, and to anyone who purifies his heart and mind, are granted through "God's love for humankind" manifested in the incarnation. "But when the goodness and loving kindness of God our Savior appeared, he saved us, not because of any works of righteousness that we had done, but according to his mercy, through the water of rebirth and renewal by the Holy Spirit" (Titus 3:4–5).[39] When the people heard Anthony speak these words many wanted to follow his way of life, to follow the "monastic way of life." Monasticism and desert spirituality are the realization of the fullness of the incarnation.

The essence of monasticism is not in the dwellings or the location; it is rather a mindset, a way of life. That is the power of desert spirituality; you carry it within you wherever you go. A monastic is a "citizen of

37. Vivian, *Life of Antony*, 92 (C); *v. Anton.* 14.

38. Ibid.

39. Bartelink, *Vie d'Antoine*, 175 n. 3.

heaven," not a citizen of the world.[40] "But our citizenship is in heaven, and it is from there that we are expecting a Savior, the Lord Jesus Christ" (Phil 3:20). Desert spirituality aspires to the heavenly kingdom and to the unceasing contemplation of God. We can be citizens of heaven anywhere in the world. "The earth is the LORD's and all that is in it, the world, and those who live in it" (Ps 24:1).

The *Life* informs us that soon monastic dwellings around Anthony increased and Anthony guided them "like a good father."[41] Two aspects of monasticism are immediately apparent from this first monastic nucleus: individualism and discipleship, that is, the father-disciple relationship. These two characteristics will influence desert spirituality greatly. The monastic dwellings mentioned above did not form a monastery as we understand it in modern terms. These dwellings were separate cells or caves clustered around a spiritual father. There was no communal life and they were not enclosed within a perimeter wall. They lived a semi-hermitical lifestyle. Each monastic was bound to the spiritual father but they were not bound to each other. Their bond with one another was the Christian bond that united them, just as they were united to the rest of the human race. The spiritual bond with the father was voluntary and was based on mutual agreement. A spiritual father who had more than one disciple would have a different arrangement with each disciple. This does not mean that the father discriminated among his disciples, but rather that the father catered to each disciple according to his needs. Thus a mature disciple would not need as much attention as a young novice, nor would he receive the same spiritual advice. Not all people are the same and not all people are at the same spiritual level. Thus there can be a variety of answers to the same question. Spiritual instructions cater to the variety of individual temperaments and spiritual levels.[42]

Work and Self-Sufficiency

Athanasius describes Anthony as being accustomed to "working hard."[43] He was not a financial burden on anyone but was self-sufficient. He worked to provide for his needs by farming a piece of land so as not to be dependent on others. The land would serve not only his needs but the

40. Ibid., 92 (C); *v. Anton.* 14.
41. Ibid., 94 (C); *v. Anton.* 15.
42. Please, refer to chapter 4 for examples.
43. Vivian, *Life of Antony,* 171 (G); *v. Anton.* 53.1.

needs of his visitors, who needed relief from their long journeys.[44] By this behavior, Anthony established a very important principle in desert spirituality: monastics have to provide for themselves and not be dependent on others. This principle earned the respect of the population, as they did not consider the monks living among them a burden on the society or a nuisance to the social and economic fabric of their towns and cities. The Apostles also supported themselves in their proclamation of the gospel and emphasized the necessity of self-sufficiency: "You remember our labor and toil, brothers and sisters; we worked night and day, so that we might not burden any of you while we proclaimed to you the gospel of God" (1 Thess 2:9; see also 2 Thess 3:6, 8). For desert dwellers, work had a biblical warrant and it became a characteristic of their desert spirituality. Work was to provide for their necessities, but they were not to accumulate money or luxury items. Monks also gave alms to the poor. Similarly, the monastic communities of Pachomius developed such elaborate work projects in their monasteries that they began trading their commodities with the larger community. They even had boats to trade their products in Alexandria, in the northern part of Egypt, which was a long journey. The wealth the Pachomian communities accumulated from their trade led to the downfall of the Pachomian federated monastic structure. Their work consumed them and swayed them from their spiritual goals. The trick is to balance work with one's spiritual life. Monastic spirituality emphasizes work should sustain life but not overwhelm, impede, or destroy lives.

Anthony Seeks Humility

Anthony's fame led people to come and line up in front of his cell. The crowds made him reflect on how this would affect his humility and if it would make people think that "he is greater than he was."[45] He decided to leave for a quieter place that would ensure his inner tranquility. This marked his move to the "inner desert," i.e., a more secluded desert area. In the present media-frenzy culture, in which everyone is seeking fame, Anthony, who intentionally avoided fame, would seem very countercultural. His motivation for withdrawal was his spiritual steadfastness. Withdrawal for the sake of humility does not mean a person hates people. He had a clear goal in his life: to please God rather than people. He did not hate people but loved God more. His care and love for people was clear as he

44. Ibid., 167 (G); *v. Anton.* 50.7.
45. Ibid., 163 (G); *v. Anton.* 49.1.

attended to the long lines of people waiting to see him to ask him spiritual questions or for prayers for healing and other needs. Anthony needed discernment to reach a balance between the unending lines of people and his own spiritual welfare. Every Christian has to decide between work and responsibility and spiritual needs.

To assert Anthony's inner humility, Athanasius explains that Anthony's healing of people was only done through the invocation of the name of Christ. So it is clear that it was God who healed and that these healings were a manifestation of God's love for humanity.[46] Athanasius is saying, in other words, that God's love for humanity was manifested through Anthony. Anthony cared about people so much that Athanasius wrote: "Anthony was like a physician given by God to Egypt, for whoever went to him sad at heart and did not comeback rejoicing?"[47] It is out of the heart's great love for God that the heart gives back love to people freely and in abundance.

"Fought the good fight" (2 Tim 4:7)

At the age of 105, Anthony delivered a farewell speech to his disciples in which he informed them of his approaching death and that he was ready to leave. He exhorted them not to neglect their ascetic discipline and become faint-hearted during their spiritual journey. He emphasized that they should live each day as if it was their last, that is, to be always ready. Anthony was famous not only after his death but also during his lifetime. His was famous not because he was a theologian or a famous writer; rather he was famous "through his love of God."[48] That is the power of Anthony's spiritual legacy.

"Listen to advice . . . that you may gain wisdom" (Prov 19:20): Anthony's Advice on the Ascetic/Spiritual Life

Anthony delivered advice to his disciples in the form of a discourse outlining his understanding of the ascetic and spiritual life based on his own personal experience. These are some of the main ideas and advice he expressed in his discourse.

46. Ibid., 237 (G); *v. Anton.* 84.1.
47. Ibid., 243 (G); *v. Anton.* 87.3.
48. Ibid., 259 (G); *v. Anton.* 93.4.

Scripture

The first comment in his discourse is about Scripture. This indicates the centrality of Scripture that we have already observed in Anthony's spiritual journey. He said, "The Scriptures are sufficient for us for instruction, but it is good for us to encourage one another in the faith and to train by means of words."[49] He recognized the importance of encouragement in the spiritual life—"Therefore encourage one another with these words" (1 Thess 4:18). The source of this instruction and encouragement is Scripture.

Practice Asceticism to Be Well Pleasing to God

Anthony warns his disciples against practicing asceticism for the sake of rewards or boasting but rather to be well pleasing to God. Asceticism is not a competition to see who can be the most ascetic. He tells his disciples to pray as part of their ascetic practice and not to demand compensation for ascetic discipline so that the Lord may help them in their journey and give them discernment to have victory over the Enemy's temptations.[50]

Spiritual Guidance

The beginner in the spiritual journey is to consult with his spiritual father or mother. Though Scripture is the primary teacher, the spiritual guide encourages and steers the person through the journey and explains how to discern the Spirit and its work. The spiritual guide shares with the disciple wisdom from her experience.

Remember Your Spiritual Goal

Anthony advised his disciples to put in perspective what they have renounced in the present, short life by comparing it to the gains in eternal life. Athanasius quotes Psalm 90:10 as a reminder that this is ancient wisdom: "The days of our life are seventy years, or perhaps eighty, if we are strong; even then their span is only toil and trouble; they are soon gone, and we fly away." The present life will soon pass away; if we spend seventy or even a hundred years in ascetic discipline, this will pale when

49. Ibid., 97 (G); *v. Anton.* 16.1.
50. Ibid., 133 (G); *v. Anton.* 34.1.

compared with the heavenly and eternal kingdom. Anthony reminds his disciples that the contest is on earth but the promises and inheritance are in heaven. We tend to lose heart because of the length of the journey here. "So let us not grow weary in doing what is right, for we will reap at harvest time, if we do not give up" (Gal 6:9). Focusing on the goal, on the heavenly kingdom, rejuvenates the spirit exhausted from constant struggle. As Paul says, "I consider that the sufferings of this present time are not worth comparing with the glory about to be revealed to us" (Rom 8:18).[51] Focusing on the goal, on the heavenly kingdom, is a means of overcoming despair, boredom, lack of motivation, doubt, and other spiritual maladies that accompany the lifelong spiritual journey. "I press on toward the goal for the prize of the heavenly call of God in Christ Jesus" (Phil 3:14).

Anthony argues that it is better not to focus on the accumulation of worldly wealth, which we will leave behind anyway (Eccl 2:18–19; 6:2), but to focus on the accumulation of virtues we can take with us, such as "clear thinking, prudence, righteousness, courage, understanding, godly love, love for the poor, faith in Christ, freedom from anger, hospitality."[52] Focusing on the "glory to be revealed to us" puts suffering in perspective and energizes spiritual eagerness. Anthony gives this analogy: "a servant does not dare say, 'Since I worked yesterday, I am not going to work today.'"[53] Applied to a present day setting this would mean that we are required to work every day if we want to receive a paycheck at the end of the week. Why should we behave otherwise towards God and towards the heavenly kingdom? Anthony concludes by the example of Judas who toiled all his life but lost everything in one night. Thus diligence and attentiveness to our spiritual life is essential for we do not know when the day of the Lord will come (see 1 Thess 5:2) and readiness requires diligence in spiritual life. This attentiveness is fostered by focusing on the spiritual goal.

Discernment of Spirits

Anthony informs his disciples—probably based on his personal experience, as he suggests it more than once during his discourse—that when the Spirit grants the gift of discernment to someone, the gift is sustained through prayer and asceticism. Discernment helps us recognize not only the evil spirit, but also what this spirit is doing and the means of casting it

51. Ibid., 99 (G); *v. Anton.* 16.4—17.1.

52. Ibid., 101 (G); *v. Anton.* 17.7.

53. Ibid. (G); *v. Anton.* 18.2.

out.[54] Athanasius explains that discerning the spirits means "recognizing their movements," how they hatch their plots against a person.[55]

Spiritual warfare is vividly depicted in desert spirituality. It is the image of the crafty serpent trying to entice our first parents to sway them away from God's commandment, the gospel narrative of Christ's temptation in the wilderness, and the Epistles' warnings "against the spiritual forces of evil in the heavenly places" (Eph 6:13), together with Athanasius' understanding of the creation and fall of humanity and the necessity of the incarnation, that formed the image of spiritual warfare. Anthony's personal spiritual warfare with the Enemy is to be understood against this biblical and theological background. For Anthony and the rest of the desert fathers and mothers, discernment was a major spiritual theme, even a spiritual weapon that helped in spiritual warfare. One of the main weapons that the enemy throws at the desert dwellers is "thought." It is the struggle of the mind and its thoughts that bedevils every Christian. Paul exhorts all Christians to "take every thought captive to obey Christ."(2 Cor 10:5). This is the struggle of the mind, the *nous*, that Athanasius has referred to, in which the aim is that the thought and the *nous* become captive to Christ.

Anthony gave his disciples concrete examples of how to discern the spirits. Evil spirits place "terror in the soul, confusion, and disordered thoughts, dejection, hatred for other ascetics, listlessness, sadness, homesickness, and fear of death; and later, the desire for evil, the neglect of virtue, and disorder in one's character."[56] He describes the inner thoughts that become "disordered." A person's thoughts become confused and stray from God. Eventually the person becomes consumed with inner fears and neglects virtue. The thoughts become preoccupied with "desire for evil." Anthony gives a description of the gradual escalation of the inner thoughts as they become captive to the "fear of death," sadness, and other destructive ideas. The disorder in one's character does not appear suddenly, and Anthony advises his disciples to watch for the early signs before the desire for evil takes over their lives.

As to the spirits from God, they take fear away. "Unutterable joy" comes, "along with tranquility and confidence and renewed spirits and calm thoughts," in addition to "courage and love for God."[57] Anthony describes this state of the soul as "peaceful and gentle." As to the inner

---

54. Ibid., 111 (G); *v. Anton.* 22.3.

55. Ibid., 245 (G); *v. Anton.* 88.1.

56. Ibid., 137 (G); *v. Anton.* 36.2.

57. Ibid. (G); *v. Anton.* 36.3.

condition of the soul, it is in a state of tranquility and calmness and is not troubled by any disturbing thoughts.[58] Anthony then gives examples of such state of tranquility and joy: Abraham rejoiced when he saw the Lord (John 8:56), and John leaped with joy in Elizabeth's womb and she was filled with the Holy Spirit (Luke 1:41). These examples affirm that the encounter with the Spirit of God leaves the person in utter joy and peace. The Spirit of God also removes all fear as in the examples of the archangel's encounter with Mary and Zachariah and when the angel appeared to the women at the tomb.[59] These concrete biblical examples are a guide to the soul to discern its inner state—whether of peacefulness or of fear—and then act accordingly. We can consider this explanation of discerning the spirit as a practical interpretation of 1 John 4:1: "Beloved, do not believe every spirit, but test the spirits to see whether they are from God."

The Path of Spiritual Struggles

Anthony starts with the struggle against "impure thoughts." He tells his disciples that these thoughts are not to be feared, "for through prayer and fasting and faith in the Lord the demons immediately fall."[60] But the Enemy does not give up very easily and attacks through more deceptive ways. "And no wonder! Even Satan disguises himself as an angel of light. So it is not strange if his ministers also disguise themselves as ministers of righteousness" (2 Cor 11:14–15). Anthony further encourages his disciples that as Christians they have power over the Enemy through the sign of the cross. The Enemy is afraid of the "Lord's cross because by it the Savior stripped them of their weapons and made an example of them" (see Col 2:15).[61] The cross's power is that it is a reminder of the Lord's crucifixion and the overcoming of death by his resurrection; it is the ultimate sign of victory over death and all evil. Anthony, in his arguments with the philosophers, says that the cross "is a sign of courage and proof that we look upon death with contempt."[62] Through the resurrection Christians have the power and "authority to tread on snakes and scorpions, and over all the power of the enemy; and nothing will hurt you" (Luke 10:19).[63]

58. Ibid., 135 (G); v. Anton. 35.4.

59. Ibid., 139 (G); v. Anton. 37.1.

60. Ibid., 111 (G); v. Anton. 23.2.

61. Ibid., 135 (G); v. Anton. 35.3.

62. Ibid., 213 (G); v. Anton. 74.3.

63. Ibid., 113, 115 (G); v. Anton. 23.4; 24.5.

Anthony concludes: "It is appropriate that we have no fear of demons; through the grace of the Lord, all their endeavors will come to nothing."[64]

Anthony advises his disciples that they need the greatest discernment because the enemies "disguise themselves as ministers of righteousness." A person might not be deceived easily when something sounds wrong or does not look right; the difficulty is when evil is clothed in the form of friendly advice or a person who seems genuine but is in truth very deceptive. This is where discernment, prayer, and faith come to the rescue. Anthony comforts his disciples: "We ought not to fear them, even if they threaten us with death, for they are powerless and are unable to do anything evil to us."[65] The Enemy is powerless before the power we acquired through the incarnation and resurrection; death has no power. By his resurrection Christ "abolished death and brought life and immortality to light through the gospel" (2 Tim 1:10). By his incarnation and resurrection "death has been swallowed up in victory. Where, O death, is your victory? Where, O death, is your sting?" (1 Cor 15:54–55). If the most frightening thing that humans face is death, and death has no power now, then we should be fearless. In the path of our spiritual struggles we should be fearless on the spiritual and physical level.

Athanasius in his book *On the Incarnation* discusses the theme of being fearless facing death. By the fourth century, Christianity had spread to many parts of the ancient world and most of the territory of the Roman Empire. Athanasius writes: "Christ alone, using common speech and through the agency of men not clever with their tongues, has convinced whole assemblies of people all the world over to despise death, and to take heed to the things that do not die, to look past the things of time and gaze on things eternal, to think nothing of earthly glory and to aspire only to immortality."[66] He goes on to explain that these are not mere words; when we look at people living a virtuous and chaste life, they did this through Christ alone. The martyrs endured suffering and did not fear death, for they thought nothing of earthly glory but were assured of and aspired to immortality by the promise of the resurrection.[67] Christian martyrs face death fearlessly because of Christ and his promises.

64. Ibid., 117 (G); *v. Anton.* 24.7.

65. Ibid., 120 (C); *v. Anton.* 27.

66. Athanasius, *On the Incarnation: The Treatise De Incarnatione Verbi Dei*, trans. and ed. by a religious of CSMV, rev. ed., Popular Patristics 3 (Crestwood, NY: St. Vladimir's Seminary Press, 1998) 85; *inc.* 47.

67. *inc.* 48.

Therefore, it is through Christ and the power of the resurrection that we live the life of virtue, which is exemplified in Anthony and which Anthony assures his disciples they can achieve no matter with what temptations the Enemy deceives them. Christians are powerful through Christ and should not fear any harm that afflicts them, whether spiritual or physical, so long as they live by virtue and do not fear death. For a Christian aspires to the immortality granted by the resurrection. Anthony's statement that the Enemy is powerless is based on the theology of the incarnation, a theology he embraced so deeply that it shaped his spiritual experience and, accordingly, his advice to his disciples.

Anthony refers to the strong connection between the incarnation and our ability to overcome the Enemy when he says to his disciples, "When the Lord [lived] among us, the Enemy was fallen and his thoughts weakened."[68] The greatest thing the Enemy fears, Anthony continues, is the weapon we have, which is "an upright life and faith in God. Without a doubt, demons are afraid of ascetic practices: fasting, keeping vigils, prayers, gentleness, tranquility, poverty, moderation, humility, love of the poor, almsgiving, the absence of anger and, above all, devotion to Christ."[69]

Anthony concludes his discourse to his disciples with words of encouragement. He exhorts them to be joyful. The source of their rejoicing is the thought of their salvation. He exhorts them to be courageous because the Enemy cannot harm them by any means. If we are in a fearful state, he will pry on us and exert more fear in our hearts. On the other hand, if the enemies find us rejoicing, having our hearts set on the Lord and his works, and the soul "secure with thoughts of this kind, they turn away."[70] Our way to the peace and tranquility of our soul is to think constantly on the Lord and not give other thoughts any chance to disturb us.

The Promise of the Savior

Athanasius expected that his description of Anthony might arouse some skepticism among his readers. Anthony is described as having reached a state of perfection that might seem to some very hard if not impossible to achieve. Anthony's response to the gospel message is well known and equal to that of the time of the Apostles. His faith in God, in addition to his rigorous asceticism, seemed to be unshakable. The description of Anthony's

68. Vivian, *Life of Antony*, 120 (C); *v. Anton.* 28.

69. Ibid., 127 (G); *v. Anton.* 30.2.

70. Ibid., 149 (G); *v. Anton.* 42.7.

sainthood is almost legendary; he healed the sick, exorcised demons, and loved his disciples and all who came to see him. His humility, calmness, unmistakable joy, meticulous self-examination, and wisdom seem to be hard to find in one single person. Athanasius response is that this "is the promise of the Savior." We are promised that if we have faith we can move mountains (Matt 17:20) and will receive what we ask for (John 16:23–24). Christ gave to his disciples and to everyone who believes in him the power to "cure the sick, cleanse the lepers, cast out demons. You received without payment; give in return without payment" (Matt 10:8).[71] Christ's promises were fulfilled in Anthony. Athanasius is telling his readers that if they do not believe the story of Anthony they do not believe in the power of the incarnation, the resurrection, and the whole of the gospel message. This is the Christian message; if we believe in Scripture and in Christ, we have to believe that all he promised in the gospel is attainable. Anthony believed and he attained it. Many of his disciples believed and attained it. It is up to us to believe and to attain it.

Epilogue to Part I: The Balance of the Heart

The three literary works of Athanasius discussed in Part I of this book form one continuous and consistent theological and spiritual idea. Though written in three books, they should be read together to understand their full meaning. The first two texts, *Against the Gentiles* and *On the Incarnation*, set the theological background for understanding the spiritual life. Anthony in the *Life* is the practical application of this theology in concrete form. Athanasius did not write theology for the sake of promoting abstract theological theories. He wrote a theology that is at the heart of the Christian life and affects the daily life of every Christian. These three books are a trilogy on how to live a Christian spiritual life grounded in sound orthodox theology.

Athanasius starts with the creation narrative. God created humanity with a mind that comprehends God and reason that is capable of contemplating God at all times. The constant contemplation of God preserves the purity of humanity, in which the heart finds its pleasure contemplating God and the mind transcends the things of the body and the senses. The pure heart sees God (Matt 5:8). This was the paradisal state of our first parents. But the soul became attached to things related to the senses and the body, and as a result the mind/*nous* was no longer able to contemplate

71. Ibid., 236 (C); *v. Anton.* 83.

on God and succumbed to the evil contrived by it. Humanity chose to contemplate themselves rather than God and turned toward their lusts and what pleases them. When the soul is not in God's presence because the mind is not preoccupied with contemplating him, it loses its ability to discern what is good from what is evil. Humanity was given the senses to know about the world and to comprehend God. But when the senses are captive to pleasures, humanity loses the ability to use its reason for its benefit and for the glorification of God.

According to Athanasius, because humanity is created in God's image, finding God starts by searching within oneself. The search starts by perceiving and contemplating the Divine in the soul and the mind or reason (*nous*) that reside within each of us. The senses perceive the world but the soul and the mind discern and decide. When the body is quiet and still, the rational soul can behold what is outside itself. The soul and the *nous* residing within it can behold and contemplate God. The rational and immortal soul and the *nous* residing within it perceive what is beyond the immediate senses and introduce it to the body. Thus humans perceive what is pleasurable to the senses, but by their reason they chose to make moral or ethical decisions, even if the decisions affect their welfare or their physical safety. This explains why some people chose to sacrifice for the sake of their families, friends, church, country, or neighbors. Societies honor people who make great sacrifices because they have proved that their reason and ethical reasoning have overcome their immediate personal or sensual gratification. The noble soul is that which is cleansed from all sensual gratification and returns to its simplicity. Fallen humanity could not do this on its own; it needed the incarnation.

God created humans as rational, endowed with reason, and this is what it means to be created in the image of the Word, the Logos, which by definition means reason. Since humans are created rational, they have the ability to choose between good and evil. God commanded them not to eat of the tree. They chose to eat and suffered the consequence of transgressing the commandment and choosing evil, that is, death and corruption. They were deprived of being in God's presence and the constant contemplation of him. With the fall, humans kept turning to corruptible things, to matter, to the gratification of their senses, and corruption began gaining more power over them; thus the necessity of the incarnation. The Son of God had to become incarnate, die, and rise again to overcome death and corruption. With the resurrection, death no longer has hold over humanity. With the incarnation, the Word renewed his image within humanity so that through him humanity can once more come to know God and be in his likeness. The incarnate Son revealed the Father to humanity, and with his resurrection humanity came to worship the Savior rather than heroes or idols. Through the resurrection, Christ, the giver of life, introduced virtue, immortality, and the desire for heavenly things. This desire enables the soul and the *nous* dwelling within it to discern and choose good over evil.

We have to keep watch over the purity of the soul so that the desire for heavenly things will guide the senses and the body to choose good. This is what all Christians should endeavor to do. Many Christians have left the comfort of their homes and withdrawn to quieter places outside their towns so as not to be disturbed or distracted from working on the purity of their soul, mind, and heart. Chapter 1 presented many examples of people trying to attain this goal. Anthony came and demonstrated by his lifestyle how to go about achieving this goal. He withdrew gradually from his home, then town, and later went to the desert seeking the path of constant contemplation of God. He started with guidance from some of the anchorites who preceded him, but eventually he had to find his path on his own. Athanasius describes the tranquility and purity of Anthony's soul, which were revealed by the movement of his body. Athanasius described Anthony's spiritual formation and his struggle with the demons to preserve the purity of his thoughts.

In Anthony Athanasius has given us a practical example of the application of his theology. Anthony's whole life shows how to keep the thoughts pure, how to subdue the senses to reason and virtue. How reason guides the soul to choose good over evil and how to conquer evil are shown in Anthony's struggle with the demons. Anthony's victory is a demonstration of the power of the incarnation, which gave him the ability to make his thoughts guide his senses. Humanity suffered the fall when its senses overcame its reason; Anthony triumphed over the demons when his thoughts overcame his senses. What sustained Anthony in his struggle was his constant contemplation of God, aided by constant reading of Scripture and constant prayer. This became the foundation of the monastic life: reading Scripture, praying, and working to support oneself and give alms. This was accompanied with various spiritual and ascetic exercises (*askēsis*). Anthony worked very hard to observe the movements of his soul, what affected it, and to learn how to purify it and what hinders the soul and thoughts from being in constant conversation with God and in his presence.

Anthony's life was written down so that others would emulate it. His life has set the pattern for and foundation of organized monasticism and desert spirituality. The monastic ideal spread beyond the boundaries of Egypt to the rest of the world. Many followed his spiritual pattern. His disciples had disciples of their own, and they too have continued the spiritual journey and enriched the Christian heritage with their experience. In Part II of this book, we will discuss the cumulative experience of the desert fathers, of Anthony and those who followed his spiritual journey. Chapter 4 will give a general background to the way the monks lived to provide the context within which the sayings are to be understood. The following chapters will discuss the sayings of the desert fathers and mothers. The sayings and lives of the desert fathers and mothers deal with the nitty-gritty of daily life and daily spiritual issues and how to confront the thoughts that bombard us all the time.

Desert spirituality is the journey of constant struggle to keep the heart and the mind pure for the sake of being in constant presence before God; to be not only in the paradisal state of our first parents when humanity was in the image of the Divine, but to be in God's presence now and for all eternity. This is a state that our early parents could not sustain, but we can through the incarnation and resurrection. That is why monastic literature is full of talk about self-examination and scrutinizing every thought that comes to the mind. This spiritual journey is accompanied by physical *askēsis*, such as renunciation and fasting, to help the soul achieve a spiritual state. Christian asceticism aims to reach the right balance between the soul and the body, to reach the state of perfect harmony. Desert spirituality is the balance of the heart.

Part Two

INTRODUCTION

Clothe Yourselves with a New Self

Daily Life in the Desert

Do not lie to one another, seeing that you have stripped off
the old self with its practices and have clothed yourselves
with the new self, which is being renewed in knowledge
according to the image of its creator.

COL 3:9–10

THE WORDS "MONASTIC" AND "monk" are derived from the Greek
word *monachos*. The Greek word carries a lot of connotations that
have been lost in the English word. *Monachos* as an adjective can mean
solitary, eremitical, having ascetical discipline, single or celibate, and
having a certain form.[1] All these nuances are relevant to understanding
desert spirituality and the life of those who practiced it. "Monk" means
a solitary person, and in early Christian writings it was interchangeable

---

1. Henry George Liddell and Robert Scott, *A Greek-English Lexicon* (Oxford: Clarendon, 1992) s.vv. μονάς, μοναχικός, μοναχός (p. 1143), ἐρημία (p. 686), ἄσκησις (p. 257), σχῆμα (1745); and G. W. H. Lampe, *A Patristic Greek Lexicon* (Oxford: Clarendon, 1961) s.vv. μοναχός (p. 878), ἐρημία (p. 548), ἄσκησις (p. 244), σχῆμα (p. 1358). Two articles that summarize the development and use of the term *monachos* are Françoise-E Morard, "Monachos, Moine. Histoire du terme grec jusqu'au 4e siècle, influences bibliques et gnostiques," *Freiburger Zeitschrift für Philosphie und Theologie* 20 (1973) 332–411; and E. A. Judge, "The Earliest Use of Monachos for 'Monk' (P. Coll. Youtie 77) and the Origins of Monasteicism," *Jahrbuch für Antike und Christentum* 20 (1977) 72–89.

with the word "hermit," which is derived from the Greek word that means solitude and desert. With the development of the communal life, those living in monasteries kept the title "monk" while desert dwellers were distinguished as "eremitical" or "hermitical" monks. Even when living in a monastery, a monk was understood to be living in solitude within the monastery in addition to being single or celibate. Solitude is an intrinsic aspect of desert spirituality and Egyptian monasticism carries the solitary ethos in its practices to this day. Though solitude is an aspect of the eremitical monastic life, in most cases hermits do not speak about physical solitude but rather refer to "a spiritual condition necessary in order to attain to union with God."[2] Physical solitude is only a path to the real thing monks want to achieve, a place that enables them to be in union with God without any distractions. The desert is the place of encounter with God. When Moses encountered God, God asked him to remove his sandals because the place was holy ground (Exod 3:5); it was the place where God was present. For the monk, the desert is that holy place.

The last two nuances of the word *monachos* are "having a certain form" and "having ascetical discipline." Their ascetical practices made the desert dwellers distinct from others; they began to be distinguished by their simple clothing, which thus developed a certain form (*schēma*). Eventually, the *schēma* began to refer to the monastic attire and is the term used in Orthodox Christianity to this day. Asceticism, from the Greek word *askēsis*, means exercise, training, or practice. Monastics are expected to engage in spiritual exercises, training, and discipline.[3] Asceticism was known among pagan philosophers, for whom the practice of philosophy entailed certain disciplines that accompanied their philosophical worldview and expressed the essence of their teachings and philosophy. The same is true of the Christian *askēsis* or asceticism. The desert fathers and mothers developed and practiced an *askēsis* that reflected the essence of the biblical message. Desert asceticism is the putting into practice of biblical teachings. The second part of the book discusses the ascetic practices by which the monastics expressed their understanding of how to live the Bible to its fullest. We will start with a short introduction describing a day in the life of a desert father. This will help us to put into context the *askēsis* or asceticism they practiced.

Anthony and his style of living attracted many admirers; many renounced everything and settled beside him, thus forming the first monastic

2. Lampe, *Patristic Greek Lexicon*, 548.
3. Ibid., 244.

settlement. His disciples spread all over Egypt, many beginning their own monastic groups. When Anthony visited Abba Amoun, one of his disciples in the Nitrian desert, Amoun informed him that the brethren had increased so much that they needed to expand the monastic settlement.[4] They expanded to Scetis. According to Abba Sisoes, by the time Anthony died the western desert of Scetis was crowded with monks.[5] Anthony's fame and discipline transformed the deserts of Egypt into a "crowded" landscape filled with people who renounced everything for the sake of God. It was only natural that Anthony's life would be written for the edification of the following generations. The written biography made Anthony famous beyond the Egyptian frontiers; he became an international figure, a global example of Christian living. Already during Anthony's lifetime, the desert monks had established some sort of a rhythm for their lives that they deemed would help them in their spiritual journey. They took their guidelines first from Anthony and then perfected the pattern according to their experience.

Anthony moved to the desert to eliminate all possible distractions— or so he thought. He thought nothing would prevent him from dedicating his life to God and being immersed in constant prayer. This is the way everyone thinks: if I just move from this place, then I can accomplish what I want. Sometimes a place can be a hindrance, but most times the hindrance is within us. Anthony did not expect to be weighed down by *accedia*, a Greek word that can be translated as "boredom" or "torpor," which causes fatigue, weariness, loss of hope, sometimes sadness, or even the feeling of wanting to leave the place altogether.[6] The fathers believed this type of weariness, sadness, and boredom, which attacked many around noon, was "the destruction that wastes at noonday" mentioned in Psalm 91:6. Some have even called it the "midday demon." Most would succumb to the feeling of *accedia*, but Anthony's strategy was to confront this feeling with fervent prayer, laying down his struggles before God. God responded to his prayer and revealed to him that he was to work as well as pray. His work should be accompanied by prayer and his prayers should be accompanied by work.[7] This established the first principle in desert spirituality:

4. *AS Ward*, 8, Anthony # 34.

5. *AS Ward*, 218, Sisoes # 28.

6. Lampe, *Patristic Greek Lexicon*, s.v. ἀκηδία (p. 61–62).

7. *AS Ward*, 2, Anthony # 1.

the importance of work accompanied by prayer. The *Life* describes Anthony as working "diligently" and "hard."[8]

All those who settled beside Anthony's cell followed his example. Athanasius describes their daily rhythm as follows:

> So there were in the mountains monastic dwellings like tents filled with heavenly choirs singing psalms, studying the Bible, fasting, praying, rejoicing in the hope of things to come, working in order to give alms, having love for each other and being in harmony with one another.[9]

This summarizes the monastic life not only during the time of Anthony but from the fourth century to the present day in Egyptian monasticism. Anthony realized from his experience that spending the day in constant prayer was very hard. Monastics divided the day among the following activities: work, prayer, studying the Bible, singing psalms, fasting, giving alms, loving your neighbor as yourself, and striving for the heavenly kingdom. Actually, all these activities are required of all Christians whether they are in the desert or not.

Each monk spent Monday to Friday in solitude in his cell or monastic dwelling. The cells were made of brick or sometimes carved into a mountain. Some of the cells were one room; others had two rooms, the inner room being for the privacy of prayer. On Saturday and Sunday, all the brothers would go to the church; some of them would walk miles to attend the Saturday and Sunday liturgies and partake of the Eucharist. After each liturgy all the brothers would have an agape meal together. Saturday night would be spent primarily in chanting psalms and prayer. After each psalm there would be a short silence for prayers. The weekend gathering was an opportunity for monks to ask the elders for advice, exchange spiritual experiences, and check on each other. These meetings were to energize the weak and young and encourage and inspire the others. They would visit any brother who did not show up lest he be ill or in distress. At the end of the weekend, each monk would exchange his weekly work for bread, water, utensils for basket weaving, and other needed supplies that would sustain him during the following week.

Once the monk returned to his cell he resumed his weekly routine. One might think that the weekend would disturb a monk's solitude and

8. Tim Vivian, trans., Athanasius, *The Life of Antony: The Coptic Life and the Greek Life*, Cistercian Studies 202 (Kalamazoo, MI: Cistercian, 2003) 170 (C) and (G) 171; *v. Anton.* 53.

9. Ibid., (G) 153; *v. Anton.* 44.2.

would seem like backsliding on his advance toward solitude. Not necessarily. The brothers were careful during their gathering not to slander, exchange news or gossip, or engage in other blunders of the tongue. Their discussions were primarily spiritual in nature and for their edification. Even during midweek visits of monks traveling from monastic settlements far away, conversation was intended for spiritual edification.

On weekdays, a monk would wake up early at dawn for morning prayers, then start weaving baskets or mats. Basket making was an industry profitable enough to cover their expenses. Baskets were a needed product; they were the only means of storing or transporting commodities for many centuries. It was the work most suitable for the monks because it did not hinder their minds and thoughts from contemplating God while they worked. John the Short, for example, "was weaving rope for two baskets, but he made it into one without noticing, until it had reached the wall, because his spirit was occupied in contemplation."[10]

While weaving their baskets, their hearts and thoughts were engaged in contemplation on biblical verses and prayer. Biblical verses were the source of their prayers and they read Scripture constantly. Abba Sisoes would read the New Testament and then he would turn to read the Old Testament.[11] They not only read but also memorized segments of Scripture so that they could recite them and contemplate on them while walking or traveling. They did not have the technology to help them retrieve Scripture on the move, so they used their memory to keep their thoughts in the constant presence of God. The Psalms was the most commonly memorized biblical text because it was the source of prayer. Anthony advises the brothers to "pray without ceasing, to say the psalms before going to sleep and after arising from sleep, to learn by heart the precepts of the Scriptures."[12]

The monastics understood their "work" on different levels. Work done to obtain food, clothing, and money to give alms did not exhaust the concept of work. Some of the brethren asked an elder monk how a monk can die every day for the love of Christ (see 1 Cor 15:31; 2 Cor 4:11). The elder responded by saying this can be done by contemplating in silence while working. Then he explained to the brethren the different levels of work: there are the "works of the body," which are fasting, vigil, recital of psalms, prayers, genuflections, weeping for one's sins, and the reading of

10. *ASWard*, 87, John the Dwarf #11.

11. *ASWard*, 219, Sisoes #35.

12. Vivian, *Life of Antony* (G) 175; *v. Anton.* 55.3.

Scripture; and, more important, there is the "work of the mind," which is constant remembrance of God, meditating on God and on his blessings and commandments. In the "work of the mind" our "gaze must always be on the Lord" and we pray without ceasing and without distractions. Also in this category are the possession of spiritual virtues, asceticism, and the "life of the mind," which he explained as death to the anxieties and the cares of the world, for a monk should care about nothing except attaining the perfect love of the Lord.[13] It is important to observe that work is not defined as what generates income. Nor is it defined as a guarantee of the heavenly kingdom. It is rather the inner and outer aspects of our life and behavior that help us set our gaze on the Lord. In another story an elder was asked: Does a person who lacks work also lack love? The elder responded that it is impossible to love God and not work, for it is absurd to teach something and not follow your own teachings. In this case the tongue is the greatest enemy, for such a person speaks life but is subject to death.[14] "But whoever obeys his word, truly in this person the love of God has reached perfection" (1 John 2:5). For how can a person be filled with the love of God and hate his neighbor, or not be compassionate, or not be a peacemaker? The person's behavior and work reflects the inner mind of the soul. That is why the main work of the monk is to attain perfect love of God and set his gaze on the Lord.

The monks would do manual work until three in the afternoon, which is when they would have their first meal. They would usually eat one loaf of bread the size of a big muffin, soaked in water, together with salt. They kept their bread for a week or more, so they had to soften the bread in water. If they received guests, they would break their fast and offer them a better meal, which would include some beans, oil, and even wine. Receiving guests was an act of love toward a brother that was more valued than any ascetical practice and was in line with biblical and monastic principles of loving your neighbor as yourself. On the weekend, when all the monks would gather at the agape meal, they would eat cooked food, which would include vegetables. They did not eat meat.

13. *SABudge*, 327, #672.

14. *SABudge*, 328, #678.

Fig 21: Older cells from the monastery of St. Macarius. (Photo by author)

Fig 22: A modern monastic cell from the Monastery of the Virgin Mary (known as *al-suryān*). (Photo by author)

Fig 23: Modern monastic cells from the Monastery of the Virgin Mary (known as *al-barāmūs*). (Photo by author)

Fig 24: An ancient monastic refectory from the Monastery of the Virgin Mary (known as *al-barāmūs*). The table and seat made of stone with the stone lectionary at the back of the picture are used for reading monastic or Biblical texts during agape meals. Some sayings took place in similar settings. (Photo by author)

Fig 25: A closer picture of the stone lectionary. (Photo by author)

Fig 26: Bread loaves baked in the same form and way as the fourth-century monastic bread. (Photo by author)

Fig 27: Modern Coptic Orthodox monk. (Photo by author)

Fig 27a: Thirteenth century painting from the Monastery of St. Anthony that exhibits monastic figures wearing the same hood (*qulunswa*) modern Coptic monastics still wear (compare with picture of Modern Coptic Orthodox monk). (Photo by author)

The fasting practices of the desert fathers were honed by experience. Abba Poemen advised Abba Joseph to eat a little every day and not to stuff oneself with food. He explained that when he was younger, he experimented with fasting two days at a time, and sometimes three or four, or even a whole week.[15] The advice of the fathers was to eat every day in moderation and not strive for excessive ascetic practices, which would lead to gluttony and vainglory. The desert fathers did not view food with contempt, as one might suspect from their austerity, but rather as a necessity that had to be taken care of with appropriate reverence. They did not cease from praying while having their meals; that is why they took their meals in silence, so as to enable contemplation and prayer. Abba Isaiah was present at one of the agape meals when the monks were not keeping their silence as they were supposed to. When their chatting became rather loud, one of the brothers said, "I have seen a brother eating with you and drinking as many cups as you and his prayer is ascending to the presence of God like fire."[16] This story indicates that the brothers got excited to meet each other on weekends. But at the same time it shows that some kept their solitude and their constant prayer life, even within such a boisterous gathering.

Most probably many of the sayings of the fathers known to us were exchanged during such gatherings when the elder would meet with his disciples. A disciple would approach the elder with the following general question: "Father, tell me a word to live by." Sometimes he would have a specific question that he would like his father to respond to. However, not all the advice was given in public settings. A disciple could visit the elder at any time of the day or night to seek urgent advice for a persistent struggle and he would be well received.

The desert sayings are not a systematic spiritual program. They are mostly personal questions asked at different times, in different situations, by different disciples, to different teachers and fathers. Thus each answer is specifically tailored to the person asking the question. Good examples are found in the stories about Abba Achilles and Abba Poemen. Three elderly men approached Abba Achilles. The first one asked him to make him a fishing net. Abba Achilles refused his request. The second pleaded for the net, claiming that it would be a souvenir from Abba Achilles and the monastery. Abba Achilles refused the second request. The request of the third person, who was of bad reputation, was granted immediately without

15. *ASWard*, 171, Poemen #31.
16. *ASWard*, 69, Isaiah #4.

hesitation. The other two men came back later asking for an explanation of what seemed to be inconsistent behavior. Abba Achilles explained that they understood that he did not have time, and they would be only a little disappointed. But as for the third man, if his request were not granted, he would have been devastated, blaming the denial of the request on his sin, and been overcome with grief and be lost.[17]

The second story is about Abba Poemen's experience. Abba Poemen asked Abba Joseph what to do with thoughts of passion that disturbed him. Abba Joseph advised him to examine his thoughts even though they might disturb and shake him. Another brother from Thebes came later and asked the same question of Abba Joseph, who responded that he should fight the thoughts immediately and not let them linger for a moment. When after some time Abba Poemen heard about such contradictory counsel, he felt betrayed and his trust in his spiritual father was shaken. He immediately confronted Abba Joseph, requesting an explanation. Abba Joseph responded that for a brother of his spiritual stature it is better to examine his thoughts; they will not injure him but rather give him more maturity. As for the other brother, such an approach could be deadly.[18]

From these two stories we understand how specific the answers could be and that they were based solely on the situation. Nevertheless, such questions are still asked by Christians anxious to find answers to their struggles in their spiritual journey. Such struggles become representative of the soul's journey in general. When the age of these early experienced spiritual and monastic athletes began to draw to a close, their disciples started to gather the sayings and put them into writing. Some suggest this started with the disciples of Abba Poemen, since he has the largest number of sayings in the collection.[19] They cherished the sayings as oral tradition for some time, but they recognized that this tradition would be valuable also for coming generations. And they were right. From the time they were uttered in the fourth century and written down in the fifth, Christians have cherished their wisdom to the present day.

Understanding the setting of these sayings is important since not all sayings will necessarily resonate with every reader. The collection of sayings is also known as "The Paradise of the Fathers," and truly it is a garden full of different spiritual fruits where each reader can pick the fruit most

---

17. *ASWard*, 28, Achilles #1.

18. *SABudge*, 198, #210.

19. Jean-Claude Guy, trans., *Les apophtegmes des Pères: Collection systématique*, vol. 1, Sources chrétiennes 387 (Paris: Éditions du Cerf, 1993) 79–84.

suitable to his or her temperament, level of spiritual growth, personal experience, and many other unique qualities that makes each of us who we are. It is this variety of approaches to spiritual experience that makes these wisdom sayings most valuable as they speak to our different stations in life. If you encounter a spiritual counsel that might be too harsh for you or just does not fit, just remember that another reader might respond to and welcome that wisdom more than you. Keep on reading until you find the spiritual fruit most suitable to your taste.

The early desert dwellers examined their hearts daily in an attempt to purify their thoughts to be in accordance with God. Their daily activity was meant to declutter their minds by living life as simply as possible. They tried not to be enslaved to habits but to free their desire from the clutches of luxurious food, clothing, and other temptations; to live in simple housing; to work so as not to burden society; and also to save enough to give alms at the end of the week. The monks did not speak about their inner contemplation; they did not boast about their spiritual success. Abba Anthony had some thoughts of pride, so it was revealed to him that there was a doctor living in the city who gave alms to the poor and attended to his prayers; what the doctor was doing was equal to what Anthony was doing in the desert.[20] The desert fathers were always reminded that their style of life was not any better than the city dwellers who lived according to God's commandments. Therefore, they did not boast about their inner spiritual work; we glean their experiences from the problems they faced and the advice they gave. To these experiences we will now turn.

20. *ASWard*, 6, Anthony #24.

4

Let the Word of Christ
Dwell in You Richly

Scripture

Let the word of Christ dwell in you richly; teach and admonish one another in
all wisdom; and with gratitude in your hearts sing psalms, hymns, and spiritual
songs to God. And whatever you do, in word or deed, do everything in the name
of the Lord Jesus, giving thanks to God the Father through him.

COL 3:16–17

SCRIPTURE IS THE CORNERSTONE of desert spirituality. Reading Scripture, retaining it in memory and in the heart, using Scripture as a
means of prayer, and meditating on and following scriptural precepts are
some of the different activities that characterize the relationship between
the Christian who follows desert spirituality and Scripture. The desert fathers and mothers understood such spiritual exercises in Scripture as the
guides that would lead them to purity of the mind, thought, and heart.[1]

1. For archaeological evidence for the abundance of biblical texts in the desert
read Douglas Burton-Christie, *The Word in the Desert: Scripture and the Quest for
Holiness in Early Christian Monasticism* (New York: Oxford University Press, 1993)
43–48. For further discussion on the abundance of literate monks in the desert and
Pachomian monasteries see Samuel Rubenson, *The Letters of St. Antony: Monasticism
and the Making of a Saint*, Studies in Antiquity and Christianity (Minneapolis: Fortress, 1995) 35 and 115–21; and Chrysi Kotsifou, "Books and Book Production in the
Monastic Communities of Byzantine Egypt," in *The Early Christian Book*, eds. William

Abba Poemen said, "The nature of water is soft, that of the stone is hard; but if a bottle is hung above the stone, allowing the water to fall drop by drop, it wears away the stone. So it is with the word of God; it is soft and our heart is hard, but the man who hears the word of God often, opens his heart to the fear of God."[2] This requires a willingness of the person to allow the bottle to hang until the stone wears away and not plug the bottle when the words seem harsh or require one to change. Change requires courage. Though a single word of Scripture is powerful enough to transform—the handiest example is that of Anthony, who listened to the gospel message one Sunday morning and immediately renounced everything and followed Christ—most people need more than one reading. Accordingly, reading Scripture "often" is crucial. The ceaseless reading of Scripture acts as a constant reminder until the words of God can be engraved in one's memory, thought, and heart. The constant reading of Scripture acts like a mental Post-it note.

One of the monks asked Abba Sisoes the Theban a word of advice. He answered, "I read the New Testament, and I turn to the Old."[3] The answer indicates that Abba Sisoes' spiritual practice was to read Scripture from beginning to end without ceasing. The best advice he could give a newcomer to the desert was to read Scripture. Scripture will teach you everything.

A certain Melania informs us that Alexandra, a hermit and ascetic woman, spent her time in seclusion, dividing her time between prayer and manual work. From morning until three in the afternoon—the usual time for the ascetics' first meal—she would weave linen while praying and contemplating on the Psalms. The rest of the day she spent memorizing some of the writings of the "holy fathers" and contemplating on the prophets, apostles, and martyrs.[4] This narrative tells us something special about Alexandra's contemplation: she contemplated not only on Bible verses, but also on the lives of the biblical figures, whether ascetics such as Elijah, John the Baptist, and Anna the daughter of Phanuel (whom she would emulate), or other prophets and apostles whom she could take as role models. She also contemplated early church martyrs who renounced everything, even their lives, for the sake of Christ. Close reflection on the lives of the biblical figures gave some of the desert fathers and mothers a

---

E. Klingshirn and Linda Safran, CUA Studies in Early Christianity (Washington, DC: Catholic University of America Press, 2007) 48–66.

2. *ASWard*, 192, Abba Poemen #183.

3. *ASWard*, 219, Abba Sisoes #35.

4. *SABudge*, vol 1, 96.

special spiritual bond with these figures, who influenced them in some of their spiritual practices.

There is another story about a certain Daniel who "memorized all the Scriptures, the Old and the New [Testaments]. . . . He had this trait of never speaking except about an important matter of necessity. Again his memory and his drill were marvelous, for he was very delightful and he was long-suffering concerning each phrase which he spoke with great accuracy . . . daily he recited ten thousand verses from memory. . . . The abundance of much mediation formed his nature as it was said in the Song of Songs, 'I sleep and my heart watches.'"[5] Another story is about a monk who memorized fourteen books of Scripture, which became his means of keeping his mind in prayer.[6] Similar stories are associated with many of the desert fathers and mothers whose constant exercise was reciting Scripture. Reciting Scripture here means retrieving the biblical texts from memory for prayer and contemplation. It does not mean reciting without understanding or for the sheer purpose of boasting of one's intellectual abilities.

One of the aims of this spiritual exercise is to reach the point where "I slept, but my heart was awake" (Song 5:2), where one's inner thoughts are constantly contemplating on God and his words as a means to attain purity of thought. It is a way to fulfill the command, "You shall love the Lord your God with all your heart, and with all your soul, and with all your strength, and with all your mind" (Luke 10:27). Many wake up with the last thoughts they went to sleep with or with the topic that most worries them. Sleeping and waking up with thoughts of resentment, worry, dissatisfaction, or frustration will render a person exhausted and depleted, without any positive outlook on the world for the following day. If the last thoughts are words of Scripture or thoughts of the Divine, then this is what we will be subconsciously thinking of during our sleep and when we first wake up. This first thought will set the mood for the day.

The fathers understood "I slept, but my heart was awake" as the total devotion of the heart to God, and that one of the means to achieve this level of devotion was by the constant contemplation on Scripture.

> Someone asked Abba Anthony, "What must one do in order to please God?" The old man replied, "Pay attention to what I tell you: whoever you may be, always have God before your eyes; whatever you do, do it according to the testimony of the holy

---

5. *SAChaine*, 77, #250; *SAHartley*, 161, #250.

6. *AParadise*, 255.

Scriptures; in whatever place you live, do not easily leave it. Keep these three precepts and you will be saved."[7]

Having God before one's eyes is aided by reading Scripture, in which one is constantly reminded of God. The second part of the saying advises acting according to the biblical precepts. This is where memorizing Scripture becomes helpful: first, because one will have knowledge of the precepts; second, because when a person is required to make a decision, Scripture will act as a guide to show the person what would be the best action to take.

An elder disclosed to his disciples his approach to life: "I never take a step without first learning where I am about to put my foot, but I stand up and look about me carefully, and I am not careless, and I do not let [my foot go] until God guideth me and leadeth me on the path to the place which pleaseth Him."[8] Scripture guides the footsteps on the spiritual path. Epiphanius said, "Ignorance of Scriptures is a precipice and a deep abyss."[9] He also said that "reading Scripture is a safeguard against sin."[10] Abba Arsenius said that one should not do anything "without the testimony of Scriptures."[11] Scripture is the guiding rod for desert spirituality; it guides prayers and actions as well as conversations.

A group of monks came to visit Abba Anthony and the subject of the conversation was what a certain text from Scripture meant. Abba Anthony started with the youngest of the group and asked everyone to give their opinion.[12] Another group of monks coming from Scetis came to visit Abba Anthony. During their trip they were sitting on the boat weaving baskets— that is, attending to their manual work—and discussing Scripture.[13] Some of the questions asked revolved around interpreting or explaining certain biblical passages. A father asked Abba Poemen, "Who is he who says, 'I am a companion of all who fear Thee' (Ps, 119.63)." Poemen responded, "It is the Holy Spirit who says that."[14] Whether the monks were in the desert, visiting, or traveling, Scripture was the topic of their conversations.

---

7. *AS Ward*, 2, Antony the Great #3.

8. *SA Budge*, 247–48, #457.

9. *AS Ward*, 58, Epiphanius of Cyprus #11.

10. *AS Ward*, 58, Epiphanius of Cyprus #9.

11. *SA Budge*, 197, #203.

12. *AS Ward*, 4, Antony the Great #17.

13. *AS Ward*, 5, Antony the Great #18.

14. *AS Ward*, 186, Poemen #136; another example is *SA Budge*, 226, #365.

Abba Macarius gave the following advice to a monk who was tormented by many thoughts: "Practice fasting a little later; meditate on the Gospel and the other Scriptures, and if an alien thought arises within you, never look at it but always look upwards, and the Lord will come at once to your help."[15] Fasting, meditating on Scripture, and prayer are three ingredients that will grant a person God's mercy to overcome his thoughts. A crucial point is asking for God's help, because if we think that we overcome everything merely through our will power then we will be trapped in arrogance. It is the Spirit working within us that makes us follow Scripture and even start to understand it. Abba Anthony was asked to explain a passage in Leviticus. He did not know the answer, so he went into the desert to pray, beseeching God to "send Moses, to make me understand this saying." Abba Ammonas, who followed him to the desert, heard a voice but could not understand it.[16] This story encourages every person who reads Scriptures but does not understand a verse or a passage to first implore God to reveal the meaning of the Scripture. This does not mean one does not refer to commentaries, but the inner and deep meaning of a verse or passage might not be understood in any way other than through prayer.

The desert fathers and mothers were very careful to assert that reading Scripture was primarily for their edification and spiritual growth and not for boasting about their knowledge or intellectual abilities. The following saying indicates the anxiety that arises when reading Scripture shifts from one's personal edification to other uses. This shift affects the mode of reading and the approach towards Scripture.

> Ammon (of the place called Raithu) brought this question to Sisois: "When I read Scripture, I am tempted to make elaborate commentaries and prepare myself to answer questions on it." He replied, "You don't need to do that. It is better to speak simply, with good conscious and a pure mind."[17]

This can be a concern to many church leaders who have to prepare for Sunday sermons, Bible studies, or talks. Because of such obligations the leaders might become so consumed with preparations for a successful delivery that they overlook their own benefit from the biblical text. There is no doubt that the person who prepares for any type of church service

---

15. *ASWard*, 12, Macarius the Great #3.

16. *ASWard*, 7, Antony the Great #26.

17. *SSWard*, 81, Nothing Done for Show #16; cf. *ASWard*, 216, Abba Sisoes #17.

reaps some benefit, but this might be a benefit that satisfies the intellect rather than enriches the spirit.

The fathers knew Scripture so well and were so engaged in Bible study and interpretation that their language was filled with biblical images and metaphors and their sentences were woven with biblical verses. In short, the desert fathers and mothers were so immersed in Scripture that they were speaking Scripture. Scripture became the center of their spiritual activities; it nourished their prayers, their contemplation and meditation, and their conversation. The constant contemplation of Scriptures consecrated their thoughts and they were able to contemplate the Divine without ceasing.

The desert fathers and mothers memorized Scriptures as an integral part of their spiritual life. Given modern technology and the high level of education of modern societies, one might ask: Why memorize Scripture? The initial reason for memorization in ancient societies was that illiteracy was the norm and only a few were capable of reading and writing. The culture was more oral than modern cultures. Memorization was the main tool for the easy and quick availability of information. The modern educational system emphasizes analytical thinking rather than memorization and honing the tools and faculties for memorization. Now, with modern technology, when literally the whole of Scripture is available digitally at our fingertips, why memorize? Memorization is still important for the spiritual endeavor. Technological tools provide Scripture on demand, but that was not what the fathers were doing. Memorization internalizes the biblical message in the heart, soul, and mind of the person endeavoring to live a spiritual life. Technology cannot internalize Scripture; it makes it available, but we have to do the inner work of interacting with the biblical verses or figures and meditating on them. Visual media enhanced by modern technology might facilitate our memorization, since we are becoming more and more of a visual culture, but we still have to inwardly interact with the Word in whatever form we receive it. The main goal is internalizing Scripture so that our heart, soul, and mind conform to God's words so that we can be in the constant presence of God. Scripture provides words for us to pray, bless, praise, and give glory to God when we are in his presence. Internalizing Scripture helps us achieve this goal.

Is this goal achievable in our busy city life? Yes. It will be more difficult, and we will never reach the high level of spirituality of the desert fathers and mothers, but we can reach a certain level of constant presence before God. This requires some decluttering of our lives, which the desert fathers called renunciation. The more we simplify our lives, the more we are able to have inner quietness, the more our heart has the space to praise, bless, and feel God and enjoy being in his presence. The decluttering and quietness should be accompanied with some memorization of Scripture—a verse a day, or a verse a week, or even a verse a month. The focus on one verse for some time quiets the heart and focuses the mind and helps prayer and praise.

Biblical Verses on Scripture for Further Contemplation

PSALM 119:11—I treasure your word in my heart, so that I may not sin against you.

LUKE 11:28—But he said, "Blessed rather are those who hear the word of God and obey it!"

HEBREWS 4:12–13—Indeed, the word of God is living and active, sharper than any two-edged sword, piercing until it divides soul from spirit, joints from marrow; it is able to judge the thoughts and intentions of the heart. And before him no creature is hidden, but all are naked and laid bare to the eyes of the one to whom we must render an account.

1 JOHN 2:14—I write to you, young people, because you are strong and the word of God abides in you, and you have overcome the evil one.

2 TIMOTHY 3:16–17—All scripture is inspired by God and is useful for teaching, for reproof, for correction, and for training in righteousness, so that everyone who belongs to God may be proficient, equipped for every good work.

EPHESIANS 6:17—Take the helmet of salvation, and the sword of the Spirit, which is the word of God.

PHILIPPIANS 1:27—Only, live your life in a manner worthy of the gospel of Christ.

COLOSSIANS 3:16–17—Let the word of Christ dwell in you richly; teach and admonish one another in all wisdom; and with gratitude in your hearts sing psalms, hymns, and spiritual songs to God. And whatever you do, in word or deed, do everything in the name of the Lord Jesus, giving thanks to God the Father through him.

1 John 2:4—Whoever says, "I have come to know him," but does not obey his commandments, is a liar, and in such a person the truth does not exist.

Further Sayings for Reflection

Abba Arsenius used to say, "Thou shalt not depart from a place without great labour, and thou shalt do none of the things which, evilly, though desirest, and thou shalt do nothing without the testimony of the Scriptures."[18]

One of the old men used to say, "The Prophets compiled the Scriptures, and the Fathers have copied them, and the men who came after them learned to repeat them by heart; then hath come this generation and [its children] have placed them in cupboards as useless things."[19]

The brethren asked an old man, saying, "How is it that God promiseth in the Scriptures good things to the soul, and that the soul desireth them not, but turneth aside to impurity?" And he answered and said unto them, "It is my opinion that it is because it hath not yet tasted the good things which are above, and therefore the good things which are here are dear unto it."[20]

When you sit in your room read [Scripture] with reason and understanding and mediate giving praise and glory to God.[21]

When you return to your cell, devote your time to reading Scriptures and prayer, for manual work solely makes you forgetful of God your creator.[22]

An elder said, "Woe to the soul that inquired about the word of God and listened to it and does not do anything of what it hears."[23]

Three brothers visited an elder. The first said to him, "Teacher, I have copied the Old and the New Testament." The elder replied, "You filled the cupboards of your cell with paper." The second said to him, "I have learned the Old and the New Testament in my heart." The elder replied, "You have filled the air with words." The third said to him, "Weeds have filled my oven." The elder said to him, "You have kicked out the love of strangers."[24]

18. *SABudge*, 197, #202.
19. *SABudge*, 56, #250.
20. *SABudge*, 166, #46.
21. *AParadise*, 131.
22. *AParadise*, 131.
23. *AParadise*, 389.
24. *AParadise*, 390.

5

Thought Captive to Christ

Thought

"Take every thought captive to obey Christ."

2 COR 10:5

He answered, "You shall love the Lord your God with all your heart,
and with all your soul, and with all your strength,
and with all your mind; and your neighbor as yourself."

LUKE 10:27

IN PART I OF this book we presented Athanasius' argument in *Against
the Gentiles* that the beginning of evil came from human thoughts and
the presence of evil is the work of the mind or *nous*. The desert fathers
and mothers, who were seeking perfection, seeking to please God, seeking to be in God's presence, and seeking to be in God's image and likeness,
understood the profound essence of Athanasius' theology and its impact
on the spiritual life. They understood that they had to struggle with their
inner demons as well as the outer demons. They had to confront and
work on their inner thoughts. Thoughts reflect the work of the mind and
the movement of the heart. "For it is from within, from the human heart,
that evil intentions come: fornication, theft, murder, adultery, avarice,
wickedness, deceit, licentiousness, envy, slander, pride, folly. All these
evil things come from within, and they defile a person" (Mark 7:21–23).

The early desert fathers and mothers understood that dealing with their thoughts was the key to overcoming many of their spiritual woes. Examining their thoughts became the center of their spiritual exercises. If they took their thoughts captive to conform them to Christ, they would preserve God's image and likeness within them. They would return to the paradisal state of the first Adam. They would be like angels on earth. They would live the newness of creation granted us by the resurrection. "They are like angels and are children of God, being children of the resurrection" (Luke 20:36). In the state of holding their thoughts captive to Christ they would not condemn and judge, they would not slander or gossip, they would not hate or get angry, they would not be tempted, they would not be struggling with thoughts of pride and arrogance, they would not suffer from jealousy, and they would not struggle with the acquisition of possessions and renunciation. Desert spirituality is centered on purifying the thoughts. According to Athanasius, thoughts can incline to either side: either to create evil or to praise God. Guarding one's thoughts creates a pure heart, and a pure heart sees God. "Blessed are the pure in heart, for they will see God" (Matt 5:8). A pure heart contemplates God and prays without ceasing. A pure heart gives praise and glory to God. A heart filled with anger, envy, or hatred cannot raise up a pure prayer, for we "call on the Lord from a pure heart" (2 Tim 2:22).

Those who went to the desert had one goal: to be with God and let nothing stand between them and God. In the desert and its silence, they confronted the major obstacle that effectively obstructs being with God: the inner thoughts. In the desert external voices cease. This is when the inner voice becomes louder and is heard. But to be with God, one must work on purity of heart. The inner voice also must be quieted so as to hear God's voice. For God is not in the earthquake or the fire, but in "a sound of sheer silence" (1 Kgs 19:12). Those who are busy with the world are too busy to analyze their inner selves and understand where their hearts and thoughts are taking them. In the desert, they examined their hearts very closely; it became the place to find the balance of their hearts and determine if purity of heart would tip the scale. The following generations of Christians benefited from their inner struggle, which paved the way for us to explore the heart and mind. Though we would have liked to know more than the pithy statements or short stories they left us, what we have is enough to guide us through the initial phases toward spiritual maturity.

The following story is indicative of the awareness of the desert fathers of the theology of St. Athanasius and his understanding of the newness of life regained by the resurrection:

> One of the Fathers used to tell of a certain Abba Paul, from Lower Egypt, who lived in the Thebaid. He used to take various kinds of snakes in his hands and cut them through the middle. The brethren made prostration before him saying, "Tell us what you have done to receive this grace." He said, "Forgive me, Fathers, but if someone has obtained purity, everything is in submission to him, as it was to Adam, when he was in Paradise before he transgressed the commandment."[1]

In paradise there was peace and harmony, and this is what humanity is always seeking. Before the fall and before transgressing God's commandment, our first parents were living in purity and the harmony of the universe was preserved. Isaiah anticipates the state when humanity will be living in righteousness and faithfulness:

> The wolf shall live with the lamb, the leopard shall lie down with the kid, the calf and the lion and the fatling together, and a little child shall lead them. The cow and the bear shall graze, their young shall lie down together; and the lion shall eat straw like the ox. The nursing child shall play over the hole of the asp, and the weaned child shall put its hand on the adder's den. They will not hurt or destroy on all my holy mountain; for the earth will be full of the knowledge of the LORD as the waters cover the sea. (Isa 11:6–9; see also Isa 65:25)

The association of the images of a child peacefully playing close to an asp's hole and the hermit confidently holding snakes cannot be missed. The hermit himself has acknowledged that it is "purity" that makes creation submit to humans.

The sayings and lives of the desert fathers and mothers are full of stories of interaction with fierce and dangerous animals being tamed at the presence of the saints. It is an outward indication of the level of purity that the saint has attained. It is the actual realization of the renewed life granted to humanity by the resurrection, a newness of life already actualized on earth in fulfillment of God's promise to be in God's image, similar to the paradisal life before the fall. Purity of heart is what all are seeking. Examining the heart and thoughts is the primary concern of desert spirituality.

1. *ASWard*, 204.

One of the desert elders said that we have to be attentive to every thought of contempt in our hearts, for "whoever shall say to his brother, 'Raca,' shall be guilty before the supreme court; and whoever shall say, 'You fool,' shall be guilty enough to go into the fiery hell" (Matt 5:22). We also have to be attentive to the least thought of lust in our hearts: "But I say to you that everyone who looks at a woman with lust has already committed adultery with her in his heart" (Matt 5:28). The seven sons and three daughters of Job would gather and hold festivities in which they would eat and drink. As for Job, he would wait until the festivities were done, and then "Job would send and consecrate them, rising up early in the morning and offering burnt offerings according to the number of them all; for Job said, 'Perhaps my sons have sinned and cursed God in their hearts.' Thus Job did continually" (Job 1:5). Job worried not only about the sins of his heart but also the sins of his children's hearts. If we know all these things, the elder continues, we have to be mindful of all "the movements of our thoughts."[2]

Abba Silvanus is a good example of the diligent scrutiny of thoughts: "Some brothers once asked Silvanus, 'What way of life did you follow to be endowed with such prudence?' He answered, 'I have never let any bitter thought remain in my heart.'"[3] The Lord accepts prayer from a pure heart. We cannot offer a gift at the altar of prayer if we remember there is something against a brother or a sister. Christ required us to reconcile with a brother and sister before offering the gift (see Matt 5:23–24). This is what Abba Sivlanus had in mind when he said he never let any bitter thought remain in his heart.

Abba Poemen "examined his thought for about an hour" before attending the communal prayer with the rest of his monastic community.[4] He took Matthew 5:23–24 very seriously and made it a priority in his spiritual life. Abba Ammoes would not talk to anyone on his way to church lest the conversation would let him slip into non-"edifying words."[5] We have to consider carefully the state of our mind and thoughts before offering praise to God as they affect our prayers. If our mind is entertaining thoughts against a neighbor, a coworker, a friend, or a family member worried about our future or concerned about a project, our mind will be clouded with thoughts of anger, hurt pride, revenge, worry,

2. *SABudge*, 81–82, #360.

3. *SSWard*, 124, Sober Living #30.

4. *ASWard*, 172, Poemen #32.

5. *ASWard*, 30, Ammoes #1.

or hopelessness. These thoughts will attack us during prayer and not let us contemplate God. "But the cares of the world, and the lure of wealth, and the desire for other things come in and choke the word, and it yields nothing" (Mark 4:19). If we stand in prayer and find no peace then it is time to examine the thoughts of our hearts.

The fathers astutely understood the connection of thoughts and emotions within us and their impact on our physical well-being. Abba Poemen's practical advice reflects the deep understanding of this process:

> Another brother questioned him in these words: "What does, 'See that none of you repays evil for evil' mean?" (1 Thess 5:15) The old man said to him, "Passions work in four stages–first, in the heart; secondly, in the face; thirdly, in words; and fourthly, it is essential not to render evil for evil in deeds. If you can purify your heart, passion will not come into your expression; but if it comes into your face, take care not to speak; but if you do speak, cut the conversation short in case you render evil for evil."[6]

Understanding the stages of the progression of evil thoughts within us is the key for many of the sayings of the desert fathers and mothers. Discerning the internal dialogue of the heart reflects the level of one's spiritual state and becomes central in desert spirituality; it indicates if one can stop the progression of evil thoughts at its roots, the heart. If the person is too late to discern the inner movement of the heart, then the person should work on the outward expressions of the soul: the countenance, and then speech. Our facial expressions unconsciously betray our feelings. But it is sometimes too late or difficult to control them. That is why dealing with the root of the problem in the heart is essential. But if we cannot manage to get to the root, we know we should and can control our speech. Slander, the tongue, and talk are going to be another focus of the spiritual journey and we will devote a chapter to them.

If the root of all our thoughts lies in the heart, how can we manage these thoughts? Abba Poemen has some wisdom on such matters:

> A brother came to see Abba Poemen and said to him, "Abba, I have many thoughts and they put me in danger." The old man led him outside and said to him, "Expand your chest and do not breathe in." He said, "I cannot do that." Then the old man said to him, "If you cannot do that, no more can you prevent thoughts from arising, but you can resist them."[7]

6. *AS Ward*, 172, Poemen # 34.
7. *AS Ward*, 171, Poemen # 28.

The key point here is that we have the free will to accept or reject thoughts that put us "in danger." The purer the heart, the less the thoughts torment us. Nevertheless, thoughts are going to haunt us and it is within our means to accept and toy with them or oppose them. Hundreds of thoughts cross our mind every day; some do not trouble us, and some we do not even notice. It is the thoughts that come and never leave that can be a starting point for our concerns, because there is good reason for them to remain and linger. The desert fathers and mothers advise us to examine these thoughts.

Abba Epiphanius said that when thoughts of pride or vainglory fill one's heart, one should oppose the thought as "fornication."[8] Epiphanius is using a biblical image mentioned in Isaiah 1 and Jeremiah 2, in which Israel and the people of Israel are accused of fornication because they have left God for other gods and because their thoughts are not devoted to God like a bride devoted to her groom. Spousal betrayal is compared to humanity's betrayal of God when our thoughts and our heart are not fully devoted to him. James uses a similar image: "Adulterers! Do you not know that friendship with the world is enmity with God?" (Jas 4:4). Befriending the worldly life is a betrayal of God's love; it is adultery. Epiphanius laments the soul's betrayal of God when it accepts thoughts of its own glory rather than God's. This could be applied to all thoughts that do not give glory to God; they are a betrayal of God's love for us. Colossians 3:5 considers the following vices to be idolatry: "Whatever in you is earthly: fornication, impurity, passion, evil desire, and greed (which is idolatry)." And Colossians 3:8 addresses vices of the mind: "But now you must get rid of all such things—anger, wrath, malice, slander, and abusive language from your mouth." Such sayings set the standard of perfection too high and some of the brothers questioned the possibility of attaining such perfection in life. For as long as we are humans with rational minds we will be always having thoughts. In response to such concerns, one of the elders said it was important not to carry the thought into deed.[9] If we cannot prevent the evil thought, we should not entertain it and put it into action.

Amma Syncletica has the following saying:

> She also said, "There is a useful sorrow, and a destructive sorrow. Sorrow is useful when we weep for our sins, and for our neighbour's ignorance, and so that we may not relax our purpose to attain to true goodness, these are the real kinds of sorrow. Our

8. *SABudge*, 246, #446.

9.. *SABudge*, 253, #502.

enemy adds something to this. For he sends sorrow without reason, which is something called lethargy. We ought always to drive out a sadness like that with prayers and psalms."[10]

Some expect if one is leading a spiritual life there must be constant joy. But sorrow has its spiritual benefits. Sorrow makes us repent and change our ways. We also need discretion to understand that not all sorrow is useful; some is destructive. The same goes with all other spiritual states we experience. Joy might not be always helpful because it can drive us to inattentiveness, pride, or spiritual idleness. Discernment of thoughts is crucial in desert spirituality. Another major component of this advice is prayer. Prayer helps us in the process of discernment and to expel unwanted thoughts.

It is up to us to accept thoughts or reject them. One of the hermits advises a brother: "Though the demons are careful to send thoughts to you, they do not force you to accept them. It is up to you to receive or reject them."[11] James 4:7–8 expresses a similar sentiment, accusing those who submit to the devil and are not pure in heart as double minded: "Submit yourselves therefore to God. Resist the devil, and he will flee from you. Draw near to God, and he will draw near to you. Cleanse your hands, you sinners, and purify your hearts, you double-minded."

Another hermit addressed specifically thoughts of lust, explaining that once we let them in and entertain them they control us and we become addicted to them.

> A hermit used to say, "A lustful thought is brittle like papyrus. When it is thrust at us, if we do not accept it but throw it away it breaks easily. If it allures us and we keep playing with it, it becomes as difficult to break as iron. We need discernment to know that those who consent lose hope of salvation and for those who do not consent, a crown is made ready."[12]

Many understand the addictive power of lust; it is as "difficult to break as iron."

With the extraordinary advancement of technology the modern person is left to work not only with his thoughts but also with the numerous visual and audible messages that bombard one every day. The modern person has a tougher struggle, which the early church fathers and mothers

10. *SSWard*, 105, Discretion #71.

11. *SSWard*, 44, Lust #32.

12. *SSWard*, 44, Lust #33.

could not even imagine. The media industry knows the addictive nature of such images and has exploited it to the maximum. The exploitation has not left any person safe, whether young or mature; the media knows how to target each age group. The media addresses and exploits human senses very effectively. Athanasius argued in *Against the Gentiles* that when Moses was delayed on the mountain, the people of Israel collected their gold and "cast an image of a calf" and offered it worship because humanity tends to make ideas concrete to satisfy the senses. While Moses was delayed by an invisible God, the people of Israel fashioned a concrete golden god, pleasing to the eye, which they could see, feel, and touch. Modern man does not need a golden calf or an idol anymore; the media has created virtual idols and celebrity idols that mesmerize the audience and hook them to the screen. The media exploit the senses with images appealing not only to sexual lust, but to lusts that satisfy all the senses. For example, commercials entice the viewer with food for the sense of taste, beauty products and luxury clothes for the sense of sight, and cars and extraordinary mansions for the lust of possession. And all these advertisements are accompanied by sounds to allure with the sense of hearing. The whole media industry exploits the senses and entices the imagination with an unreal world. The media has mastered the art of exploiting and appeasing human senses.

The early desert fathers understood the power of the senses Athanasius discussed and knew they were the gate to the mind and heart. The following saying expresses this succinctly:

> One asked an elder, "Why does my mind [heart] wander when I reside in my dwelling place?" The elder answered him, "Because the outer senses—sight, hearing, smell, speech—are ill. As for these, if you exercise their functions in purity, the inward senses are at rest and healthy."[13]

To control the thoughts and the wandering of the mind, one must control the senses. Abba Anthony was once asked about thoughts and he said, "Do not carry them into effect, but let them settle down and down until they breed worms and perish."[14] This was Anthony's approach to thoughts in general—"not to carry them into effect." If a person persists in not submitting to a thought it will eventually disappear. On another occasion, Abba Anthony suggests one should "not even entertain" the thought.[15]

13. *SAChaîne*, 2, #5; *SAHartley*, 27, #5.

14. *SABudge*, 249, #474.

15. *v. Anton* 19.5.

Abba Poemen advised Abba Joseph to examine his thoughts even though they might disturb and shake him.[16] Poemen does not advise Joseph to comply with the thought, but to examine it to be more effective in restraining it. Abba Poemen spoke about thoughts of lust and slander together, saying, "he should not in any way whatsoever incline towards these two thoughts, and he should not utter them, and he should not meditate upon such things in his heart. And if he desires to think about them and to turn them over in his heart, he will not benefit thereby but will rather suffer damage."[17] The desert fathers generally suggest that it is better to avoid thoughts of lust and not to negotiate with them because lusts hold the thoughts captive with their allures and the thoughts spiral down and take control of the person. As much as possible one is to avoid exposing the senses to outward stimuli; experience indicates that the more a person exposes himself to such thoughts, the more addictive they become and the more difficult it is to resist them.

Thoughts of arrogance and pride are the ones that the desert fathers and mothers considered most perilous to the spiritual life. In a culture where getting hired requires a well-crafted resume that sings one's praises and shows off one's achievements, and where advancement up the corporate ladder requires self-promotion, cultivating thoughts of humility and combating thoughts of pride might seem at first to be counter cultural. But on a closer look, humility is still a well-respected and appreciated trait. When you choose a friend you do not choose a proud, arrogant person, but rather a humble person who cares about others rather than her- or himself. A humble person might not climb the social and corporate ladder as fast, but there is always the cross that one has to bear and sacrifices that one has to offer for the sake of following Christ. Humility stems from a strong life of faith and a strong character that is not captivated by the glamor of outward appearances. Humility is not a sign of weakness but rather of a self-assured person with a strong, secure character who is not swayed by the attraction of satisfying the senses. People with mature life experience will know that pride has been the downfall of many. Pride blinds one from assessing one's true self and does not provide an opportunity for self-improvement.

The desert fathers and mothers gave advice regarding thoughts of pride:

16. *SABudge*, 198, #210.
17. *SABudge*, 206, #253.

An elder said: "If a thought which exalts arrogance comes to you, examine your thoughts (to see) if you have been keeping the commandments: if you love your enemies; if you rejoice at the praise of your enemies and are grieved at their needs; if you consider yourself a useless servant and a sinner greater than everyone. In these things you do not think on greatness [i.e. self importance] as though you are perfect in everything, for you know that this thought destroys every work."[18]

In this saying, the elder is examining his thoughts in light of Matthew 5:44; Romans 12:15; and 1 Timothy 1:15. No one is perfect, yet we judge everyone else, requiring perfection of them. The simple spiritual exercise of examining our self against some of the Bible verses reveals that we ourselves have not fulfilled all the commandments and we are not as perfect as we think. This exercise will make our criticism of others less harsh, if not vanquish it completely. Thoughts of pride will just disappear.

Another monk came to Abba Peter the Pionite and said, "'When I am in my cell, my soul is at peace, but if a brother comes to see me and speaks to me of external things, my soul is disturbed.' Abba Peter told him that Abba Lot used to say, 'Your key opens my door.' The brother said to him, 'What does that mean?' The old man said, 'When someone comes to see you, you say to him, "How are you? Where have you come from? How are the brethren? Did they welcome you or not?" Then you have opened the brother's door and you will hear a great deal that you would rather not have heard.'"[19] This is an account of a person who is at peace when alone, but when he meets others, the conversation seems to disturb him. The advice he receives is that we can steer the conversation to our benefit by not asking questions that prompt gossip, slander, or disturbing information about others. If we do not want to listen to disturbing gossip, we can steer the conversation in another direction.

Some of the younger monks came to test Abba John the Short to see if he would let his thoughts be scattered by gossip and idle conversation. So, the brothers came and said to him, "We give thanks to God that this year there has been much rain and the palm trees have been able to drink, and their shoots have grown, and the brethren have found manual work."[20] They were careful to begin the discussion with thanksgiving, since this would open the door for other conversation. Abba John steered the

18. *SAChaîne*, 29, #128; *SAHartley*, 83, #128; and *SSWard*, 162, Humility #54.

19. *ASWard*, 200, Peter the Pionite #2.

20. *ASWard*, 87, John the Dwarf #10.

conversation to a discussion on the Holy Spirit. The brothers understood that Abba John had no intention of continuing the conversation and preferred to talk about more spiritual topics.

Memorizing Scripture has been one of the ways of keeping the mind contemplating on God and not deviating to other thoughts. Thus it is said about a certain Abba Daniel that he memorized all Scripture, Old and New Testament, with other church writings, and he contemplated and recited the biblical texts continuously. He is also described as a person who was "delightful," who "spoke with great accuracy." Because his mind was continuously meditating on the words of God, "meditation formed his nature as it was said in the Song of Songs, 'I sleep and my heart watches.'"[21] The constant preoccupation of the mind with words of Scripture displaces other thoughts that linger in the mind. When a person is concerned with an urgent matter and it preoccupies his mind, he tends to forget other matters, ones that might even be important, because his mind is worried or preoccupied. The desert fathers made Scripture their urgent matter. With constant study, memorizing, contemplation, and discussion during Bible studies, it became the overriding thought whether awake and asleep.

Abba Hyperichius said, "Spiritual hymns and persistent mediation lessen for us the war which comes against us."[22] When one sets his sights on something, one thinks of it constantly until one achieves his goal. Thus "Hyperichius said, 'Let your mind be always on the kingdom of heaven, and you will soon inherit it.'"[23] Career-motivated people devote all their time, energy, and life towards their career goals. They are commended by the society for their achievements. If God is our goal and living a spiritual life is one of our aims, we have to devote time and energy towards that goal. The desert fathers and mothers took that goal very seriously and chose to dedicate all their lives to it. Our goals define how we behave and determine our priorities. If the heavenly kingdom is our goal, this goal will shape our decisions, our relationships, and how we choose to spend our time. If God is our goal, then our mind will be preoccupied with him and examining our thoughts to conform to him will become more and more effortless.

The previous sayings have been primarily focused on how to oppose thoughts, either to not let them enter our minds or, if they have entered, to not let them nest there and occupy our minds. Other sayings

21. *SAChaîne*, 77, #250; *SAHartley*, 160, #250.
22. *SAChaîne*, 9, #43; *SAHartley*, 43, #43.
23. *SSWard*, 125, Sober Living, #35.

are concerned with the activities we do to help us preserve pure thoughts and a pure heart. "Abba Theonas said, 'When we turn our spirit from the contemplation of God, we become the slaves of carnal passions.'"[24] Abba Theonas has summarized Saint Athanasius' theology in a simple, succinct statement. Athanasius argued that when the human soul, which was created rational in order to contemplated God, became attached to sensible things—the things that are near to the body and senses—it was no longer able to contemplate God. When people were deceived by their surroundings, and preferred to contemplate themselves rather than God, they forgot the power they originally had from God. Athanasius emphasizes that when people were pure they contemplated God and could see God; when they contemplated their own bodies and all that belongs to the senses, they were stripped of the contemplation of the divine things. It was then they knew that they were naked. When humans discovered they were naked, they clung to their desires and became comfortable in their desires; it became a habit, and they became subject to the fear of death. Their fear made them unable to be satisfied with anything and they learned to commit wrong.[25] Many of the sayings of the desert fathers and mothers affirm the deep theological roots of desert spirituality; they are not flowery sayings but rather spring from deep theological and biblical reflection.

Another father recapitulates the essence of this same theology when he says, "It is necessary for a man to place a work inside himself. If he is occupied with the work of God, the enemy comes to him from time to time, but he does not find a resting place in him. Again if he is ruled by the captivity of the enemy, the Spirit of God comes to him frequently, but if he does not leave a place for him, he departs because of evil."[26] When a person is "occupied with the work of God," by which he means the inner spiritual work of the contemplation of God and meditation on divine Scriptures, the Holy Spirit finds a place to dwell within him or her. But when the person is preoccupied with thoughts from elsewhere, the Spirit does not find a welcoming place in the heart because the person is busy with other concerns. Similarly, Abba Macarius said, "If we keep remembering the wrong which men have done us, we destroy the power of the remembrance of God."[27] In this case the heart is so preoccupied with anger and hurt from another person that God's love becomes a stranger to it.

24. *ASWard*, 80, Theonas #1.

25. *gent.* 3.

26. *SAChaîne*, 15, #67; *SAHartley*, 56, #67.

27. *ASWard*, 136, Macarius the Great #36.

"Abba Alonius said, 'If a man does not say in his heart, in the world there is only myself and God, he will not gain peace.'"[28] Only God can grant us peace; distraction with other concerns will preoccupy a person's thoughts and will not leave a place for the Spirit to dwell within. When the heart is filled with God and God's love, the heart does not care to carry thoughts that drive the divine presence away. Thoughts of hatred, anger, revenge, worry, or any other thoughts evaporate before the divine love. It is only when we let go of all these thoughts that the heart finds peace.

Some of the monastics reached such a level of constant contemplation on the Divine that they became totally absorbed in their meditation. John the Short reached such a level of constant contemplation that while his hands were working on basket weaving, "his spirit was occupied in contemplation" and he did not notice that he had weaved the rope of two baskets into one.[29] We do the same thing when our minds are so preoccupied with something that we do not realize the mistake we have done at work; the difference is that his mind was preoccupied with God, while ours is preoccupied with our daily worries, frustration, anger, or other consuming thoughts.

The following story suggests that inner spiritual discipline should be accompanied by bodily discipline. It highlights the importance of both practices. We cannot consider the spiritual to be superior to bodily discipline; both should go hand in hand since they interact with and affect one another.

> Agatho was asked, "Which is more difficult, bodily discipline, or guard over the inner self?" He said, "Man is like a tree. His bodily discipline is like the leaves of the tree, his guard over the inner self is like the fruit. Scripture says that 'every tree which bringeth not forth good fruit is hewn down and cast into the fire' (Matt. 3:10). So we ought to take every precaution about guarding the mind, because that is our fruit. Yet we need to be covered and beautiful with leaves, which is bodily discipline." Agatho was wise in understanding, earnest in discipline, armed at all points, careful about keeping up his manual work, sparing in food and clothing.[30]

For Abba Poemen, good thoughts are like good company. He says that, externally, we should work, keep silence, meditate, and live

28. *AS Ward*, 35, Alonius #1.

29. *AS Ward*, 87, John the Dwarf #11.

30. *SS Ward*, 90, Discretion #11.

moderately. Internally, we should keep the hours of prayer, and keep "a watch on the secret thoughts of the heart."[31] Poemen considers both of these activities good company. Poemen also thinks bodily activity provides a tranquil setting for the inner spirit to be at peace. Like Agatho, he thinks inner and outward activities should go hand in hand. For Poemen, as long as the heart is engaged in an inner activity then the heart is engaged in good thoughts and good company. He considers preserving inner peace, giving thanks to God in illness, and having a pure mind to be three equally commendable inner works.[32] On another occasion Poemen warns that outward silence is not sufficient; what counts is inner peace and tranquility. He says, "A man may seem to be silent, but if his heart is condemning others he is babbling ceaselessly. But there may be another who talks from morning till night and yet he is truly silent; that is, he says nothing that is not profitable."[33]

When we say that purity of thought associated with inner quietness is essential for the life of prayer and spirituality, we might think that this is only for the solitaries in the desert. Because of their solitary lives they are able to practice purity of thought. Living in the desert however, does not guarantee a pure heart or pure thoughts. This is best captured in the saying of Amma Syncletica:

> Amma Syncletica said, "There are many who live in the mountains and behave as if they were in the town, and they are wasting their time. It is possible to be a solitary in one's mind while living in a crowd, and it is possible for one who is a solitary to live in the crowd of his own thoughts."[34]

All these sayings actually address the "crowd" and clutter of one's thoughts. Everyone lives with thoughts; it is inevitable. The real issue is: What type of thoughts occupy our minds? Are they the "thought captive to obey Christ" (2 Cor 10:5)? Are they the thoughts that make us blessed ("Blessed are the pure in heart, for they will see God," Matt 5:8)? Faith in the incarnation and the power of the newness of life granted to us by the resurrection enable us to believe that this is attainable. Christ would not have demanded for us to be pure in heart if this were not possible. He has granted us the power of the Holy Spirit to make this attainable.

---

31. *SS Ward*, 103, Discretion #64.
32. *AS Ward*, 171, Abba Poemen #29.
33. *AS Ward*, 171, Abba Poemen #27.
34. *AS Ward*, 234, Amma Syncletica #19.

The desert fathers and mothers took Matthew 5:8 very seriously. They believed in the promises of the resurrection and that the way to see God is to have a pure heart. They struggled with thoughts of envy, hatred, judgment, lust, and slander, just to mention a few. Their sayings are practical and emerged from an inner struggle that all human beings experience. The sayings in this chapter can apply everywhere and to anyone. What the desert fathers and mothers did paves the way for us to identify the struggles of our hearts and thoughts much easier. They left guideposts to help us navigate through the maze of thoughts that bombard us all day long and leave us exhausted at the end of the day and wondering why we can't pray. Purity of thought is attainable. Amma Syncletica is right to say that it is not our location that dictates our inner thoughts. Each one of us has met someone in our church or family, or a neighbor or coworker, whom we can identify as a person who has a pure heart. We know it is possible to be pure in thoughts because we met people whom we know well who have achieved this status of purity of heart. To be pure in heart and thoughts is for everyone. "It is possible to be a solitary in one's mind while living in a crowd."

Biblical Verses on Thought for Further Contemplation:

COLOSSIANS 1:21-22—And you who were once estranged and hostile in mind, doing evil deeds, he has now reconciled in his fleshly body through death, so as to present you holy and blameless and irreproachable before him. . . .

PHILIPPIANS 4:7—And the peace of God, which surpasses all understanding, will guard your hearts and your minds in Christ Jesus.

TITUS 1:15—To the pure all things are pure, but to the corrupt and unbelieving nothing is pure. Their very minds and consciences are corrupted.

SIRACH 42:20—No thought escapes him, and nothing is hidden from him.

PSALM 77:6—I commune with my heart in the night; I meditate and search my spirit:

GALATIANS 5: 24-25—And those who belong to Christ Jesus have crucified the flesh with its passions and desires. If we live by the Spirit, let us also be guided by the Spirit.

EPHESIANS 2:3—All of us once lived among them in the passions of our flesh, following the desires of flesh and senses, and we were by nature children of wrath, like everyone else.

EPHESIANS 4:17—Now this I affirm and insist on in the Lord: you must no longer live as the Gentiles live, in the futility of their minds.

EPHESIANS 4:22–23—You were taught to put away your former way of life, your old self, corrupt and deluded by its lusts, and to be renewed in the spirit of your minds.

PHILIPPIANS 2:5—Let the same mind be in you that was in Christ Jesus.

COLOSSIANS 2:8—See to it that no one takes you captive through philosophy and empty deceit, according to human tradition, according to the elemental spirits of the universe, and not according to Christ.

COLOSSIANS 3:9–10—Do not lie to one another, seeing that you have stripped off the old self with its practices and have clothed yourselves with the new self, which is being renewed in knowledge according to the image of its creator.

HEBREWS 4:12—Indeed, the word of God is living and active, sharper than any two-edged sword, piercing until it divides soul from spirit, joints from marrow; it is able to judge the thoughts and intentions of the heart.

DEUTERONOMY 11:18—You shall put these words of mine in your heart and soul, and you shall bind them as a sign on your hand, and fix them as an emblem on your forehead.

ROMANS 7:23—[B]ut I see in my members another law at war with the law of my mind, making me captive to the law of sin that dwells in my members.

PHILIPPIANS 3:19—Their end is destruction; their god is the belly; and their glory is in their shame; their minds are set on earthly things.

Further Sayings for Reflection:

Abba John said, "I am like a man sitting under a great tree, who sees wild beasts and snakes coming against him in great numbers. When he cannot withstand them any longer, he runs to climb the tree and is saved. It is just the same with me, I sit in my cell and I am aware of evil thoughts coming against me, and when I have no more strength against them, I take refuge in God by prayer and I am saved from the enemy."[35]

The same old man used to say, "The life and conduct of a monk are these: He must not act iniquitously, and he must not look upon evil things with his eyes, and he must not hearken with his ears unto things which are alien to the fear of God, and he must not utter calumnies with his mouth, and he must not seize things with his hands, but must give especially to those who are in need, he must neither be exalted in his mind nor mediate with wicked thoughts, and he must not fill his belly. All these things he must perform with intelligence, for by them is a monk known."[36]

One of the fathers said, controlling the mind and heart comes from an attentive person. Do not neglect your thoughts, if the enemy attacks with thoughts do not pay attention to him because his aim is to distract you from conversing with God.[37]

The brethren said, "If a man attaineth unto purity of heart what is the sign thereof? And when will he know himself if the heart is coming to purity?" The old man said, "when he seeth that all men are fair, and when no man appeareth to him to be unclean or polluted; whosoever is thus indeed standeth in purity. And if this be not the case, how can he fulfill the word of the Apostle which saith, 'When a man standeth wholly in purity, he will think that every man is better than he in heart and in truth,' unless it be that he attaineth to the state of him of whom it is said, 'He whose eyes are pure seeth not wickedness.'"[38]

Question: What does the Scriptures mean: "If someone has faith like a mustard seed"? [Matt 17:20]
Answer: A farmer plows the earth and sows seed, and when the seed finds free space in the earth it puts forth roots and produces branches above ground so that the birds of the air make their nests in them [Matt 13:32].

35. *ASWard*, 87, John the Dwarf #12.
36. *SABudge*, 244, #436.
37. *Aparadise*, 399.
38. *SABudge*, 309, #641.

In the same way, if a person purifies his heart and receives the word of God and it resides there, it produces good thoughts so that the commandments of God reside in him.[39]

It was said of the same Abba John that when he returned from the harvest or when he had been with some of the old men, he gave himself to prayer, meditation and psalmody until his thoughts were re-established in their previous order.[40]

Amma Syncletica said, "Therefore one must guard against remembering past injuries, for many terrible things follow from this: envy, grief, backbiting talk. . . . But these do not kill by the greatness of the blow, but through the carelessness of the wounded ones, for while disregarding the backbiting and the rest, little by little one is killed by them."[41]

Abbâ Epiphanius said, "He who revealeth and discovereth his good work is like unto the man who soweth [seed] on the surface of the ground, and doth not cover it up, and the fowl of the heavens cometh and devoureth it; but he who hideth his good works is like unto the man who soweth his seed in the furrows of the earth, and he shall reap the same at harvest."[42]

And he also said, "O monk, take thou the greatest possible care that thou sin not, lest thou disgrace God Who dwelleth in thee, and thou drive Him out of thy soul."[43]

Amma Syncletica said, "Therefore it is necessary always to be watchful. For he [the devil] does battle by means of external acts, and subdues by means of internal thoughts. And he does much more by means of the internal; for night and day he approaches spiritually. Therefore what is useful in the present war? Clearly, painful ascetic practice and pure prayer; these have emerged generally as able to keep off all destructive thoughts."[44]

---

39. Tim Vivian et al., *Words to Live By: Journeys in Ancient and Modern Egyptian Monasticism*, Cistercian Studies 207 (Kalamazoo, MI: Cistercian, 2005) 14, #20.

40. *ASWard*, 92, John the Dwarf #35.

41. *Sync.*, 292, #65.

42. *SABudge*, 77, #337.

43. *SABudge*, 77, #338.

44. *Sync.*, 279, #28, 29.

The same old man also said, "The chief of all wickednesses is the wandering of the thoughts."[45]

The same old man said, "A man is not able to know outside himself the thoughts which are in him, but when they resist him from within, if he be a warrior, he will cast them out from him."[46]

An old man was asked by a brother, "How should a monk dwell in his cell?" The old man said unto him, "Let him dwell by himself, so that his thoughts may be with God."[47]

Amma Syncletica said against thoughts of despair: "He places all sins before the eyes of the novice and insecure souls. For he suggests to it: 'What kind of forgiveness will there be for you who has fornicated?' And he says to another, 'You were so covetous, it is impossible for you to have salvation.' Therefore one must speak gently to weakened souls, for it is necessary to say to them: 'Rahab was a prostitute, but was saved through faith; Paul was a persecutor, but he became a chosen instrument; Matthew was a tax collector, but no one is ignorant of his grace; and the robber pillaged and killed, but he was the first one who opened the door of paradise. Therefore contemplating these, do not despair for your own soul.'"[48]

Amma Syncletica said regarding counting the thoughts and knowing its source: "Certainly I know a certain servant of God living in accordance with virtue, who, when sitting in her cell, looked out for the introduction of thoughts; and she kept count of which was the first, which was the second, and for how much time each one of them held her; and whether she fell short of or exceeded the day before. Thus she knew accurately the grace of God and her own endurance as well as her power, in addition to the defeat of the enemy."[49]

Amma Syncletica said, "To be angry is a lesser of the evils; but the remembrance of injuries is the weightiest of all. For anger, like smoke, having disturbed the soul for a little while, is dissolved. But the remembrance of injuries, fixing in the soul, performs more terribly than a wild beast. . . . But the one ruled by memories of past injuries is not persuaded by

45. *SABudge*, 83, #370.

46. *SABudge*, 202, #227.

47. *SABudge*, 222, #345.

48. *Sync.*, 288, #52.

49. *Sync.*, 301, #88.

consolation, nor tamed by food, and time that changes everything does not cure this emotion. Therefore, these people who suffer this emotion are the most atheistic and impious of all. For they do not obey the Savior who says: 'Go, first be reconciled to your brother; then bring your gift' (Matt 5:24). And elsewhere: 'Do not let the sun go down,' it says, 'on your anger' (Eph 4:26)."[50]

50. *Sync.*, 291, #63.

6

Pray without Ceasing

Prayer

Rejoice always, pray without ceasing, give thanks in all circumstances;
for this is the will of God in Christ Jesus for you.

1 Thess 5:16–18

WHEN KING DARIUS THE Mede promoted Daniel and appointed him over the whole kingdom of Babylon, the two "presidents"—the highest-ranking officials of the kingdom—out of jealousy, wanted to file complaints against him but discovered that he was blameless in all of his administrative decisions and actions for the kingdom. The men said, "We shall not find any ground for complaint against this Daniel unless we find it in connection with the law of his God" (Dan 6:5). They conspired to enforce a new law, signed by the king, that the entire kingdom was to pray to and worship the king. "Although Daniel knew that the document had been signed, he continued to go to his house, which had windows in its upper room open toward Jerusalem, and to get down on his knees three times a day to pray to his God and praise him, just as he had done previously" (Dan 6:10). Abba Poemen, one of the desert fathers, comments on this biblical story that the only accusation they could find against Daniel was in regard to his prayers to God. This was in response to the question by one of his disciples of how "to walk in the path of righteousness."[1]

---

1. *SABudge*, 26, #114.

Daniel represented an example of a righteous man whose righteousness was demonstrated in his integrity and his prayer life, which he practiced even under the threat of losing his life. If Daniel, the highest-ranking state official in Babylon, was able to find time during his busy schedule to offer prayers to the Lord three times per day, he has set the standard very high for all working people.

Abba Ephrem set the bar even higher: not the three times per day of Daniel, but at the seven times the busy King David managed to pray to the Lord: "David the prophet prayed late at night; waking in the middle of the night, he prayed before the day; at the dawn of day he stood before the Lord; in the small hours he prayed, in the evening and at mid-day he prayed again, and this is why he said, 'Seven times a day have I praised you' (Ps 119:164)."[2] Based on this verse, monastics in Egypt scheduled seven hours of prayer, setting the standard also for the laity to follow, as is customary to this day in the Church of Egypt. The desert fathers used the two statesmen as examples of people who found the time to pray several times a day even with their busy schedules. Another desert father gave the examples of Huldah the prophetess, who resided in Jerusalem, and Anna the prophetess, who "never left the temple but worshiped there with fasting and prayer night and day" (Luke 2:37; see also 2 Kgs 22:14; 2 Chr 34:22), as women who devoted their lives to prayer.[3] These examples represent two patterns of prayer: the two working men prayed at certain intervals of the day, while the two prophetesses devoted their life to unceasing prayer.

Abba Macarius the Great made the point that it is not the number of times or number of prayers that matters but rather the purity of the heart and mind offering the prayer as well as the simplicity of the prayer. A certain monk by the name of Paul used to pray without ceasing, three hundred prayers every day. Paul heard about another woman who had been an ascetic for thirty years who used to pray five hundred prayers per day. He was so distraught when he heard this that he went to Abba Macarius tormented by his failure to reach such a high state of prayer. Abba Macarius responded that he had been an ascetic for sixty years and only prayed fifty prayers a day; he also worked, received guests who sought his spiritual advice, paid all his debts, and did not feel guilty about treating God lightly. Abba Macarius then addressed Paul and suggested that his guilt was either from not praying with a pure heart or not praying as

---

2. *ASWard*, 58, #7.

3. *SABudge*, 256, #520.

much as he could.[4] Abba Macarius did not focus on the number of prayers but on purity of heart. So whether it is Daniel's three prayers, or David's seven, or Paul the monk's three hundred, what is important is the purity of the heart offering the prayers. On another occasion Abba Macarius was asked how we are to pray. He replied: "There is no need to talk much in prayer. Reach out your hands often, and say, 'Lord have mercy on me, as you will and as you know.' But if conflict troubles you, say, 'Lord, help me.' He knows what is best for us, and has mercy."[5] A simple and short prayer is usually very profound (see Matt 6:7).

The desert fathers and mothers left us samples of short, simple prayers. Abba Macarius was once heard praying, "Jesus, Jesus, if my cries do not ring in your ears when I call out day and night to you in heaven to have mercy on me and to pity me on account of my sins, I will still not grow tired of imploring you."[6] Other desert fathers also emphasized the short, simple prayer. It is said about Abba Serapion that he would advise new monks to pray one simple prayer: "Lord, teach me to do Thy will."[7] Another father used to pray, "Lord, how am I to acquire Thee? Thou, even Thou knowest that I am a beast, and that I know nothing. Thou hast brought me to the highest point of this life, O redeem me for Thy mercy's sake. I am Thy servant and the son of Thine handmaiden. O Lord, by Thy wish make me to live."[8] John the Short said, "If you stand before God for prayer first of all say: Holy, Holy, Holy Lord of Hosts, heaven and earth are full of your praise. Then say: Lord, grant us by your grace the honor you prepared for us in the new world. [By your mercy] do not let your righteousness condemn us at your great coming. Lord grant me to truly know you and grant me union through your perfect love. Then conclude your prayer with the prayer that our Lord taught us and always articulate it in meditation."[9]

One of the fathers was asked, "How ought we to pray before God?" To this question he responded that we should pray

---

4. *SABudge*, 224, #356.

5. *SSWard*, 132, Unceasing Prayer #10; *ASWard*, 131, #19.

6. Tim Vivian, trans., *Saint Macarius, the Spiritbearer: Coptic Texts Relating to Saint Macarius the Great*, St. Vladimir's Popular Patristics (Crestwood, NY: St. Vladimir's Seminary Press, 2004) 72.

7. *SABudge*, 231, #386.

8. *SABudge*, 245, #441.

9. *AParadise*, 249.

For the return of sinners, and the finding of the lost, and the bringing near of those who are afar off, and friendliness towards those who wrong us, and love towards those who persecute us, and a sorrowful care for those who provoke to wrath; if a man doeth these things verily there is repentance in his mind, and sinners will often live, and their soul[s] be redeemed in life. For the prayer which our Lord delivered unto us for the need of the body is a word which covereth the whole community, and was not uttered solely for those who are strangers to the world, and who hold in contempt the pleasures of the body. For he in whose dwelling the kingdom of God and the righteousness thereof are found lacketh nothing, even when he asketh [not].[10]

This prayer is devoted to the lost, the travelers, and to those who have wronged or provoked us. It is also from a repentant mind. We should observe that in this prayer and the previous ones just quoted all supplications give glory to God and are directed toward God's mercy. They are about others, and none includes petitions or demands from the person offering the prayer. No petitions for personal material needs are included because the fathers believed that if we have faith when praying the Lord's Prayer, the Lord who knows what we need will provide for us (see Matt 6:11; Luke 11:3). This attitude requires a deep faith that God provides for all our material needs even when we do not ask for them, just as God takes care of the birds of the air (see Matt 6:26). Petitions for needs are not considered part of the main goal of prayers. Prayers are for the praise and glory of God. If urgent needs arise, the fathers believed, they should be mentioned at the end of a prayer, as an appendix. God already knows about them, as he knows the deep secrets of our hearts, and he will attend to them even without our asking. On the other hand, the fathers and mothers constantly asked God for spiritual needs.

The question was asked, "What is the kind of prayer which is not acceptable before God?" The elder responded, "The destruction of enemies, and asking for evil things [to come upon] those who do harm to us, and the health of the body, and a multitude of possessions, and abundance of offspring – prayers for these things are not acceptable before God. . . . It is not right for us to ask for the things which belong to the body, for the wisdom of God provideth all things."[11] The first half of the saying is reasonable enough; we do not pray for the harm of others, even our enemies. But what about praying for our needs? We were instructed to "Ask, and it will

10. *SABudge*, 267, #568

11. *SABudge*, 267, #565.

be given you; search, and you will find; knock, and the door will be opened for you" (Matt 7:7; see also Luke 11:9; 13:25). The desert fathers and mothers considered even pondering such petitions unacceptable because of the faith and confidence they had in God and his promises. They reached a level of relationship with God where they experienced everyday examples of how God sustained them in the desert. We all have experienced God's care for us on occasions and in ways that are sometimes minute and sometimes so huge that we get overwhelmed by the grace that we have received from God. The desert fathers and mothers found it unacceptable to ask for their bodily needs lest they acknowledge that they had forgotten God's work for them. Scripture reminds us that God took care of thousands of his people in the wilderness for forty years. There was a daily test of their faith; they had to believe that God would provide the manna for them the next day and not take more than their immediate needs required. Their faith was tested for forty years, and for forty years God provided daily for his people in the wilderness (Exod 16:35).

The inspiration of the fathers' prayers was primarily Scripture. On his way to church Abba John the Short used to reflect on Scripture "in his heart with unceasing prayer " (see 1 Thess 5:17).[12] As mentioned in the chapter on Scripture, the fathers and mothers of the desert memorized Scripture to have it for constant contemplation and reflection, not only during their prayers at set times, but also during their work, while eating, and while walking, as in the case of John the Short on his way to church. The fathers meditated on the Prophets, Gospels, and Epistles, but the book most used for prayers and contemplation was the Psalms.

The fathers were concerned about their state of mind before starting prayer and while praying. One of the desert fathers was asked how the fathers sang the Psalms without their minds wandering.[13] A wandering mind is a concern of our modern times; it was also the concern of the fathers and Athanasius. The wandering mind represents the pull of the mind away from God. Rather than thinking of God, the mind is more attracted to its personal thoughts, thoughts of worry, anger, judgment, pride, and other thoughts that cloud the mind of our heart in our meditation on God. As Athanasius argued, the presence of evil is the work of the

---

12. Tim Vivian et al., ed. and trans., Zacharias of Sakha, *The Holy Workshop of Virtue: The Life of John the Little*, Cistercian Studies 234 (Collegeville, MN: Liturgical, 2010) 76, #8.

13. *SABudge*, 306, #637.

mind; thoughts that are not evil do not distract us from God but preserve the purity of our heart. A pure heart can pray (see Matt 5:8).

In his response to the question of how to praise with the Psalms without a wandering mind, the father responds by saying that while standing for prayer the fathers try to collect their minds as much as they can and start praying with the Psalms without letting "one word (*or* verse) escape them without their knowing the meaning".[14] He specifically mentions ways of thinking that are not conducive to prayer, such as looking at the Psalms as "history." In this case the prayer seems to be about someone in the past and we become detached from the words and do not internalize them as our own. Another way he finds unhelpful is reading or praying the Psalms as an interpreter or translator. In this case we are consumed with matters of grammar and vocabulary or are distracted with modes of eloquence in speech and how best to interpret the verse, and we forget that God is at the center of the prayer and the psalm itself. His advice is to pray the Psalms "spiritually, according to the interpretation of the Fathers, that is to say, they applied all the Psalms to their own lives and works, and to their passions, and to their spiritual life, and to the wars which the devils waged against them."[15] This is done according to the capacity of each person.

Rather than being distracted with interpretation or grammar or other linguistic matters, even if they seem genuine because they are related to the Psalms themselves, the father suggests a method of praise and paying attention to the deeper meaning of the Psalms. Through frequent use of this method a person acquires the "daily faculty of singing a song mingled with the meditation of God and with the gaze [which is fixed] upon Him."[16] The key element here is the frequent use of the method, so that the mind constantly delves into the deeper meaning of the Psalms and the eye of the mind is "gazing" on God. With time the mind and the heart become so overwhelmed with the deep meaning of each verse that one cannot move as quickly through a psalm; one lingers and meditate on the meaning of one or two verses only. At this point, the mind does not want to move through the whole psalm, for the heart sings "a song which is superior [to that of] body and flesh, and which is like unto the angels."[17] This deep immersion into the meaning of the Psalms takes years to achieve. The practice requires patience. Spirituality is not a quick fix. Though the

14. *SABudge*, 306, #637.
15. *SABudge*, 306, #637.
16. *SABudge*, 306, #637.
17. *SABudge*, 307, #637.

father in this saying is speaking specifically about the Psalms, the same method can be applied, and was applied by the desert fathers and mothers, to any verse in Scripture. So when Abba John the Short walked to church meditating on Scripture, he was applying the same method, taking every single verse at the spiritual and personal level and making it a prayer of his own heart, thus aiming to attain the "gaze on God." At this point the mind conforms to that of God, and we praise without ceasing. Humanity cannot achieve this level without the incarnation and the renewal of creation and God's image within us. Such prayer is the work of the Spirit within us.

The fathers speak not only about prayer itself but also about the attitude in which we approach prayer and stand before God while praying. Abba Epiphanius gave some advice for a person who wants to stand before God in prayer. That person should have a pure heart. He said we should receive everyone without distinction. If a person admonishes or criticizes us, we should bless him or her even if this is not to our benefit. Abba Epiphanius gave the example of Abba Arsenius, who stood before the Lord with tears like the sinful woman. Abba Epiphanius added that this humble attitude is the suitable way to stand before the Lord, because when we raise our hearts to God in prayer he is present before us, and this is the most suitable way to be in his presence. We should examine our "mind most minutely, both in respect to the things which are above, and those which are below." We should stand before God as blameless.[18] In this saying Abba Epiphanius gives different aspects of standing before God in purity of heart: being on good terms with others, respecting them and blessing them, and with oneself by examining one's "mind most minutely."

Another brother asked why it was that when he started to pray his mind was "empty of spiritual thoughts." The elder answered that it was because he had not followed Psalm 34:1: "I will bless the LORD at all times; his praise shall continually be in my mouth." Blessing God should be done in action, word, and mind, for God is not confined to one place; he is the one who sustains the whole world and all things and is capable of all things.[19] This is a profound theological understanding of the omnipresence of God and how we are in God's presence all the times. Since we are constantly in his presence, we should constantly bless and praise him. We do not praise God only when the liturgy or other communal prayer starts. We do not attend a meeting and start by saying, "Well, let me see where to start; I am not sure what I should be speaking about!" Rather we

18. *SABudge*, 28, #125, also 246, #450.
19. *SABudge*, 29, #128.

prepare for the meeting in advance and then just before the meeting starts we gather our thoughts to be ready for the discussion. The same should be true with prayer. If we pray only when we go to church on Sunday morning, we face the same dilemma of the brother; we stand "empty of spiritual thoughts." That is why the fathers considered praying without ceasing to be the entry point to start our prayers. Praying without ceasing is preparation for prayer.

John the Short contemplated Scripture on his way to church to put himself in the state of prayer before he arrived to attend the liturgy. The Eucharistic liturgy was the center of the prayer life in the early church, as it still is in Orthodox Churches. Personal prayer and reading Scripture prepare the mind and heart of the person to be in the presence of God and partake of the heavenly banquet. If, when we start prayer, we are not "in the prayer of the spirit," the fathers advise that we stay with "the prayer of the body." That is, we do not abandon prayer because we do not feel the warmth and the fire of the spirit, but we persevere in prayer; if we knock at the door we shall receive (see Matt 7:7; 21:22)[20] This is the time when the fathers feel it is pleasing to petition God.

When we live with the understanding that God is present everywhere and that we are constantly in his presence, prayer without ceasing becomes second nature. We know we are in God's company all day and we engage him in conversation. Conversing with God all the time is unceasing prayer. God becomes our very personal and intimate friend with whom we are constantly conversing; he always listens and is never busy. When we understand that we are in God's company all the time, we develop an appetite and desire for talking to him more and more. The awareness of God's presence everywhere and at all times leads to unceasing prayer. Abba Isaiah speaks about a monk who was eating at a table with other brothers after the liturgy. The monks were eating and talking, except for one who was eating and "whose prayer [was] going up to God like a darting flame."[21] We can be eating and in others' company and still be offering a very powerful prayer.

There is another story about the fathers' understanding of praying without ceasing. A group of monks claimed that they prayed without ceasing. So a certain Lucius asked them about their manual work, to which they responded that they did not work, following Paul's advice to pray

20. *SABudge*, 192, #174.

21. *SSWard*, 131, Unceasing Prayer #7; also *SABudge*, 25, #112; and *SABudge*, 26, #117.

without ceasing (1 Thess 5:17). Lucius asked them, "Don't you eat? . . . Don't you sleep?" They responded yes to both questions. So Lucius asked them who is praying while they are eating and sleeping. They could not answer. Lucius then explained to them that he prayed while working, saying, "'Have mercy upon me, O God, after thy great mercy: and according to the multitude of thy mercies do away with mine iniquity' (Ps 51:1). He asked them, 'Is that prayer, or not?' They said, 'It's prayer all right.'" He responded that by working and praying with all his heart, he earned his wages. He spent some of it on his food and the rest he put outside his door for whoever passed and needed money. The person who took alms from him while he was sleeping was praying and giving thanks to God; in this way prayer was raised while he was asleep.[22] To those who do not want to work, giving the excuse of prayer and devotion, Lucius explains that work does not necessarily keep a person from praying; even when one is not able to pray, alms giving and other charitable works are considered a form of praise to God. He is actually responding to certain ascetic groups that emerged who advocated ceaseless prayer and not working.[23]

Anthony himself started his monastic life with this attitude of ceaseless prayer without work. He was corrected when God showed him a man "like himself, who was sitting at work, getting up from his work to pray, then sitting down and plaiting a rope, then getting up again to pray."[24] The message of desert spirituality from its inception emphasized the importance of work and the importance of prayer while working.[25] Working constantly depletes a person spiritually, psychologically, and mentally. Praying while working is the way to keep the balance between the soul and the way we earn our living. If praying without ceasing is not accompanied by work, we become a burden on society. Desert spirituality finds the balance between work and prayer.

We have observed that ceaseless prayer prepares the mind and the spirit for praying during set times, like the liturgy or the prayer of the hours. Prayer at set times and ceaseless prayer are not mutually exclusive but they feed on each other. They should be viewed as one continuous dynamic of prayer. A group of monks sent to Abba Epiphanius informing

22. *SS Ward*, 132, Unceasing Prayer #9.

23. For an exposition of Messalians read Daniel Caner, *Wandering, Begging Monks: Spiritual Authority and the Promotion of Monasticism in Late Antiquity*, Transformation of the Classical Heritage 33 (Berkeley: University of California Press, 2002).

24. *AS Ward*, 1, Antony the Great #1.

25. Refer to chapter 3 under the heading "Work and Self-Sufficiency."

him that they were praying the hours diligently. Abba Epiphanius blamed those who sent the message and responded: "Ye must know that ye are indeed neglectful of the services and prayers which belong to the other eight hours which are in the day."[26] For the fathers and mothers of the desert, prayer is not only the structured liturgical prayers or personal prayers that are either structured or spontaneous; it is the state of mind that is in the constant presence of God. Prayer is not limited to formal prayers, which are markers throughout the day serving as a constant reminder of being in God's presence. These prayers keep the mind, the heart, and the spirit in the constant contemplation of God.

Prayer generates prayer. Prayer preserves the mind in the contemplation of God. The more we contemplate, the more our mind is focused on God, the less distracted it is, and the more we pray. "A brother asked Abba Poemen concerning the thoughts which invaded his mind." Abba Poemen answered that it is like water and fire; fire is the thoughts that invade our minds, and we extinguish it with water, which is "the pouring out of the soul before the Lord."[27] The constant pouring out of our souls before God diminishes and even extinguishes the fire of invading thoughts. Quenching the fire of invading thoughts with prayer purifies the heart. Prayer fetters invading thoughts.

One of the desert fathers said that if our work does not correspond with our prayers then we labor in vain. He explained further that if we pray for the remission of our sins we must not be negligent.[28] In other words, when we pray for the forgiveness of our sins our behavior has to correspond with our prayers. We do not behave in a sinful way, saying that we will ask for forgiveness of these sins anyway so that it does not matter if we sin or not. Prayer affects our life and vice versa. One of the elders said, "Do nothing without prayer, and afterwards thou wilt never be sorry."[29] Prayer guides us in all our decisions. This assures us that we are doing God's will and gives us confidence in whatever decision we have taken.

But what if our prayers have not been answered? This is a question that everyone has asked for centuries. When Abba Ammon was asked this question, he said that Jacob toiled and did not marry the woman he sought after; he kept on laboring again for the woman he loved (Gen 29).[30] Thus

26. *SABudge*, 26–27, #118.
27. *SABudge*, 29, #129.
28. *SABudge*, 180, #123.
29. *SABudge*, 196, #192; and *SABudge*, 252, #493.
30. *SABudge*, 171, #68.

we keep on "laboring," that is, praying, for what we want and this requires patience. Abba Ammon provides a good example of this when he says, "I have spent fourteen years in Scete in making supplication unto God by day and by night that He would grant me to overcome anger."[31] The import of this saying is that God trained Ammon in persistence and also in patience, which is an antidote to anger. He learned not to get angry when his prayers were not answered. Ammon's spiritual experience also shows that whatever spiritual level we reach, it is only through God's grace.

The early desert fathers and mothers were absorbed in prayers. One of the monks visited another. In preparation for his hospitality the second monk cooked some lentils. When the monk arrived they decided to begin with prayer, as was their custom, and they started praying with the Psalms. They were so absorbed in prayer that they prayed the whole book of Psalms and the guest recited "two books of the Great Prophets" (that is, Isaiah, Jeremiah, or Ezekiel, not one of the shorter prophetic books). The guest then departed.[32] They were so consumed in their prayers that they forgot to eat, though it was supposed to be a short prayer before their meal. Absorption in prayers is possible in the same way we get so absorbed in any activity that we like. We simply forget or do not care about food. When the mind is absorbed in thought we can forget basic things in life like food. It is up to us to choose the activity we want our minds to be absorbed in. Do we choose to contemplate God? Or do we choose to be absorbed in our work, a shopping spree, the next meal, possessions, or anything else that we think is important for us and actually ends up defining us? We are what we think about. The sayings describe John the Short working on sewing a plait into a basket; instead he sewed two plaits into one basket, making a mistake in his work because "his mind was led captive by the sight of God."[33] Similarly, Abba Arsenius "would pray [with his hands stretched out toward heaven] until the sun rose in his face."[34] He was so absorbed in prayer that he did not notice the passing of time—sunset to sunrise—or change his body posture. Also, Abba Sylvanus saw the "glory of God" so that he did not notice his disciple Zachariah entering and leaving.[35] In all these sayings, the fathers demonstrated by their own lives that deep immersion in Scripture and prayer can be so powerful that the "glory of

31. *SABudge*, 210, #257.
32. *SABudge*, 16, #64.
33. *SABudge*, 30, #132.
34. *SABudge*, 24, #105.
35. *SABudge*, 201, #220.

God" and the "gaze on God" can totally absorb our senses and mind to the extent that we lose all awareness of our surroundings.

This is exactly what St. Athanasius was describing in his *Against the Gentiles*. Our mind chooses to contemplate either good or evil. Contemplating God, contemplating the divine name—as in the case of Abba Macarius—is to contemplate reality itself. When we contemplate God, we contemplate goodness and what is good. When we contemplate evil we contemplate what is not, what does not exist; we contemplate the false imagination in human thought. Athanasius explains that when the soul contemplates evil the mind is averted from contemplating God and what is good and turns towards its lusts and what pleases it.[36] We are all aware of the power of being totally consumed by a thought. While we are in this state we lose touch with our surroundings and everything else at this moment of time becomes trivial. We choose what will consume our mind: either the contemplation of God or compulsive absorption in our work, excessive attention to physical beauty, absorption in hurt pride, anger, or any powerful thought that each one of us has experienced that totally consumes us and even sometimes paralyzes us. Deep prayer is the choice the desert fathers and mothers made; they chose to "gaze on the glory of God."

We all decided how we want to divide our thoughts between contemplation of God and attention to worldly concerns. Earning a living is required of everyone—the fathers and mothers of the desert were constantly working—so the point is how to balance our life between work, entertainment, and prayer. We can choose the number of hours, and sometimes days, we spend playing with electronic gadgets and the number of hours we want to spend reading the Scriptures, meditating on them, and praying. Prayer is choosing to contemplate the good and God. It is the conscious decision to devote more time to God than watching television. That does not mean there is no time for entertainment and relaxing. There is a story about a hunter who saw Abba Anthony having some fun with the brethren. He was shocked because he was under the impression that the ascetic life was a strict form of life. Abba Anthony noticed his confusion. He asked him repeatedly to shoot an arrow from his bow until the hunter objected that any further use of the bow would break it. Abba Anthony responded that it is the same with the "work of God"; we have to attend to our needs.[37] Spirituality does not prohibit leisure activity, but it is the choice of recreation and the amount of time spent on it that requires

36. Please refer to chapter 2.
37. *ASWard*, 3, Antony the Great #13.

balance. Desert spirituality guides us to balance our spirituality and daily life necessities. Our happiness is in finding this balance. It is the balance between our contemplation on Scripture, prayer, work, attending to our daily needs and, finally, some time to relax so that the bow does not break.

Prayer is the "gaze on God." Prayer is being in the constant presence of God. We acknowledge being in his presence by speaking to him. Praying is to have our thoughts contemplating God, the divine name, and all goodness. Prayer leads to more prayer. When we pray, our mind, thoughts, and heart are captive to God. The more the mind is held captive to God, the less distraction and wandering the mind experiences, the more easily it becomes to pray without distraction, to pray without ceasing. Being in God's presence during the whole day, while we work, eat, and move around, makes it easier to be in his presence when we stand and raise our hands in prayer. Praying without ceasing prepares us for prayer. For the desert fathers and mothers the transition from one mode of prayer to the other was seamless. They were in the constant presence of God.

Biblical Verses on Prayer for Further Contemplation:

MATTHEW 5:44—But I say to you, Love your enemies and pray for those who persecute you.

SIRACH 28:2—Forgive your neighbor the wrong he has done, and then your sins will be pardoned when you pray.

MARK 14:38—Keep awake and pray that you may not come into the time of trial; the spirit indeed is willing, but the flesh is weak.

1 CORINTHIANS 14:15—What should I do then? I will pray with the spirit, but I will pray with the mind also; I will sing praise with the spirit, but I will sing praise with the mind also.

2 CORINTHIANS 13:9—For we rejoice when we are weak and you are strong. This is what we pray for, that you may become perfect.

SIRACH 37:15—But above all pray to the Most High that he may direct your way in truth.

ROMANS 12:12—Rejoice in hope, be patient in suffering, persevere in prayer.

Colossians 4:2—Devote yourselves to prayer, keeping alert in it with thanksgiving.

James 5:15—The prayer of faith will save the sick, and the Lord will raise them up; and anyone who has committed sins will be forgiven.

1 Peter 3:12—For the eyes of the Lord are on the righteous, and his ears are open to their prayer. But the face of the Lord is against those who do evil.

Further Sayings for Reflection:

Blessed is the person who will be found tending the blessed name of our Lord Jesus Christ without ceasing and with contrition of heart.[38]

Abba Nilus said, "Everything you do in revenge against a brother who has harmed you will come back to your mind at the time of prayer."[39]

He also said, "Prayer is a remedy against grief and depression."[40]

If a man's deeds are not in harmony with his prayer, he labours in vain. The brother said, "What is this harmony between practice and prayer?" The old man said, "We should no longer do those things against which we pray."[41]

Isidore, the priest in Scetis, said, "When I was young and stayed in my cell, I set no limit to the number of psalms which I said in the service of God. Night and day alike were spent in psalmody."[42]

The same old man used to say, "If thou criest unto God in prayer with a pure heart thy prayer shall not return unto thee fruitless.[43]

Question: How can a person know that his prayer is acceptable to God? [1 Pet 2:5]

38. Vivian, *Saint Macarius*, 111–12.
39. *ASWard*, 153, Nilus #1.
40. *ASWard*, 153, Nilus #3.
41. *ASWard*, 141, Moses #4.
42. *SSWard*, 121, Sober Living #17.
43. *SABudge*, 254, #505.

Answer: When a person makes sure that he does not wrong his neighbor in any way whatsoever, then he can be sure that his prayer is acceptable to God. But if someone harms his neighbor in any way whatsoever, either physically or spiritually, his prayer is an abomination and is unacceptable. For the wailing of the one who is being wronged will never allow this person's prayer to come before the face of God. And if indeed he does not quickly reconcile with his neighbor, he will certainly not go unpunished his whole life by his own sins, for it is written that "whatever you bind on earth will be bound in heaven" [Matt 18:18].[44]

Abba Macarius Teaches about Relying upon the Name of Christ

Abba Macarius the Great said, "Concentrate on this name of our Lord Jesus Christ with a contrite heart, the words welling up from your lips and drawing you to them. And do not depict him with an image in your mind but concentrate on calling to him: 'Our Lord Jesus, have mercy on me.' Do these things in peace and you will see the peace of his divinity within you; he will run off the darkness of the passions that dwell within you and he will purify the inner person [2 Cor 4:16; Eph 3:16] just as Adam was pure in paradise. This is the blessed name that John the Evangelist pronounced: 'Light of the world and unending sweetness, the food of life and the true food'" [John 6:48, 6:55, 8:12].[45]

Abba Macarius Teaches about Attending to the Lord in Prayer

Abba Macarius the Great said, "If you pursue prayer, pay careful attention to yourself lest you place your pots in the hands of your enemies, for they desire to steal your pots, which are the thoughts of your soul. These are the precious pots with which you will serve God, for God does not look for you to glorify him only with your lips, while your thoughts wander to and fro and are scattered throughout the world, but requires that your soul and all its thoughts wait upon the sight of the Lord without distraction, for he is the great physician, the healer of soul and bodies, our Lord Jesus

44. Tim Vivian, with Apostolos N. Athanassakis, Maged S. A. Mikhail, and Birger A. Pearson, *Words to Live By: Journeys in Ancient and Modern Egyptian Monasticism*, Cistercian Studies 207 (Kalamazoo, MI: Cistercian, 2005) 17, #31.

45. Vivian, *Saint Macarius*, 117.

Christ. Let us beseech him to heal the illnesses of our souls and illumine our thoughts and the perceptions of our hearts that we may understand his great love for humanity and the suffering that he undertook in the world of us and the good things he has done for us day after day, although we are unworthy, for he is our master and savior, our Lord Jesus Christ."[46]

Abba Zenon said, "Who wants God to listen to his prayers quickly, when he stands for prayer, first let him raise his hand, then he is to ask for his enemies with all his heart before he prayers for himself, with this virtue God responds to all his concerns."[47]

Abba Isaac said, "On one occasion I was sitting with Abba Poemen and noticed he was in a state of *theoria* [the contemplation of God]. As I had some influence on him I asked him, 'What are you thinking of my father?' After insistence he said, 'I was contemplating on the cross where Saint Mary the Theotokos was standing weeping beside the cross of our savior, I wished I would feel like this at all times.'"[48]

One of the brothers said to some monks: "Have you seen a liar more than me?" They responded, "How is that?" He replied, "When I stand for prayer I raise my hand and eyes upward and weep and ask that he hear my petition and have mercy on my weeping, at the same time when I sin I say he does not see me. For this reason I know that I lie to myself."[49]

46. Ibid., 133.
47. *AParadise*, 267.
48. *AParadise*, 268.
49. *AParadise*, 262.

7

Treasure in Heaven

Renunciation

Jesus said to him, "If you wish to be perfect, go, sell your possessions,
and give the money to the poor, and you will have treasure in heaven;
then come, follow me."

MATT 19:21

RENUNCIATION IS THE RESPONSE to Christ's advice to the rich young
man in Matthew 19:21. After the young man "went away grieving,
for he had many possessions," Peter, feeling good about himself, continued the conversation: "we have left everything and followed you" (19:27).
Christ made sure that Peter and those standing by understood that renunciation is not limited to material possessions: "[E]veryone who has
left houses or brothers or sisters or father or mother or children or fields,
for my name's sake, will receive a hundred fold, and will inherit eternal
life" (19:29). Christ extended renunciation beyond material possessions
to include all family ties, with the promise of eternal life. Following
Christ includes not burying your father: "[F]ollow me and let the dead
bury their dead" (Matt 8:22). Renunciation includes being ready to die
or be betrayed by one's family and leave one's town at very short notice
for Christ's name (see Matt 10:21–23, 39). One cannot follow Christ unless there is complete inner renunciation, for "whoever loves father or
mother more than me is not worthy of me; and whoever loves son or

daughter more than me is not worthy of me; and whoever does not take up the cross and follow me is not worthy of me" (10:37–38). Again, there is a strong interconnection between renunciation and following Christ. Renunciation is not for the sake of an ideology or feeling inadequate to carry a responsibility or other personal reasons but rather for Christ's sake. Recognizing the difficulty of leaving a "child" for the sake of Christ, monastics renounced familial bonds and opted for celibacy for the sake of Christ. Renouncing sexual activity is not to denounce it or to criticize family life, but rather stems from an inner theological and spiritual desire to free the inner self of all bonds to be ready to follow Christ. It is a supreme act of renunciation for the sake of God's love.

Renunciation is an outward as well as an inward spiritual activity. Renunciation is the frame of mind of not being attached to anything. Renouncing one's possessions is an exercise of freeing oneself from material possessions with all their obligations and constraints. Renunciation is not limited to material possessions, but definitely includes them. In monastic literature, as in Christian literature in general, renunciation is sought after for the sake of God. It is a voluntary decision and action. Renunciation is an inner spiritual exercise that manifests itself in the outer aspect of renunciation. Without inner renunciation, outer renunciation is meaningless. It is the inner renunciation that the desert fathers and mothers were seeking, and the spiritual exercises they practiced were for the sole purpose of inner spiritual freedom. Renunciation is freedom from all constraints that hinder us from being fully in Christ and in his constant presence.

Renunciation is an inner as well as outward letting go. In the early church some proclaimed their renunciation by selling their possessions and giving it to the poor; others opted (for various reasons) to practice renunciation while living in society and pursuing their day-to-day activities. Renunciation was an early Christian way of life and not limited to monastics. It was the way to follow Christ's commandments regardless of rank or wealth. Thus Emperor Theodosius the Younger (408–450) lived in his palace and commanded the armies and empire while pursuing an ascetic life, a life of renunciation. He endured physical hardships such as heat and cold. He fasted beyond the commitment of Wednesdays and Fridays. He transformed the palace into a monastery and kept early morning prayers with his sisters. He sang and memorized hymns and Scripture.[1] Another example is that of Macrina, who came from a wealthy family. She kept all her possessions, which included a large estate and a comfortable, expensive

---

1. Socrates, *Eccl. Hist.* 7.22.

home, but she lived an ascetic life. Her brother, Gregory of Nyssa, came to witness the last moments of her life and eventually had to attend to her funeral. He expected to find suitable clothing for the burial of his wealthy sister but discovered that "she had so little concern for dress that she owned nothing during her lifetime and stored none away for the present situation [her death], so that, even if we desired it, there is nothing more to use than what is already here . . ."[2] And when Gregory asked to look into her closets he was told, "You have everything she possessed in your hands. Look at her dress, look at the covering of her head, her worn sandals. This is her wealth, this is her property. There is nothing beyond what you see put aside in hidden places or made secure in treasures houses."[3]

From these two examples—and there are plenty of others—we see that even the rich and powerful members of early Christian societies understood that living the life of renunciation is an integral part of following Christ and fulfilling the Christian message. They did not renounce their fortunes or positions publically, but rather lived a life of inner renunciation. Renunciation is not restricted to monastics but rather was understood to be the Christian way of life. In the early church, whether you were an emperor or a citizen, you lived frugally and did not have more than what you needed. You ate little and fasted more than was required by church ordinances, you dressed modestly, you possessed only what you needed. You always gave alms or did charity work. You lived a "hidden" or inner life of renunciation; Macrina's brother was not aware of his sister's lifestyle until the day of her death. You renounced possessions, food, comfort, and even sleep in order to attend to prayer, and whatever else you could. Renunciation is a lifestyle that exceeds and extends beyond letting go of material possessions. It is an inner spiritual exercise by which you live and consume what is absolutely essential and are satisfied with basic necessities; having anything beyond what we need is not considered renunciation. Early Christians were careful not to show off their inner spiritual exercises, even if that exercise included a physical or outward expression, such as that of renunciation.

Renunciation springs from a deep theological reflection on the incarnation. Philippians 2:7–8 describes the incarnation as Christ "empt[ying] himself, taking the form of a slave, being born in human likeness. And being found in human form, he humbled himself and became obedient

2. Virginia Woods Callahan, trans., Gregory of Nyssa, *Ascetical Works*, The Fathers of the Church 58 (Washington, DC: Catholic University of America Press, 1967) 184.

3. Ibid.

to the point of death—even death on a cross." Christ emptying himself for our sake, renouncing his exalted status and condescending to take the form of a slave and be born in human likeness, is one of the most powerful images of renunciation. It is the renunciation of status, power, and even self, to be ready to die for those whom God loves. It is this deep and strong understanding of the incarnation that supported the conviction of renunciation. Obedience to God is one aspect of renunciation. To achieve the state of renunciation one cannot be attached to personal glory, ego, or material wealth. Renunciation cannot be achieved either inwardly or outwardly if it is not motivated by this theological vision. The theological vision safeguards against the possibility of renouncing one's possessions for the sake of vainglory, as in the case of Ananias and Sapphira (see Acts 5). When the soul is in awe, overtaken and overwhelmed by the realization of the magnitude of the Son of God's renunciation for our sake, renunciation becomes an act of love, gratitude, and recognized unworthiness before God. The greater the love that engulfs the heart and mind, the greater the act of renunciation, though no act of human renunciation is ever equal to the act of divine renunciation that the Son has undertaken for the sake of humanity. It is the constant contemplation of the incarnation, crucifixion, and resurrection—the fullness of the Son's renunciation—that sustains and strengthens the one who renounces in this endeavor that seems beyond human understanding and capacity.

Second Corinthians 8:9 expresses Christ's renunciation in these terms: "For you know the generous act of our Lord Jesus Christ, that though he was rich, yet for your sakes he became poor[4], so that by his poverty you might become rich." Again the early Christians were aware that for our sake and to enrich humanity the Son became incarnate, accepting extreme poverty, owning absolutely nothing, and living in a state of beggarliness. Confronted with this realization, they understood that no aspect of renunciation could match the divine renunciation. But emulating his extreme poverty enriches us. Egyptian desert monastics understood that the enriching did not mean material riches, just as they understood that

---

4. "Poor" is the translation of πτωχείᾳ, which means extreme poverty, literally "beggarliness." See Walter Bauer, *A Greek-English Lexicon of the New Testament*, 2nd ed. (Chicago: University of Chicago Press, 1979) 728. We can compare this to πένης, which means poor or needy (ibid., 42), and also a day laborer who works for his daily labor. This should be distinguished from a beggar (πτωχός). Also see Henry George Liddell and Robert Scott, *A Greek-English Lexicon* (Oxford: Clarendon, 1992) 1550. Thus Christ did not just choose mere poverty for our sake but extreme and abject poverty, he became a beggar. "Generous act" is the translation of χάριν, meaning grace.

renunciation did not mean only renunciation of material goods. Though 2 Corinthians 8:9 describes the abject poverty of the incarnate Son, Egyptian monasticism never advocated excessive poverty or asceticism that debilitates a person; the emphasis was always on moderation.

Their profound understanding of the incarnation and what it entails gave the monastics a deep spiritual understanding of renunciation, which is not only renunciation of material things but renouncing oneself, imitating Christ, emptying oneself. This emptying includes renunciation of family as well as physical and intellectual things. Because Christ's emptying and impoverishment was for the sake of our enrichment, it is through Christ, through his grace, that renunciation can take place. This does not leave any room for self-glorification by attaining a level of extreme renunciation. Renunciation is rather a matter of striving to imitate Christ and reach the fullness of the incarnation. "I can do all things through him who strengthens me" (Phil 4:14). It is not through personal endeavor or intellectual exercise that one can achieve renunciation. Rather it is through Christ and by Christ that we can achieve true renunciation.

Renunciation is an act of faith. When the Israelites crossed the Red Sea they complained against Moses because he deprived them of their fill of bread and the fleshpots of Egypt. The Lord then said to Moses, "I am going to rain bread from heaven for you, and each day the people shall go out and gather enough for that day. In that way I will test them, whether they will follow my instructions or not" (Exod 16:4). The instructions were to gather enough to meet their daily needs of bread and quails, without excess, and on the sixth day to gather twice as much to observe the Sabbath. Not all the Israelites had faith that God would provide the manna the next day, so they gathered more than their needs and kept it for the next day. This manna "bred worms and became foul" (16:20). They did not have faith that God would provide the next day. The Israelites ate the manna for forty years until they arrived at the borders of the promised land. This was an exercise of faith and renunciation. Gather only what you need and not more; those who gathered more discovered that their acquisitions went to the worms.

The Israelites learned to have faith that God would provide for their daily needs. The early Egyptian monastics were constantly tested in their exercise of renunciation and tempted to wonder if God would forsake them. "Therefore I tell you do not worry about your life, what you will eat, or about your body, what you will wear. For life is more than food, and the body more than clothing" (Luke 12:22–23). Abba Doulas was traveling beside the sea with his spiritual father Abba Bessarion when he felt very thirsty. Abba Bessarion prayed on some of the seawater and when Abba Doulas drank of it he found it sweet. Abba Doulas poured the rest of his water in a leather bottle to which his spiritual father objected, explaining, "God is here, God is everywhere."[5] The disciple Doulas behaved like any cautious, responsible person; let's save some of the sweet water for later use. His father Abba Bessarion considered this a lack of faith, for if God provided them sweet water beside the sea, then we must learn that God will provide again, for he is everywhere. God provided the manna daily; God is capable of providing sweet water beside the sea.

In another narrative, a brother wanted to keep some money "as a provision for the needs of the feebleness of the body." The elder who was guiding him consented to that. But the brother was tormented in his mind and began debating whether his spiritual father spoke truthfully to him. When he returned, the elder explained that he consented because he noticed that he wanted to keep it. The father continued, "Why do you have your hope on money? Do you think God will not take care of you?"[6] It is really the same question of trust and faith in God as one who takes care of those who depend on him. Abba Anthony said, "Do not keep beyond your need, and do not pay beyond your ability."[7] Renunciation is an act of faith. It is tested every day and the resolution to renunciation has to be renewed every day. It is not a one-time resolution; it is a resolution that requires faith and constant and continuous spiritual vigilance.

It is not sufficient to renounce your possessions only once; rather, renunciation is a constant exercise that is repeated throughout our life. That is one of the major differences between renunciation and poverty. Poverty is a state into which one might be born or enter; it denotes a lack of material possessions. In the first case it is an unwelcomed state and involuntary. In the second case it can be either voluntary, by renouncing one's possessions, or involuntary after the loss of one's possessions due to a natural disaster, war, a financial recession, health issues, or any other change in one's fortunes. Involuntary poverty is not welcomed and those afflicted by it tend to do their best to escape its clutches because of its physical as well as social and psychological hardships. People afflicted with poverty tend to aspire to riches and attempt to find the first way out of poverty. When we speak about poverty, the discussion is usually restricted

5. *ASWard*, 40, Abba Bessarion #1; *SAChaîne*, 63, #216; *SAHartley*, 140, #216.

6. *SABudge*, 37, #169; also *SSWard*, 59, Possessing Nothing #22.

7. *AParadise*, 168.

to material wealth; renunciation includes the renunciation of money and physical objects, but also includes spiritual, emotional, and intellectual renunciation. Renunciation includes renouncing oneself for the sake of Christ. It is a mindset, a voluntary way of life. It is for the sake of Christ and in imitation of Christ.

Monastics were constantly practicing renunciation by giving away their Bibles and books, their food, their clothes, their utensils, and whatever else they owned. They renounced out of their need and not from their overstocked wardrobes or food closets. A certain Abba Dioskoros was said to have one hood and two linen robes, one of which was used for liturgical purposes. When someone asked him for clothes, he immediately gave away one of his robes. On another occasion, someone came to ask him for clothes and he gave him the good robe that was lying there and kept the poor one he was wearing. When asked why he did not give him the poor garment, he answered, "Would you give the poor one to Jesus?"[8] Abba Dioskoros did not renounce his clothes just once, but every time he was asked. His cell contained the bare necessities, only salt and bread without any oil, and he slept on the ground.[9] He was a scribe and when he wrote a book he exchanged it only for bread.[10] Scribes usually were well paid for their work since it required special skills, but he accepted only what was essential for him, bread. If a brother arrived at the mountain where Dioskoros' monastic dwellings were, he would invite him to his cell, show him his bread basket, and tell him he could take as much bread as he wanted until he could provide for himself.[11] On another occasion, a brother came to ask him for a door to use in his cell. Abba Dioskoros said to him, "Remove this one for yourself," and the brother took the door and left. It took Abba Dioskoros some time to replace the door with one of palm branches.[12]

"An elder said: 'If one asks you for something do not compel yourself, but give it to him willfully, because your mind is persuaded to give whatever you will give to him just as it is written: "If one compels you (to go) a mile, go with him two." That is, if one asks you for something, give it from all of your heart and your spirit."[13] An important aspect of renun-

8. *SAChaine*, 79, #260; *SAHartley*, 164, #260.

9. *SAChaine*, 78, #254; *SAHartley*, 162, #254.

10. *SAChaine*, 79, #256; *SAHartley*, 163, #256.

11. *SAChaine*, 79, #256; *SAHartley*, 163, #256.

12. *SAChaine*, 79, #258; *SAHartley*, 163, #258.

13. *SAChaine*, 36, #161; *SAHartley*, 98, #161. The quote is referring to Matt 5:40–41. Also in *SSWard*, 180, Charity #15.

ciation is that it has to be done with complete willingness from the heart and spirit. Any grudging giving away is not renunciation. It was told that Abba Theonas baked some bread. Some poor people came and knocked at his door and he gave them the bread. Others came and he gave them his baskets. Others came and he gave them his garment, and he entered his cell covered with some rags.[14] Abba Arsenius said, "It is a great thing for a man not to bind himself with any matter."[15] Such acts of renunciation emerge from a heart full of love for the other and a generous heart that gives freely. To give generously requires love, and love is nourished by the constant contemplation of God's love for us, which in turn is nourished by constant contemplation of the incarnation and Christ's self-emptying. Renunciation comes from a heart overflowing with love from God, for God, and for our neighbor. Love of neighbor and a life of renunciation generate generosity. We cannot be attached to our worldly possessions and be able to give freely and easily to whoever asks us. It is only a heart that has renounced everything that is capable of fulfilling Matthew 5:42: "Give to everyone who begs from you, and do not refuse anyone who wants to borrow from you."

Renunciation is not easy whether we are poor or rich. Two monastics were living in community and the elder was applying his understanding of renunciation and "was giving bread to everyone who came." The brother got worried about his sustenance and asked to take his share of bread and live on his own. The elder continued his charitable work and did not let anyone who came to his cell asking for bread leave empty handed. The story says that "God saw his joy of heart and blessed his bread." Giving with joy brings God's blessings on our sustenance, indeed, on our whole lives. The careful and cautious brother, on the other hand, did not receive the same blessings; he was eating his bread alone, not giving any away in charity, and he ran out of bread. He returned to his elder and said, "Since I have a little bread, accept me to yourself, and let us again share (things) in common." The elder accepted him back. The elder continued his practice of renunciation and again they ran out of bread. The brother went to his Abba to say there was no more bread. The elder, filled with faith in God's blessings, instructed the brother to give bread to anyone who asked. When the brother returned to the pantry, he found it full of bread. He gave bread to a poor brother and "recognized the faith and the virtue of the elder, and

---

14. *SAGuy*, 108; Theodore of Pharme #18; also *AParadise*, 175 (but attributed to Abba Theophilus, the archbishop, rather than Theonas).

15. *SABudge*, 120, #527.

he glorified God."[16] It took a long time for the younger brother to understand the idea that blessings accompany renunciation, that God enriches us with his incarnation.

Not everyone who is charitable will be blessed materially, as in this story. Those who receive such extraordinary blessings receive them after many years of practicing renunciation in which their faith in God's ability to sustain everyone has been tested. Most receive spiritual blessings. We all observe God's blessings in families who have a limited income and seem to survive, and we wonder how this is possible! It is possible with God's blessings; he sustains humanity. But Scripture does not ask us to give up everything for God just that we may receive rewards and blessings, but rather to give us freedom from everything in order to be with God. It is freedom that gives courage to the spirit to follow God wherever God wants us to be. Renunciation guarantees our freedom.

Abba John the Short said we should renounce everything that occupies our mind; not only possessions but also sight, hearing, and talk as much as we can, for the senses tether the inner person.[17] This saying is at the core of understanding the true essence of renunciation. Athanasius spoke about God privileging humanity with an intellectual power to acquire knowledge of God, to have fellowship with God, and to communicate with God. With these faculties humanity was capable of contemplating God constantly and never letting the thought of God depart from their mind. Constant contemplation of God preserved the purity of humanity. Our first parents were created in this pure state; they transcended the senses and the things of the body and preserved their purity. But when the soul began to be attached to sensible things that are near the body and the senses, people were no longer able to contemplate God. This theological background illuminates the profound meaning of John the Short's saying. Renouncing everything that occupies the mind, including things perceived by sight and hearing and the faculty of speech, liberates the soul and puts it in its original state of purity, as at the beginning of creation, in the state of being in the image of God.

On another occasion, John the Short spoke about freedom; he asked his listeners not to be slaves to their master's will. They are not to be slaves to vainglory or any other spiritual agony. They are to regain the freedom granted to them by Christ's salvation and acquire the freedom of the new world by not inventing new laws that enslave them. Be free and do

---

16. *SAChaîne*, 21, #96; *SAHartley*, 69, #96.

17. *AParadise*, 378.

what you want; do not be a slave to something and do not be attached to anything.[18] Again, John the Short is connecting inner freedom with outer freedom. Outer freedom is not only from attachment to things, but also from attachment to laws, habits, and other traditions that humanity invents for itself. Be free of that. John the Short explains renunciation as freedom of the senses from all that enslaves them. He also speaks about the social binds that hinder our inner freedom. John the Short further explains that if we are not free we cannot work for Christ.[19] Renunciation is freedom, and freedom is for the sake of working for Christ.

One of the desert fathers explains that if you want to obtain peace, make sure that your possessions are poor. If you own a book, do not spend much energy decorating it. In short, do not possess things that will pain you if you lose them. Your shoes, clothes, and utensils should be poor enough so that thieves do not find them worth stealing.[20] It was told about Abba Agatho that he built a cell with his disciples and then after one week he left it because it was revealed to him that it was harmful for him. His disciples were infuriated by his decision for they felt they had wasted their time and energy on something Abba Agatho intended to renounce. They also worried that people would think monks were crazy, that they never settled, and that they would build something and leave it once it was finished. In response to their fury, Abba Agatho responded, "Although some may be shocked, there are others who will be edified and say, 'Blessed are they, for they have moved their abode for God's sake, and left all their property freely.' Whoever wants to come with me, let him come; I am going anyway." When his disciples understood that he was moving for his spiritual good and that this was an act of renunciation, they left with him.[21]

Renunciation is hard to execute and sometimes even harder to understand, even by some monks, because it sometimes defies logic and good economics. But once the spiritual goal is clear, then material profit and economic logic fade and become incomparable with spiritual profit. It really speaks about how we view and connect with material possessions and the objects we use. Are we so attached to them that, if we lose them for any reason, we are devastated? Does discarding material possessions make us furious like the disciples of Abba Agatho? Do we view material

18. *AParadise*, 378.
19. *AParadise*, 378.
20. *AParadise*, 169.
21. *SSWard*, 53, Possessing Nothing #4.

possessions as objects that define us? Or do we view them as functional objects that serve us? Renunciation speaks to the core of our value system.

"Abba Moses said: the love of possessions disturbs the mind, and renouncing it enlightens the mind."[22] Our peace of mind is affected by our material attachments; if the mind is affected, so is our prayer and spirituality. Abba Agathon said that the love of possessions is exhausting because it causes great disturbances to the soul. We have to get rid of it right away; if it becomes addictive, it becomes difficult to uproot.[23] The desert fathers and mothers are clearly aware of the addictive power of possessions and advise us to tackle the problem the moment we become aware of it. An elder said that when we become fond of material objects, we have to cast them away in order to teach our thoughts to love only Christ.[24] Another elder said that he who does not hate possessions cannot hate himself according to the Christian commandment.[25] He is referring to Luke 14:26, where becoming Christ's disciple and following him includes hating oneself. For this elder, love of possessions will not let us be free to follow Christ. Similarly, Abba Agathon said that if a person mourns the loss of something, he is not perfect, for if we are ordered to hate ourselves, how much more should we hate our possessions?[26] In all of these sayings the interconnection between renouncing material possessions and the spiritual and prayer life is indicative of the inner state of the soul in its relationship to God. If the soul does not care about material possessions, then it has reached a certain level of spiritual freedom that enables it to roam the heavenly realm unfettered by matter. But if the soul is bound by matter and the senses, then it is pitched like a tent and anchored to the soil because the senses are clouded by possessions. An elder commented that the harm is not in material possessions but rather in the way we are obsessed with them.[27] But Scripture, with its understanding of human nature, and the fathers, from their experience, speak about renunciation as a litmus test that reveals the level of our attachment to possessions and material objects and our readiness of follow Christ.

The mental struggle of renunciation can be more difficult than the actual decision to renounce and the act of renunciation. The early Christians

22. *AParadise*, 168.

23. *AParadise*, 168.

24. *LQ*, 161, #77v4.

25. *AParadise*, 169.

26. *AParadise*, 174.

27. *AParadise*, 176.

renounced everything and gave their possessions to the apostles (Acts 4:32–37). Ananias and Sepphira gave only a portion of their possessions to the apostles. Outwardly, it appeared to be an act of total renunciation, but in their hearts and in reality it was not. Peter asked, "Why has Satan filled your heart to lie to the Holy Spirit and to keep back part of the proceeds of the land? While it remained unsold, did it not remain your own? And after it was sold, were not the proceeds at your disposal? How is it that you have contrived this deed in your hearts? You did not lie to us but to God!" (Acts 5:1–4). Ananias and Sapphira renounced part of their property, but they lied and deceived not only God and the community but also themselves. They could not renounce their pride and be seen as inferior to other members of the community who had renounced all their possessions. If they had renounced their pride and kept their possessions, they would have been acceptable to God.

It is always tempting to renounce half and convince yourself as well as others that it is total renunciation. "A brother renounced the world and gave his goods to the poor, but he kept back a little for his personal expenses. He went to see Abba Anthony."[28] When Abba Anthony heard this he gave the newcomer an unconventional spiritual exercise. He asked him to buy meat and put it on his naked body and walk back to him. On his way back he was torn by dogs and birds. Abba Anthony's lesson was as follows: "Those who renounce the world but want to keep something for themselves are torn in this way by the demons who make war on them."[29] This newcomer, like Ananias and Sapphira, claimed total renunciation. Not everyone is capable of total renunciation, nor is it required of everyone. But deceiving a community with that claim is an indication of deep-seated pride that wants to gain unworthy acclaim. In these examples, mental renunciation of pride or other spiritual impediments is the core of the problem, not the renunciation of material goods.

Mental renunciation is letting go all the thoughts that hinder one's spiritual growth. If we renounce all our material possessions and family (see Matt 19:27, 29) but still sit in the desert thinking of what we have given up, our renunciation is in vain. The more we renounce, the more thoughts haunt us with the question, what if? Emperor Theodosius achieved a higher level of renunciation than a monk sitting in the desert whose mind is captive to his possessions, even if his possessions are worthless. This is what Anthony experienced when he first went to the

28. *ASWard*, 5, Antony the Great #20; also *SSWard*, 53, Possessing Nothing #1.
29. *ASWard*, 5, Antony the Great #20.

inner desert.[30] If material possessions and family ties still possess us, then we have not achieved renunciation. The desert fathers and mothers, to achieve mental renunciation, guarded very carefully their inner thoughts of pleasure, lust, covetousness, envy, judgment, etc. Any thought that possesses us and hinders our ability to love God or neighbor indicates that we have not achieved renunciation. Renouncing family ties, which would include marriage and children, is intended to liberate the person from the obligations and constraints that would obstruct one's total commitment to God. It is a scripturally based celibacy for the sake of God. Mental renunciation is also exemplified by renouncing the will, with the aim of achieving humility and freedom from the burden of the ego and from sorrows, cares, and anxiety. Through the examination of the thoughts of the mind and heart we make sure that none of these thoughts consume us to the extent that they cloud our way of thinking and paralyze our sense of judgment or hinder our righteous behavior and ability to make sound spiritual decisions.

What to renounce and how to renounce vary as much human nature is varied. What seems important and becomes obsessive for one person might be totally irrelevant to another. What we are to renounce should be tailored to our individual spiritual and inner self, and no two people are the same. That is the difficulty of spirituality; there is no one spiritual exercise that fits all. Should people living with their families and desiring to provide for all their family's needs, because they are good parents, adopt the spiritual exercise of renunciation? Most parents will oppose such a proposal because it is not good parenting and against paternal obligations. Thus for the sake of their family's comfort parents buy larger and larger houses, more toys and modern electronic gadgets to entertain their children, more clothes, more food, cars, in short, more of everything. The toys and gadgets distract the young, which results in less and less communication with parents, poor acquisition of many social skills, and less attentiveness to their spirituality. We have to acknowledge, though, that they gain other unexpected skills, such as handling electronic gadgets with great ease. Indulgence in possessions can cause exceptional financial burdens on families and raise the expectations of the young for an unsustainable standard of living. The result of such a lifestyle may be good for market consumerism but places families in debt. This mindset affects society on all levels, from the small social unit of the family to the larger economic units of banks, companies, states, and even nations. The result is

30. Refer to chapter 3 under "Temptations, Purity of Thought, and the Incarnation."

an economic meltdown. It is an unsustainable way of living that can affect the whole world.

At the time of the writing this book, in the second decade of the twenty-first century, "budget cuts," "spending cuts," and "austerity measures" have become common terms in media headlines. The world is going through the spiritual exercise of renunciation unknowingly. Renunciation is not a life of recklessness, of "let us spend now for we will die later," but rather a lifestyle of responsibility. On the microeconomic level of the family, the advice is to work hard to pay off family and personal debts. The only way to achieve this is by sitting around the kitchen table and examining family and personal bills and categorizing them under labels such as "essential," "necessity," and "not necessary." The question shifts from "What do we want?" to "What do we need?" People, as well as countries, make decisions of renunciation grudgingly, with great spiritual, social, and economic discomfort.

While forced renunciation creates resentment and discontent, Christian renunciation reaps spiritual benefits because it is done with an inner examination of the soul and with reflection on Scripture and Christ himself. The early desert fathers and mothers renounced everything willingly for the sake of Christ, who exemplified the ultimate renunciation by emptying himself for our sake and becoming incarnate. True spiritual renunciation emerges from a loving heart and creates social empathy, generosity, and healing from social and economic greed. Renunciation is an inner letting go before it is an outer letting go of material things. If there is no inner renunciation, outer renunciation is meaningless and might even cause resentment. True renunciation starts in our heart and mind before it is manifested in its outer form. Desert spirituality aims at inner renunciation rather than the outer. Desert spirituality's main concern is the salvation of the soul not the world economy. On the other hand, if each soul reflects renunciation within itself it will have a ripple effect on the larger social units that surround it, such as family, friends, and coworkers, and this in turn will affect the still larger units and eventually the whole social order. Christ has changed the world.

The spiritual exercise of renunciation is really an exercise of reflecting on how we interact with our possessions and examining the psychological, social, and intellectual issues that limit our freedom, the spiritual freedom that enables us to be in God's presence at all times without hindrance, to pray and contemplate without the distraction of material worries. Being in God's presence conforms us more and more to God's image and illuminates our inner soul. In this process we confront our pride, insecurities, greed, lack of love, even the extent of our love toward God. "Do not love the world or the things in the world. The love of the Father is not in those who love the world" (1 John 2:15). The desert fathers and mothers practiced renunciation but did not preach poverty. Renunciation goes beyond poverty since it is not restricted to the material but encompasses the essence of the person. Poverty, in the strict sense of the word, can be achieved (if anyone really wants to be poor) by an outward absence of possessions, whether voluntary or not. But most of the time it leaves a grudging soul with an ailing mental condition, suffering under its pressures. Renunciation is achievable after being confronted with God's profound love for the individual person and for humanity, and with a deep understanding of the incarnation. When this love engulfs our soul, mind, and spirit, everything else in the world pales in importance. It is at this moment that we can achieve renunciation, on the material, intellectual, and spiritual level. The importance of material wealth diminishes before God's benevolent care for us; our faith in him is heightened when we contemplate on God's care for the people of Israel in the desert for forty years, for the monastics who dwelled in the desert living in complete renunciation, and for billions of people since. John the Baptist lived in utter renunciation because he was preparing the way for the Lord. To prepare for the coming of the Lord into our heart, the example of John the Baptist paves the way for us. Renunciation opens our heart to others, and the love for our neighbor and generosity to others become natural. Renunciation begins with the contemplation of God and ends by making us captive to God's love but free toward all others. It frees us from all our inner insecurities so that we do not fear anything. We become free from the senses that, as Athanasius explained, make us captive. It is this complete inner freedom, the freedom of the spirit, that the early desert fathers and mothers were seeking.

Christ spoke about renunciation to the rich young man in Luke 18:18–24: "'There is still one thing lacking. Sell all that you own and distribute the money to the poor, and you will have treasure in heaven; then come, follow me.' But when he heard this, he became sad; for he was very rich." Many of the bystanders rightly asked the question, "Then who can be saved?" The bystanders then and we now are both asking the same question. What Christ is speaking about is unattainable. But Christ answered the bystanders and all those who have read the message through the centuries: "What is impossible for mortals is possible for God" (Luke 18:27). This powerful pronouncement is followed by another promise:

"Truly I tell you, there is no one who has left house or wife or brothers or parents or children, for the sake of the kingdom of God, who will not get back very much more in this age, and in the age to come eternal life" (Luke 18:29-30).

Biblical Verses on Renunciation for Further Contemplation:

LUKE 12:31-34—Instead, strive for his kingdom, and these things will be given to you as well. Do not be afraid, little flock, for it is your Father's good pleasure to give you the kingdom. Sell your possessions, and give alms. Make purses for yourselves that do not wear out, an unfailing treasure in heaven, where no thief comes near and no moth destroys. For where your treasure is, there your heart will be also.

LUKE 14:26-27—Whoever comes to me and does not hate father and mother, wife and children, brothers and sisters, yes, and even life itself, cannot be my disciple. Whoever does not carry the cross and follow me cannot be my disciple.

1 TIMOTHY 6:6-8—Of course, there is great gain in godliness combined with contentment; for we brought nothing into the world, so that we can take nothing out of it; but if we have food and clothing, we will be content with these. (Read 1 Tim 6:6-12)

MATTHEW 6:28—And why do you worry about clothing? Consider the lilies of the field, how they grow; they neither toil nor spin. (Read Matt 6:25-33)

GALATIANS 5:24-25—And those who belong to Christ Jesus have crucified the flesh with its passions and desires. If we live by the Spirit, let us also be guided by the Spirit.

GALATIANS 6:8—If you sow to your own flesh, you will reap corruption from the flesh; but if you sow to the Spirit, you will reap eternal life from the Spirit.

HEBREWS 13:5-6—Keep your lives free from the love of money, and be content with what you have; for he has said, "I will never leave you or forsake you." So we can say with confidence, "The Lord is my helper; I will not be afraid. What can anyone do to me?"

JOHN 12:25—Those who love their life lose it, and those who hate their life in this world will keep it for eternal life.

COLOSSIANS 2:20—If with Christ you died to the elemental spirits of the universe, why do you live as if you still belonged to the world? Why do you submit to regulations?

1 TIMOTHY 6:17—As for those who in the present age are rich, command them not to be haughty, or to set their hopes on the uncertainty of riches, but rather on God who richly provides us with everything for our enjoyment. (Read 1 Tim 6: 17–19)

2 TIMOTHY 2:11—The saying is sure: If we have died with him, we will also live with him.

1 CORINTHIANS 1:28—God chose what is low and despised in the world, things that are not, to reduce to nothing things that are.

Further Sayings for Reflection:

He [Abba Isidore of Pelusia] also said, "this desire for possessions is dangerous and terrible, knowing no satiety; it drives the soul which it controls to the heights of evil. Therefore let us drive it away vigorously from the beginning. For once it has become master it cannot be overcome.[31]

A great man came for a distance to Scetis carrying gold, and he asked the presbyter of the desert to distribute it among the brothers. But the presbyter said to him, "The brothers do not need it." But he was very pressing, and would not give way, and put a basket of money in the church porch. So the presbyter said, "Whoever is in need may take money from here." No one touched it, some did not even look at it. The presbyter said, "God has accepted your offering to him. Go away and give it to the poor." He went away very much edified.[32]

An old man was asked, "What is the straight and narrow way?" And he answered and said, "The straight and narrow way is for a man to constrain his thoughts, and to restrain his desires for God's sake, and this [is

---

31. *ASWard*, 99, Isidore of Pelusia #6.
32. *SSWard*, 58, Possessing Nothing #19.

intended to be understood when] it is said, "Behold, we have left everything and followed Thee.""[33]

Blessed Syncletica was asked if poverty is a perfect good. She said, "For those who are capable of it, it is perfect good. Those who can sustain it receive suffering in the body but rest in the soul, for just as one washes coarse clothes by trampling them underfoot and turning them about in all directions, even so the strong soul becomes much more stable thanks to voluntary poverty."[34]

Abbâ Isaac, the priest of the Cells, used to say that Abbâ Pambô said, "The manner of the apparel which a monk ought to wear should be such that if it were cast outside the cell for three days no one would carry it away."[35]

The blessed woman Eugenia said, "It is right for us to beg, but only we must be with Christ. He who is with Christ becometh rich, but he who honoureth the things of the body more than the things of the spirit shall fall both from the things which are first and the things which are last."[36]

Daniel told this story about Arsenius. An official once came to bring him the will of a kinsman who was a senator and had left Arsenius a large bequest. Arsenius took the will in his hands and wanted to tear it up. But the official fell at his feet, and said, "Please do not tear it up; they will blame me." Arsenius said to him, "I died before he did. Now that he is dead, how can he make me his heir?" He gave back the will, and would accept nothing.[37]

He [Hyperechius] also said, "A monk's treasure is voluntary poverty. Lay up treasure in heaven, brother, for there are the ages of quiet and bliss without end."[38]

Someone asked a hermit to accept money for his future needs but he refused, because the produce of his labour was enough for him. When the giver persisted, and begged him to take it for the needs of the poor, he

33. *SABudge*, 198, #209.

34. *ASWard*, 231, Syncletica #5; also *SAChaîne*, 5, #29; *SAHartley*, 36, #29. "Perfect good" because it generates other virtues.

35. *SABudge*, 37, #168.

36. *SABudge*, 37, #172.

37. *SSWard*, 53, Possessing Nothing #2.

38. *ASWard*, 238, Hyperechius # 6. Also, *SSWard*, 56, Possessing Nothing #14.

replied, "If I did that my disgrace would be twofold, I do not need it, yet I would have accepted it: and when I gave it to others, I would suffer from vanity."[39]

The old man [John the Short] also said, "You know that the first blow the devil gave to Job was through his possessions; and he saw that he had not grieved him nor separated him from God. With the second blow, he touched his flesh, but the brave athlete did not sin by any word that came out of his mouth in that either. In fact, he had within his heart that which is of God, and he drew on that source unceasingly."[40]

Amma Syncletica said, "The cross is the trophy of victory to us. For our profession is nothing but the renunciation of life, the rehearsal of death."[41]

Amma Syncletica said, "Therefore voluntary poverty is good for those who are in the habit of goodness. For having made a renunciation of all their unnecessaries, they bear the sign towards the Lord, singing purely that divine word: 'Our eyes hope in you; and you give food in good season to those who love you (Ps 145:15).'"[42]

Amma Syncletica said, "But also the enemy is defeated to a very great extent by those who are voluntarily poor; for he does not hinder what he does not have. For the greatest part of grief and temptations lies in the removal of riches; what can he do to the impoverished? Nothing. Set fire to their lands? They have none. Kill their beasts? But they do not have any of these. Attack their most beloved things? But they said farewell to these a long time ago. Therefore voluntary poverty is a great punishment against the enemy and a highly honored treasure to the soul."[43]

39. *SS Ward*, 57, Possessing Nothing #17.
40. *AS Ward*, 95, John the Dwarf #45.
41. *Sync.*, 296, #76.
42. *Sync.*, 281, #33.
43. *Sync.*, 281, #35.

8

The Discernment of Spirits

Discernment

> To one is given through the Spirit the utterance of wisdom, . . .
> to another the discernment of spirits . . ."
>
> 1 COR 12:8, 10

DISCERNMENT IS A GIFT of the Holy Spirit. In 1 Corinthians 12:8–11, Paul speaks about varieties of gifts, services, and activities of the Holy Spirit, which he lists as follows: wisdom, knowledge, faith, gifts of healing, working miracles, prophecy, discernment of spirits (*diakriseis pneumatōn*), tongues and interpretation of tongues. The discernment of spirits is a gift of the Holy Spirit.[1] The term *diakriseis* in its many forms is rather difficult to pin down. It can mean discriminating or differentiating between things, especially spirits. It can mean determining and deciding, which also implies interpreting dreams and omens. It can also mean to distinguish or the ability to distinguish.[2] We will use the word "discernment" to indicate our meaning. There are other Greek words that are usually translated as "discernment," as in the following examples, which are relevant to our understanding of discernment. When the Lord appeared to King Solomon at Gibeon, Solomon asked for "an understanding mind"

1. The only other time the term διακρίσεις is used in the New Testament is in Rom 14:1 to indicate distinguishing or differentiation of thoughts and opinions.

2. Henry George Liddell and Robert Scott, *A Greek-English Lexicon* (Oxford: Clarendon, 1992) 399, s.v. διάκρισις.

that would enable him to govern the people of Israel and "to discern between good and evil" (1 Kgs 3:9). God granted him "a wise and discerning mind" (3:12), the gift by which he has been known through history. The term used in 1 Kings 3:9 is *krinein*, which has the meaning of distinguishing, deciding, or judging. The term that describes the same gift given to Solomon in 1 Kings 3:12 is *phronimos*, which indicates wisdom and prudence.[3] King Solomon asked for the gift of discernment, to judge between good and evil, and Scripture says he was given wisdom and prudence. Paul prays on behalf of the Colossians that God would fill them with "knowledge of God's will in all spiritual wisdom and understanding" because this is the way they can live a life worthy and pleasing to God that will bear the fruit of good work and growth in the knowledge of God (Col 1:9–10). Paul is praying for a special gift to be granted to the Colossians, "the faculty of understanding (*synesis*)." Job also prayed to God regarding any wrong done for he could not "discern (*synesis*) calamity" (Job 6:30).[4] Pharaoh chose Joseph, a most "discerning and wise" man, to guide Egypt through a looming famine (Gen 41:39). The text uses terms derived from *phronimos* and *synesis*, for which wisdom is the common meaning with additional nuances of intelligence and prudence. In Romans 12:2 all the faithful are required to discern the will of God: "Do not be conformed to this world, but be transformed by the renewing of your minds, so that you may discern what is the will of God—what is good and acceptable and perfect." Discerning here is *dokimazein*, which carries the understanding of testing and examining.[5] This verse requires all Christians, regardless of their status in life, to be transformed and not to conform to the world with all its demands. The means of this transformation is the renewal of the mind, the *nous* of which Athanasius spoke. This mind must be endowed with the gift of discernment so as to understand and follow God's will. All Christians living this transformed life, who do not conform to the world, are living a spiritual life, which gives them spiritual discernment, for "those who are spiritual discern all things" (1 Cor 2:15). The term in there is *anakrinein*, the same gift asked for by King Solomon.

3. William Arndt, F. Wilbur Gingrich, Frederick W. Danker, and Walter Bauer, *A Greek-English Lexicon of the New Testament and Other Early Christian Literature* (Chicago: University of Chicago Press, 1979) 451, s.v. κρίνειν; and Liddell and Scott, *Greek-English Lexicon*, 1956, s.v. φρόνιμος.

4. Liddell and Scott, *Greek-English Lexicon*, 1712, s.v. σύνεσις; includes intelligence, perception, and knowledge.

5. Ibid., 442, s.v. δοκιμάζω.

From these few verses it is very clear that the virtues of discernment, wisdom, judgment, understanding, prudence, and intelligence are interconnected. In many biblical verses, especially in wisdom literature, they are used synonymously. The book of Proverbs and the book of Wisdom are full of verses exalting these virtues. Biblical figures and churches, such as the Colossians, prayed for such a gift. We pray to God for the gift of wisdom and discernment. The gift of discernment enables us to discern the spirits (the Spirit of God or evil spirits), to understand, distinguish, separate, and decide between good and evil, to discern dreams (like Joseph and Daniel), to make right judgments for others as well as for ourselves, and to discern the will of God. The desert fathers and mothers prayed for the gift of discernment and the wisdom to be able to "discern all things." This spiritual gift is crucial for desert spirituality. It is involved in every single action the desert monastics undertook, whether reading Scripture, praying, fasting, or any other activity of the spiritual life. This virtue assures balance in the spiritual life and moderation in all spiritual activities. It is the antidote of pride. It safeguards the health of the spiritual journey. It is always woven into the discussion of other spiritual gifts; many readers might miss it since it is usually highlighted or praised in connection with other virtues and especially ascetic practices. It is a gift of the Spirit, but is connected with themes of wisdom, understanding, intelligence, judgment, prudence, and other activities of the mind. The presence of discernment is a sign of a "renewed mind" (Rom 12:2). The renewed mind is at the heart of Athanasius' theology. The incarnation and resurrection have granted humanity a renewal of life, a renewal of God's image within us, and a renewed mind that conforms to God's mind so as not to incline toward evil under the pressure of the senses and their immediate satisfaction. Discernment is a virtue most valued and esteemed among the desert fathers and mothers.

> A group of desert fathers gathered around Anthony and began discussing which of the virtues was most capable of preserving the monk from the snares of the enemy. Some said fasting and prayer preserve thought, poise the mind, and help the person to be closer to God. Others said humility and renunciation of earthly matters enable the mind to be calm and pure from worldly worries and to approach God. Others said that mercy is the noblest of virtues because the Lord promised those who practice mercy, "Come, you that are blessed by my Father, inherit the kingdom prepared for you from the foundation of the world." (Matt 25:34). . . . When they concluded their discussion

> Abba Anthony said, "Indeed, all these virtues are beneficial and are needed by all those who seek God and want to be in his presence. We have seen many perish physically from excessive fasting, vigilant prayers, seclusion in the desert, and asceticism so great that they kept only what they needed for one day and gave alms with the rest of their possessions. In spite of all these ascetic practices, many lost their way and lost their virtues because they did not practice discernment."[6]

This lengthy discussion among the Abbas in the desert indicates that if discernment is not practiced with all the other spiritual activities we might lose our way. Excessive or unwise fasting and vigilance can make a person susceptible to vainglory and sometimes to physical harm. Abba Anthony is advising those assembled that any spiritual practice, though it might seem totally spiritual, if practiced without moderation, guidance, and discernment, can lead to counterproductive and sometimes harmful consequences.

On another occasion, Abba Anthony summarized his advice in these succinct terms: "Some wear out their bodies by fasting; but because they have no discretion this only puts them further away from God."[7] The desert fathers also say that discernment preserves a person from vainglory and from languor.[8] They also say that discernment exposes inner deception when sometimes we do not discern whether the light within is not darkness (see Luke 11:35).[9] Discernment obliges a person to be self-reflective and examine his or her actions and sayings; it enables a person to comprehend the difference between good and evil. The desert fathers gave the example of King Saul, who did not comprehend what the Lord said to him through Samuel and did not follow his instructions; he kept the best of the enemy's spoils with the excuse of offering them as sacrifice. He did not know that the Lord delights more in obeying his voice than in burnt sacrifices and offerings (see 1 Sam 15:5–23).[10] King Saul lacked discernment and did not understand that God would not be satisfied with keeping the best of the enemy's spoils. He lacked discernment and did not heed Samuel's advice. The repercussions of not having discernment for

6. *AParadise*, 409.

7. *SS Ward*, 88, Discretion #1; *AParadise*, 412; *AS Ward*, 3, Antony the Great #8.

8. *AParadise*, 410.

9. Ibid.

10. Ibid.

Saul were the harsh words, "Because you have rejected the word of the LORD, he has also rejected you from being king" (1 Sam 15:23).

The desert fathers and mothers often spoke about obedience. They always meant obedience to God. The young and uninitiated in the spiritual life obeyed their spiritual father or mother because they trusted that God would speak to them through him or her. Discernment in obedience is of vital importance, as the following story explains: A monk was known for his discernment. When he arrived to Scetis he could not find a solitary cell to live in. While roaming the desert trying to find a place to live, he met one of the elders who invited him to use one of his cells until he could have his own place. He was very thankful for the elder's generosity. Soon other monks flocked to his cell to ask his advice and learn from his wisdom. They also brought many gifts. The elder became very jealous and said to his disciple, "We have been living in this place for many years and none of these monks ever visited us and in a few days this imposter has drawn all these monks to him. Go and throw him out of the cell."[11] This very human reaction from the elder indicates that no matter how experienced a person can be we are not immune to jealousy or other weaknesses of the soul. Observe the discernment of the disciple as the narrative progresses; he always judged orders from his spiritual father through a biblical lens to see whether or not what he advised or ordered conformed to God's word. The disciple was very aware of having personal responsibility for every action; there was no blaming others because it was an order or because he was observing obedience.

The narrative continues as follows: The disciple went to the monk and said, "My teacher is asking about your health and requests your prayers for he is sick. He is also inquiring if there is anything I can do toward your needs." The monk was taken aback by the generosity and lovingkindness of his neighbor and asked the disciple to give the elder his greetings and inform him that he was doing well with the elder's prayers on his behalf and was not in need of anything. The disciple returned to the elder and said that the monk conveyed his greetings and asked for the elder's prayers on his behalf and requested a few days to find a new cell. After three days the elder was disturbed with thoughts of jealousy and said to his disciple, "Go tell him that I have waited for too long, leave the cell." The disciple went to the monk and said that his teacher sent greetings and this blessing and requested the monk to accept it for the sake of Christ, and to pray for him for he was rather sick; otherwise he would have come personally.

11. *AParadise*, 411.

When the monk suggested that he would visit the elder, the disciple said that his teacher would not accept that such a distinguished monk should accompany him; he would deliver the greetings. The disciple returned to his teacher and informed him that the monk would leave his cell by Sunday. When Sunday arrived and the monk did not leave, the elder's mind was consumed with rage; he went out and said to his disciple, "Let us go to this imposter monk, for if he does not leave willingly, I will kick him out with my rod like a dog." When the disciple saw the fury of his teacher and realized that rage consumed his mind, he pleaded to his teacher to let him go ahead of him to the monk lest he be embarrassed before any guests. The teacher thought it was a good advice and waited for the return of his disciple, gnashing his teeth. The disciple arrived at the monk's place and told him that his teacher sent greetings; he was impatient to come and see the monk but because of his weakness was unable to come. When the monk heard these words he immediately left his cell and headed toward the elder to take his blessings. The disciple ran quickly before him to announce to his teacher that the monk had left his cell and was on his way to take his blessings before leaving. When the elder heard this he remembered his previous communications with the monk; the cloud of jealousy faded away and he became perplexed and was so embarrassed to meet the monk that he could not raise his eyes toward the monk and began retreating. When the disciple realized that the elder had awakened to his mistake, he told his teacher that he had never relayed any of his messages. The elder was elated to know this and met the monk with great delight and a pure heart. When the elder was alone with his disciple he bowed to his disciple and said to him, "Now you are my father and I am unworthy to be your disciple. Because of your wisdom, pure conscience, and great discernment, you have saved me from a scandal."[12]

The story raises questions about honesty in relaying messages, but the moral of the story is about discernment. The disciple could not disobey the commandment of love and it was very clear to him that throwing out a blameless fellow monk from his cell could not be justified by any biblical commandment. The monk had done nothing wrong, except being loved by all. The disciple understood that his obedience was first to God before any other person. And because he was wise, perceptive and discerning, he probably understood that his teacher would regret his episode of jealousy, as in fact he did. It is said that Abba Anthony once said, "If you are ordered with something that conforms to the will of God then observe

12. *AParadise*, 411–12; my translations.

it, and if you are ordered with something that does not conform with the commandments say that obedience to God is before obedience to man."[13]

The story of the disciple makes it clear how important discernment is in all walks of life. From the time we are born we are required to obey parents, grandparents, or teachers, and when we mature and start holding jobs we are required to obey many bosses and rules, depending on the number of jobs we hold during our lifetime. Probably we have found ourselves in the situation of the disciple many times. That does not necessarily mean that our bosses are evil or mean; they are human beings who have moments of weakness and give orders that they might regret. In many difficult situations our hearts and minds have asked the question: What do we do? We also give orders to many people, our children, our employees and many others. How often have we reflected on our decision making? The story reflects our different roles in life; we are sometimes the elder and sometimes the disciple. How many times have we been jealous of a new colleague? What was our reaction—generosity of heart or fuming jealousy and vengeance? Discernment makes us reflect on our role in various positions, on our decision making, and on our attitudes toward others. Discernment is a responsibility with repercussions. In our story all things turned out well. Often, however, we have to pay for our courageous stance. No matter what the repercussions are, many prefer doing what is right over a guilty conscience.

A certain brother came to Abba Joseph unable to decide between living a solitary life and living in the monastery, for he was content either way. Abba Joseph responded, "If thou art content to live in the monastery, and art [equally] content to lead a solitary life, do this: Weigh thy thoughts as it were in a balance, and the thought which outbalances the other, that fulfill."[14] Discernment helps us to navigate difficult decisions. It helps us weigh our thoughts in a balance. Another elder said, "Unto every thought that riseth up in thee say, 'Art thou of us, or of our enemies?' And the thought will always make confession unto thee."[15] Scrutinizing the thought and the motives behind each thought requires prayer with discernment. If we are attentive, God reveals his will to us.

The desert fathers and mothers were very ascetic and fasting was an important theme in their spiritualty. Practices varied; some fasted for

13. Anthony, saying 17, from a revised edition of Manuscript 5 and Manuscript 6 in the Monastery of St Macarius in Wadi al-Naṭrūn, complied by the monk Epiphanios of St. Macarius. [My translation]

14. *SABudge*, 212, #266.

15. *SABudge*, 220, #314.

a week, others for two days, others for a day, and still other until three each afternoon, with many variations in between. Their diet was primarily bread and salt with some added vegetables and beans. Others preferred to abstain from certain foods altogether. The practice of fasting was left to each individual with their spiritual advisor. On one occasion Abba Joseph asked Abba Poemen, "How should one fast?" Abba Poemen responded that it is "better that one should eat every day, but only a little, so as not to be satisfied." Abba Poemen had experimented with fasting two days, three days, and also a whole week at a time. He concluded, "The Fathers tried all this out as they were able and they found it preferable to eat every day, but just a small amount. They have left us this royal way, which is light."[16] The importance of the sayings of the desert fathers and mothers is that they convey to us in pithy statements the experience of generations of asceticism. There was a lot of experimentation to find the best practice of fasting, and the conclusion was moderation. They discovered that lengthy fasting, such as for a week, made people binge when they ate at the end of the week or proud of their human achievement—the worse spiritual conclusion one could reach. These experiences led the fathers always to suggest moderation and insist that asceticism was not an aim but a spiritual aid.

It is said that when Abba Nitira was a monk, he practiced moderate asceticism to enable him to pursue his work and prayers. After he became a bishop he became very ascetic. His disciple asked him why he changed his ascetic practices. He responded that in the desert no one would take care of him if he fell sick but that is not the case in the city. In addition, he needed to be more ascetic since city temptations are greater.[17] In this story Abba Nitira adapts his ascetic practices to his changing monastic needs. There is really no one rule even for each person; discernment requires flexibility, constant self-examination, and spiritual awareness. We need to adapt our spiritual practices to work and family demands and be alert to change our spiritual patterns with changing social and family needs. Discernment leads to spiritual flexibility and moderation.

Abba John the Short learned an important lesson about moderation when he was still young. He asked his elder brother to free him from all care, "like the angels," so he might worship God ceaselessly. He left everything and went to the desert. A week later he returned to his brother.

16. *ASWard*, 171, Poemen #31.

17. *SAChaîne*, 14, #62; *SAHartley*, 53, #62; also *ASWard*, 156–57, Netras #1; *SSWard*, 96, Discretion #36, where the name of the monk is Nathyra.

When he knocked at the door, the brother knew it was John but replied, "John has become an angel, and henceforth he is no longer among men." The elder brother refused to open the door in spite of John's pleading. The distressed young John remained outside the door till morning. His brother then opened the door and said, "You are a man and you must once again work in order to eat." Abba John learned his lesson and asked for his brother's forgiveness.[18] John was too young to have developed the gift of discernment and to have learned that moderation and balance and attending to all aspects of life are important for a healthy spiritual life. All the desert fathers and mothers of the early church prayed while working, memorizing Scripture for that purpose. Anthony learned that he must work and he could not just pray without finding sustenance for his physical needs. The desert fathers and mothers discerned through their long spiritual experience to balance work and prayer.

Amma Syncletica said, "Everything which is extreme is destructive."[19] The desert fathers and mothers have given us this important spiritual lesson lest we go through all the agony they went through before discovering the secret of discernment, balance, and moderation in spirituality. The notion of reaching perfection is always tempting and the fathers warn us against such thoughts. Abba Isaiah of Scetis advises young monks who are tempted by the devil with thoughts of perfection and the practice of a rigorous ascetic life beyond their capacity not to accept such thoughts, for such thoughts will lead them to hopelessness and spiritual frustration because they are unable to reach the high spiritual levels they arbitrarily set for themselves.[20] In another story one of the fathers was so weakened by ascetic practices that he fell sick. Another monk discovered him, got some help for him, and advised him that the body is like a garment: if we take care of it, it will last, but if we neglect it, it will perish.[21]

Some of the monks of Scetis wanted to entertain themselves and have a meal together. A respected priest among them moved among the monks to offer them drinks. Out of humility and respect for him, nobody accepted a drink, except for John the Short. Everyone was surprised and asked John the Short how he, the youngest of those present, could be the only one to accept a drink from the priest. His response was that if he were serving others he would like them to accept a drink from him, so he did

18. *ASWard*, 86, John the Dwarf #2; and *SABudge*, 172, #70.

19. *SSWard*, 106, Discretion #75.

20. *AParadise*, 142.

21. *SABudge*, 158, #20.

not want to grieve the priest since no one was accepting a drink from him. Those present were edified by his discernment.[22] In this story everyone was focused on himself and how to act in a proper way toward a respected priest. Only John the Short had the courage to behave differently. He was discerning enough to think of another, that is, the priest, rather than himself, even if the social norm would condemn his behavior since everyone questioned his action and expressed surprise. It takes courage to stand against the tide.

On another occasion, Abba John the Short was traveling back to Scetis with some of the brothers. Their guide lost his way during the night. In the fourth and fifth century people traveled in caravans and the guide, who was trained to navigate by the stars at night and the sun by day, would lead the way. When they lost their way, Abba John did not want to embarrass the guide so he pretended to be sick, and thus the whole caravan had to stop until daybreak, when the direction of the sun would put them on the right track.[23] By saving the caravan guide from embarrassment, John gives us another example of gentleness toward others. By leading others not to reprimand the guide, he gives an example of tactfulness toward others. We need to be tactful toward our colleagues when they err for any reason and not parade their mistake with the intention of highlighting our own intelligence. Being tactful with others speaks about our humility and our self-confidence at the same time; we do not need the mistakes of others to prove ourselves.

Under the title of discernment there is a lot of discussion about asceticism because it is a difficult topic that requires moderation and keeping the right balance is rather tricky. But the fathers also understood clearly that though asceticism has its value, it is never a goal. "A hermit was asked by a brother, 'How do I find God? With fasts, or labour, or vigils, or works of mercy?'" The hermit responded that it can be through any of these, but also through discernment. Without discernment, if "our mouths stink from fasting, and we have learnt all the Scriptures, and memorized the whole Psalter, we may still lack what God wants, humility and love."[24] Discernment enables the spiritual person to put things in perspective. Physical asceticism, if not accompanied by humility and love, is worthless. One of the brothers asked an elder why some of the monks followed austere ascetic practices but "have not obtained favor as the ancients." The

22. *ASWard*, 86–87, John the Dwarf #7; *AParadise*, 83.
23. *ASWard*, 89, John the Dwarf #17; *AParadise*, 83.
24. *SSWard*, 111, Discretion #94.

elder said that the ancients had more love toward each other but now each was trying to "pull his neighbor downwards."[25] Asceticism without love of neighbor gets one nowhere.

Asceticism leads some to vainglory and this is what happened to the great Abba Anthony, who was not immune from spiritual weaknesses. It was revealed to Abba Anthony that there was a physician in the city who gave to the poor everything he had beyond his needs and every day he sang the hymn "Holy, Holy, Holy" with the angels.[26] Anthony learned that the physician dwelling in the city lived in a holier way than he, the most famous ascetic, did. Anthony learned that asceticism without other spiritual virtues is not pleasing to God. Discernment enables us to balance our spiritual activities, for excess in one activity, as in the case of Anthony's asceticism, may lead to our spiritual downfall. Discernment guides a person to do what is suitable for him- or herself. It is for each reader to discern what would be pleasing to God, just as the physician discerned his spiritual path and reached the spiritual state of singing with the heavenly choir. Discernment, prayer, and inner contemplation reveal the most suitable spiritual path.

Abba Nastir was asked by one of the fathers about the best work for him. Abba Nastir replied, "[T]he book saith that Abraham was a lover of strangers, and that God was with him; and Elijah was a lover of a life of silent contemplation, and God was with him; and David was a humble man, and God was with him; therefore whatsoever work thy soul wisheth to do, provided that it be of God, that do, and keep thy heart from evil things."[27] Each of the biblical figures mentioned discerned the spiritual work that best fit his gifts, character, and temperament. Discernment is a spiritual exercise that we should practice often to examine our progress in the spiritual life and to check if we are on the right path and if what we are pursuing really fits our gifts and God's will. Discernment also requires courage to make necessary changes and to take active steps toward our spiritual advancement, which might require renunciation and the forgoing of many of the things we are attached to, whether spiritual or physical.

Discernment is a theme that is intertwined with all other themes of desert spirituality. It might sometimes seem illusive, but it is the cornerstone of spiritual moderation and wisdom. Discernment requires us to step

25. *SAChaîne*, 37, #165; *SAHartley*, 100, #165.

26. *ASWard*, 6, Antony the Great #24; and *SAChaîne*, 39, #172; *SAHartley*, 104, #172.

27. *SABudge*, 159, #21.

back and reflect on—that is, discern—our lives, our behavior, our goals, our relationships, and all other aspects of what we deem important. Discernment requires change and courage to face the requirements of change. Discernment is a gift that we pray God would grant us, but it is also a gift honed with experience. Many of us reap the benefits of discernment with the maturity of age, but when the young acquire it we truly understand what a gift the Holy Spirit has granted humanity. Solomon, Joseph, and Daniel were known for their discernment, which was manifested in their political decisions. Discernment is a spiritual gift that is used not only in spirituality but also to manage our households, businesses, and personal lives. We cannot be discerning in one aspect of life and not in another; discernment permeates our way of thinking, our thoughts, and our approach to life. Discernment engages our intellect and mind to reflect on our conduct, choices, relationships, and spirituality. The desert fathers and mothers valued discernment as a spiritual gift that moderated their ascetic practices in relationship to other spiritual exercises. As for us, discernment is a spiritual gift that lets us discern the spirits, what is good and what is evil; it gives us wisdom—spiritual wisdom and worldly wisdom—like Solomon. Discernment opens our hearts to discern and receive the word of God. Discernment gives us understanding and prudence in all aspects of our lives. Spiritual discernment should permeate all our activities.

Biblical Verses on Discernment for Further Contemplation:

PSALM 16:7—I bless the LORD who gives me counsel; in the night also my heart instructs me.

PSALM 139:2—You know when I sit down and when I rise up; you discern my thoughts from far away.

WISDOM 9:13—For who can learn the counsel of God? Or who can discern what the Lord wills?

DEUTERONOMY 4:6—You must observe them diligently, for this will show your wisdom and discernment to the peoples, who, when they hear all these statutes, will say, "Surely this great nation is a wise and discerning people!"

WISDOM 2:22—And they did not know the secret purposes of God, nor hoped for the wages of holiness, nor discerned the prize for blameless souls.

PROVERBS 21:30—No wisdom, no understanding, no counsel, can avail against the LORD.

ISAIAH 11:2—The spirit of the LORD shall rest on him, the spirit of wisdom and understanding, the spirit of counsel and might, the spirit of knowledge and the fear of the LORD.

ISAIAH 5:20—Ah, you who call evil good and good evil, who put darkness for light and light for darkness, who put bitter for sweet and sweet for bitter!

Further Sayings for Reflection:

Abba Poemen said that Abba Ammonas said, "A man can spend his whole time carrying an axe without succeeding in cutting down the tree; while another, with experience of tree-felling brings the tree down with a few blows. He said that the axe is discernment."[28]

She [Amma Syncletica] also said. "There is a useful sorrow, and a destructive sorrow. Sorrow is useful when we weep for our sins, and for our neighbour's ignorance, and so that we may not relax our purpose to attain to true goodness, these are the real kinds of sorrow. Our enemy adds something to this. For he sends sorrow without reason, which is something called lethargy. We ought always to drive out a sadness like that with prayers and psalms."[29]

Hyperichius said, "He who teaches others by his life and not his speech is truly wise."[30]

A hermit said, "All chatter is unnecessary. Nowadays everyone talks but what is needed is action. That is what God wants. Not useless talking."[31]

---

28. *ASWard*, 174, Poemen #52.
29. *SSWard*, 105, Discretion #71.
30. *SSWard*, 106, Discretion #78.
31. *SSWard*, 108, Discretion #80.

A hermit said, "We are not condemned if bad thoughts enter our minds, but only if we use them badly. Because of our thoughts we may suffer shipwreck, but because of our thoughts we may also earn a crown."[32]

Amma Syncletica said, "Therefore, discernment, I think, lies in the head. It says 'suffering' because every bud of virtue is established in sufferings. But by means of 'grief in the heart' it signified the unstable and wretched ethos [of the world]. For some have said that the heart is the dwelling place of anger and grief. Not being glorified, people become aggrieved; desiring for others, they waste away; toiling, they become impatient; being rich, they are driven mad, because on account of guarding their property, they do not sleep."[33]

32. *SS Ward*, 110, Discretion #89.

33. *Sync.*, 284, # 41.

9

God Is Love

Love

God is love, and those who abide in love abide in God, and God abides in them.

1 JOHN 4:16

GOD IS LOVE. GOD'S love has been manifested to humanity in his incarnation. The true love we experience starts with God's love for us; this love emanates from God and is reciprocated toward God and others. The incarnation, God's willingness to give up his Son for our sake and for the sake of our salvation, is the manifestation of God's immense love for humanity. Contemplating the incarnation with all our mind and heart reminds the feeble and forgetful human heart of God's love. With the constant immersion in God's love, true love toward others is experienced. Love toward another for the satisfaction of sensual, physical, and emotional needs or for the satisfaction of the ego or for financial or other benefits we receive represents human love. Divine love does not ask for anything in return. God does not benefit from our love; it is rather we who benefit from God's love for us. We love God because he loved us first and because of this love we ought to love others (see 1 John 4:10–11). When we love God and love our neighbor, God abides in us (see 1 John 4:16). The Old Testament, especially in the Psalms, describes God's love as "steadfast love." "O my strength, I will sing praises to you, for you, O God, are my fortress, the God who shows me steadfast love" (Ps 59:17). Psalm 136 is one of the psalms that present this constant contemplation and praise of God's steadfast love. The whole psalm is a thanksgiving and every one of its twenty-six verses ends with "for his steadfast love endures forever." The world cannot exhaust God's love, nor will this chapter. This chapter is about the desert fathers and mothers communicating their profound immersion in God's love in their thoughts and actions toward God and others. It is about the practical implications of God's love in our lives. It is about the manifestation of God's love overpowering human hearts and thoughts.

There were three monastics who went to work in the fields during the harvest season. It was customary among the desert fathers to spend the harvest season in the fields, earning wages. It was one of their main sources of income, over and above their basket weaving, to sustain them during the year. During the harvest season they would also obtain the wheat for their yearly bread consumption. The three monastics chose to harvest sixty acres of land. On the first day of the harvest one of the monks fell sick and returned to his cell. One of the remaining brothers told the other, "Constrain your thoughts a little," meaning do not let any thoughts of anger or discontent, or any other thoughts, rule the mind because of their brother's illness. When they calmed down they decided to complete the work of the whole field as planned because "we believe that by his prayers we shall harvest his part." They completed the work and called on their sick brother to come and collect his share of the wages. The brother asked, "What wages? I have not harvested." They responded that they completed the work of three persons because of his prayers and insisted that he come to collect his wages. The argument escalated and they had to go to one of the elders seeking his judgment. When the elder heard their story he assembled all the brothers and all marveled at their story. They judged that the brother should take his share of the wages and the brother accepted it reluctantly because it was the assembly's judgment.[1] This is a story of love among three monks. The reluctant brother could not accept to take wages that were not his; he felt it was not his right to take what he had not earned. The two other monks out of love and compassion decided that sickness should not be a hindrance and they very truly believed that the prayers of the monk enabled them to do the work of three. They did not believe they were giving the monk charity, for his prayers were effective in helping them accomplish a task beyond their physical efforts. It is a story of unworthiness and honesty, from the side of the sick monk; from

1. *SAChaine*, 37, #166; *SAHartley*, 101, #166.

the point of view of the two monks who harvested the field it is a story of love, honesty, and true faith in the power of prayer.

A fourth-century visitor to Nitria describes how the monks lived in complete isolation from each other while still caring about each other—a conundrum that baffles the modern mind. Our modern understanding of love is about conversing with the other, knowing their news, sharing meals, and engaging in other social activities that expresses interest in the other. The desert fathers and mothers understood love in a different way. It was about contributing bricks and labor toward building a new cell in one day for the newcomer to the desert.[2] It was about inviting the newcomer to the church, during which time they placed in his cell everything he needed so that the brother would not know who brought him these gifts.[3] It was about a selfless and hidden means of helping another without any expectation of return, since the newcomer did not know who brought what or did what. It was about the sensitive heart that anticipated the needs of the other. In another story, when Abba Macarius received some fresh grapes he thought of his sick brother and sent them to him. This brother in turn sent them to another brother. The grapes where sent from one brother to the other, each thinking of the needs of his brother, without anyone of them eating a single grape. The grapes circulated among the monks until they made their way back to Abba Macarius.[4] In these two stories, there do not appear to be any words exchanged, but a lot of self-sacrificing love is exchanged. Everyone is aware that when people move to a new place they need things. It requires a sensitive heart full of God's love to sit and reflect on what the new comer will need. The monastics in the story acted on their reflections. In the second story, fresh fruits are not available in the desert, and everyone knew it was a great blessing to have fresh fruit. Yet each brother thought of his neighbor, sacrificing his own personal desires to eat fresh produce. This is practical love that emanates from a sensitive heart that thinks of the other and not of oneself. As the Son of God sacrificed himself for us, so we also sacrifice for others. In times of economic hardship all over the world, it is not difficult to recognize the needs of our neighbors. In fact, the media have been bringing to us refreshing stories of people who without obligation have taken their homeless neighbors into

---

2. Norman Russell, trans., *The Lives of the Desert Fathers: The Historia Monachorum in Aegypto*, Cistercian Studies 34 (Kalamazoo, MI: Cistercian, 1981) 106; *Hist. monach.* 20.10.

3. Russell, *Lives of the Desert Fathers*, 106; *Hist. monach.* 20.11.

4. Russell, *Lives of the Desert Fathers*, 109; *Hist. monach.* 21.13–14.

their houses. These are examples of not talking about but demonstrating true love toward the neighbor.

Abba Agathon went to the city to sell his handiwork. He found a sick stranger who had no one to take care of him. Agathon carried him and rented a house and remained with him to serve him. For four months he paid the monthly rent and the rest of his expenses. After four months Abba Agathon returned to the desert.[5] At the end of the parable of the Samaritan (Luke 10:25–37), Christ asked us to "go and do likewise," and Abba Agathon did. For him it was not a parable but an injunction to take care of whoever needed care.

Two hermits shared their living quarters without ever quarreling. One proposed that they quarrel like other men do, but they never did.[6] Their love, selflessness, and respect to each other conquered any attempt to disrupt their harmony. What is interesting about this narrative is that it acknowledges that the normal behavior of people sharing their living quarters is to quarrel. We find this in campus dorms, in shared apartments, and even in shared work space. It is very hard not to hold resentment when one party is determined to make things difficult. But it is sometimes possible to break the cycle of bad behavior by an opposing act of love, which sometimes can convert hearts. There is a story of a Manichean priest who while traveling became distressed and was delayed and had no place to stay in the desert except at a monk's dwelling.[7] He was hesitant to knock at the monk's door, fearing he would recognize his religious affiliation from his dress and would not let him in. But since he did not have much choice, he knocked anyway. The monk received him very well and even asked him to pray. He was given food to eat and was refreshed from his travel and given a place to sleep. At night the Manichean priest could not but reflect on the loving reception he had received from the monk and concluded he must be a man of God. He was so overwhelmed by the monk's love that he asked him about his belief, and at the end the Manichean told the monk, "I will believe in what you believe."[8] The monk did not preach or even

---

5. *AParadise*, 67.

6. *SSWard*, 182, Charity #22; *SAChaîne*, 38, #168; *SAHartley*, 102, #168.

7. Manichaeism was founded by the Persian Mani. One of the main tenets of his teaching was that the struggle between good and evil is the struggle between the spiritual worlds of light and darkness. Mani founded his religion by taking teachings from Christianity, Zoroastrianism, and Buddhism. Manichaeism thrived between the third and the seventh century.

8. *SABudge*, 230, #384.

attempt to preach to the Manichean; he just behaved as a good, loving Christian. That was powerful enough to cause a change of heart.

Acts of love speak louder than words. In a similar story, a pagan priest met one of the disciples of Abba Macarius the Great on his way. The disciple insulted the pagan priest, most probably because of his pagan belief, and the priest responded by beating the disciple, leaving him almost dead. When the priest continued his journey he met Abba Macarius himself, who greeted him well. The priest was so astonished and he stopped and asked Abba Macarius, "What good do you see in me that you honor me by speaking to me?" Abba Macarius responded that he saw how hardworking the priest was and decided to commend him for that. The pagan priest said, "your greeting made me realize that you have a great god on your side not like the other monk who I beat almost to death." Abba Macarius realized that he was speaking about his disciple. The pagan priest remained with Abba Macarius and was eventually baptized and became a monk. Abba Macarius concluded by saying, "One evil word causes other good words to be bad, just as one good word causes other evil words to become pleasing."[9] Again, there was no preaching involved; it was the simple act of greeting another person with respect and courtesy regardless of who the other person is. It was an act of love that had the power to convert a heart. That is the power of love.

The desert fathers and mothers understood the commandment is to love everyone equally and without distinction. They struggled with their heart about loving one person more than another. Abba Epiphanius said to some monks who were visiting him that whoever does not receive all the brethren without distinction cannot be perfect.[10] Another brother was struggling with his thoughts and asked a hermit for advice. He told the hermit that when he hears something about a monk that indicates that he is living in a sinful way he does not invite him to his cell, but when he hears about a good monk he invites him gladly. The hermit advised the brother that he should "give double charity" to the first brother since the good brother does not need good to be done for him.[11] This story demonstrates how closely the desert fathers and mothers scrutinized their thoughts. They examined their hearts not for hatred, but rather for total and absolute

---

9. Tim Vivian, trans., *Saint Macarius, the Spiritbearer: Coptic Texts Relating to Saint Macarius the Great*, St. Vladimir's Popular Patristics (Crestwood, NY: St. Vladimir's Seminary Press, 2004) 59–60.

10. *SABudge*, 246, #448.

11. *SSWard*, 182, Charity #23; *SAChaîne*, 38, #169; *SAHartley*, 103, #169.

love for the other. They examined their thoughts for the slightest thought that would hinder perfect love toward their neighbor.

Love ought to permeate our decision making in all aspects of life. One of the hermits said, "I never wanted work to be useful to me while causing loss to my brother, for I have this hope that what helps my brother will bring fruit to me."[12] This saying is countercultural. The general rhetoric is that the market is competitive and survival is for the fittest. We have to be aggressive if we want to get what we want and advance in our careers. When it comes to work we have to think only of ourselves. Some defenders of the market even rationalize that what is good for me will bring fruit to the other. But the commandment of love asks us to choose the work that is useful to my brother as well as me. It is a very hard decision to take; it requires sacrifice for the sake of my brother, as Christ sacrificed for my sake. Abba John the Short said that to build a house we have to start from the foundations and work our way up. He further explained, "The foundation is our neighbour, whom we must win, and that is the place to begin. For all commandments of Christ depend on this one."[13] Winning our neighbor is the foundation of love and love is the foundation of all commandments. We have to think of this when we are at work, at home, and during our leisure time. Winning our neighbor requires laying down our lives for him or her. Abba Poemen said, "There is no greater love than that you should lay down your life for your neighbour. When you hear a complaint against you and you struggle with yourself, and do not begin to complain in return, when you hear an inquiry with patience and do not look for revenge, that is when you lay down your life for your neighbour."[14] How can we not respond to complaints or rumors against us? Christ was accused falsely and he did not respond and he laid down his life for our sake. The commandment of love is the most difficult of commandments to follow if we do not constantly contemplate God and Christ, the incarnation and the cross. The commandment of love cannot be fulfilled by human effort; if the Holy Spirit does not dwell in our hearts and our hearts are not filled with God's love, fulfillment of the commandment is unattainable. For God is not asking us for outward love, but love from our hearts and inner thoughts.

Desert fathers and mothers practiced asceticism as an exercise to help them focus more on their spiritual devotions, never as an aim in itself. This was discussed under discernment. Here is another example

12. *SSWard*, 182, Charity #24; *SAChaîne*, 38, #170; *SAHartley*, 103, #170.

13. *ASWard*, 93, John the Dwarf #39.

14. *SSWard*, 178, Charity #10.

that clarifies how much more important love is than any ascetic practice: Bishop Epiphanius wanted to see Hilarion before he died. "When they had met and had greeted each other, part of a chicken was set before them. The bishop took it and gave it to Hilarion. The hermit said to him, 'No, thank you, abba. From the time I took the habit, I have not eaten anything that has been killed.' Epiphanius said to him, 'From the time I took the habit, I have let no one go to sleep who still had something against me. And I have never gone to sleep with an enemy in the world.' Hilarion said to him, 'I beg your pardon. Your devotion is greater than mine.'"[15] Epiphanius, before he died, wanted to see his close friend and to celebrate their getting together with a nice meal. Hilarion, on the other hand, was more concerned with his ascetic practices, though many of the fathers would have eaten the chicken as a last meal with a close friend. Hilarion boasted about his ascetic practice; since he became a monk (took the habit) he never ate any animal products, which was customary for most of the desert dwellers. Epiphanius, on the other hand, considered love for the neighbor as the most important commandment. The story has more than one dimension: for the sake of love you should eat the last meal with a dying friend, no matter what that meal is; it is also the message that asceticism recedes before other spiritual virtues, especially love, since asceticism is never an aim but an aid. Similarly, Abba Agathon said, "I have never gone to sleep with a grievance against anyone, and, as far as I could, I have never let anyone go to sleep with a grievance against me."[16] Abba Agathon also said, "If I win my brother, I have offered a sacrifice [at an altar]"[17] Loving our neighbor is the highest type of worship we can offer to God. Loving our neighbor is compared to a sacramental offering, so highly is the virtue of love prized in desert spirituality.

Those experienced in spirituality understand the difficulty of fulfilling the commandment of love and truly living according to the virtue of love. One of the young brothers asked Abba Matoes how the fathers of Scetis loved their enemies beyond themselves. Abba Matoes answered, "As for me I have not yet managed to love those who love me as I love myself."[18] It is a response full of humility, but it also expresses full awareness that loving others is difficult, even loving those who love us. This is speaking about loving those who love us "as myself," which upon serious reflection is very hard to fulfill because it requires enormous sacrifice. It

15. *SSWard*, 21, Self-Control #15.
16. *ASWard*, 20, Agathon #4; *AParadise*, 66.
17. *AParadise*, 66.
18. *ASWard*, 143, Matoes #5.

is for this reason that a mother's love is always treasured as the most pure of loves because it always involves loving the child above oneself. Nothing can compare to the love of God, who became incarnate and died for our sake, and in his death forgave those who killed him. Abba Matoes is telling the brother that before aspiring to the greatest of love—that is, loving our enemies—we have to learn first to truly love those who love us to the greatest extent. We can then proceed to love our enemies because we have set a foundation for understanding true love. We can learn to love our enemies to the same degree we love those who love us.

One of the desert fathers said that if one is reviled one should not respond with revenge but with blessing. If the person accepts the blessing then it is good for both people. This will break the cycle of hatred. If the person does not accept the blessing, then each will take a reward for their actions; the one will take the reward of reviling, and the other the reward of blessing.[19] Thus we should not always expect a person to respond nicely toward us even if we respond with blessing when insulted. We are not responsible for the other reviling us if we are innocent of his accusations. God requires us to bless and we follow God's commandments regardless of the consequences, not only when it is beneficial for us. Abba Poemen also understood the difficulty of the commandment of love and explained the difficulty by saying, "[W]e do not care about our brother whom Scripture tells us to receive. Moreover we do not remember the woman of Canaan (cf. Matt. 15.22) who followed the Lord crying and begging for her daughter to be cured, and the Lord heard her and gave her peace."[20] If we do not care for our brother, how can we take care of those who revile us? But, he adds, through "crying and begging" as the Canaanite woman did for her daughter, we should plead for God to grant us the peace of love.

The desert fathers and mothers examined the development of anger and hatred in the heart. They advise us that if we do not examine in ourselves the feelings of anger and hatred toward the other, and if we keep these thoughts in our hearts, this anger will brood and turn us into savage animals that cannot be tamed. This will lead us to every road of wrongdoing and every manner of error. It is, one elder says, like one who buries "fire in chopped straw," like a den of enraged serpents, and like a wild boar that gnashes its teeth as soon as it sees a man. He uses many other metaphors for uncontrolled rage.[21] Those who do not correct themselves

19. *SABudge*, 246, #449.

20. *ASWard*, 195, Poemen #204.

21. *SABudge*, 261, #539.

quickly with regard to their inner thoughts of anger and hatred toward the other will reach a point of uncontrollable anger. This saying is addressing anger in its infancy. The elder explains that if we do not deal with thoughts of anger toward the other at an early stage, the anger will take hold of our thoughts and minds and will evolve into uncontrollable rage and destruction like a savage animal that cannot be controlled or a fire that cannot be quenched. We all have experienced these feelings at one time or another. The advice is to be spiritually alert to our inner feelings and tackle anger before it gets out of control, for "the good person brings good things out of a good treasure, and the evil person brings evil things out of an evil treasure" (Matt 12:35).

Abba Poemen was asked what the command "Do not repay anyone evil for evil" (Rom 12:17) means. Abba Poemen said there are four ways to fulfill the meaning of this verse: through the heart, the eye, the tongue, and the deed. If your heart is filled with anger your complexion will betray the anger within you, and if you do not calm yourself you will lose control of your tongue. If your tongue gets out of control, know that you will act and repay evil for evil in a way that is against Christ's commandments.[22] Abba Poemen advises us to pay close attention to the movement of our heart and thoughts and try to control the evil thoughts with each movement in our heart before they get out of control, that is, before we act on our anger in a way that is against Christ's commandments.

A brother came to Abba Silvanus and told him that he hated someone so much that he was going to deliver him to the authorities to punish him and have revenge for himself. Abba Silvanus told him that he could do as he wished. Then, while praying the Lord's Prayer before the brother left, Abba Silvanus said, "Do not forgive us our sins as we do not forgive those who sin against us." The brother interrupted him and told him not to say that. Abba Silvanus responded, "If you want to avenge whoever sinned against you this is what is supposed to be said in prayer." The brother learned a great lesson and forgave his enemy.[23] Praying carefully and thoughtfully reveals our inner thoughts. Prayer changes hearts. If we do not mean what we pray, we are lying to ourselves. It indicates that we do not know what we are praying for and that we are not praying truthfully.

Abba Macarius explained that if we are concerned with what is above we will not see what is below, and if we are occupied with what is below we will not have knowledge of what is above, for whoever understands

22. *AParadise*, 94.

23. *AParadise*, 454.

what is above does not care about other things.[24] What Abba Macarius is saying is that when we are occupied with thoughts about God and thinking about the heavenly kingdom we do not think much about the things of this world, but if we are so consumed with our daily lives and never give any time to things belonging to God, not only do we not know, we also do not understand things about God. Whatever our mind is preoccupied with shapes our worldview. If we are preoccupied with thoughts of God, if we are preoccupied with the contemplation of God's love for humanity and for us personally, then we will see God's love around us and be able to love others. We will see others through God's eyes. But if we are preoccupied with our self-indulgence, what Athanasius calls satisfying our senses, we will be so preoccupied with ourselves that we will not have time for others, we will not think about them, and we will not know their pain or joy. We become totally disconnected from others. When we know the pain and needs of others, God's love within our hearts binds us to do good. Thus one of the fathers said that love does not know how to keep a storehouse full of possessions.[25] The fathers emphasized that giving should be done with love and not grudgingly. One of the fathers explained that to go with someone for two miles rather than one is to give with all your soul and spirit.[26] Giving should be with no ulterior motive, only love.

We all consider true love to be unconditional; but the fathers had some warnings regarding love toward our neighbor. Abba Theodore said that if you love someone who falls into temptation you should stretch your hand to him and lift him up. But if the person is in heresy and is not persuaded by your advice then it is better that you not stay with him lest you sink to a great depth.[27] At first reading this might seem cruel, because this is the time when a friend's true colors appear. But Abba Theodore is also concerned about the safety of the person himself. If we put this in modern terms, if a family has a child who is in the company of friends involved in drugs or violence or any conduct that leads to trouble, wise parents will pull their child out from this company by any means; they will not say it is better to leave their child in this environment so as to convince the others not to take drugs. No one is sure that the child will not be the one convinced to take drugs rather than the other way around. Parents cannot afford risking the safety of their children. Abba Theodore is saying that if

24. *SABudge*, 185, #150.
25. *SABudge*, 248, #467.
26. *SABudge*, 79, #349.
27. *SABudge*, 70, #315.

your love for your friend will endanger your safety, and words have not brought this friend to reason, then it is better to save yourself. This is not against the commandment of love because we cannot be sure we are strong enough not to be drawn toward doing wrong. There are a few sayings that give some restrictions to love and all have the same theme: we cannot be sure that staying with the friend will save him or her, since we are all weak and we may be the ones tempted to act against the commandment.

Abba Isaiah of Scetis summarizes the theology of Athanasius regarding the preservation of the mind (*nous*) in the thought of God in these eloquent words:

> Therefore, if the intellect is strengthened and prepared to follow the virtue of love that quenches all the passions of the soul and the body, by showing long-suffering and goodness, by hating envy and pride, by not considering evil in the heart, and by not allowing anything that is contrary to nature to dominate the intellect, then the intellect resists that which is contrary to nature with the power of love until it is filled with that which is according to nature.[28]

The mind (*nous*) is expressed in the quote as "intellect." Athanasius spoke about purifying the mind (*nous*) from the power of the senses. Abba Isaiah summarizes this as "not allowing anything that is contrary to nature to dominate the intellect," giving specific examples. Letting thoughts of love dominate our mind will eliminate many of the evil thoughts in our heart toward others and restore the image of God within us, which is the ultimate goal of our spiritual longing. For when we abide in love we abide in God and God abides in us (see 1 John 4:16).

Love is a way of life. It does not have a recipe and does not follow strict guidelines. God is love and all love is from him and through him. If God is not at the center of our love toward others then we should question our motivation. Abba Elijah says that love toward a friend "which is caused by some temporal matter is, in the process of time, turned into fierce enmity."[29] If we love a person for a "temporal matter" then when the real motive is fulfilled or when the temporal circumstances change we no longer have any link that binds us to this friend and the friendship turns lukewarm and sometimes into enmity. When this happens it hurts and leaves a wound in the heart. There is no person immune to such an experience. The desert fathers and mothers were constantly examining

28. *Is. Scetis*, 136.
29. *SABudge*, 232, #390.

their thoughts and hearts for the true motivation for their love toward any person. They wanted to experience the true love that God commands of us, that is, love that does not expect any reward or gain. The desert fathers and mothers were not immune from the pain of not being loved. They examined their hearts and thoughts for feelings of hatred, anger, envy, revenge, and other thoughts that cloud the mind against another. Not only that, they also examined their thoughts for discrimination in love—why do I prefer one friend over another? In all of this scrutiny of the mind and heart they were guided by the divine love for humanity. For God loved the world without discrimination; he died for everyone, the sinner and the holy. He died for those who loved him and for those who hated him and put him to death on the cross. God's love for us is without motive and without reward. It was this love, which was exemplified in the incarnation and crucifixion, which was without reward and full of sacrifice, that the desert fathers contemplated and was the pattern they strived to emulate. This is the pattern that all Christians are required to follow.

Love is the virtue most spoken about and the most difficult to follow. It is difficult because it is a matter of the heart and also of the mind. When our mind thinks ill of another person, our heart is contaminated. The way to cleanse our mind and heart of all grudges against others is to constantly contemplate Christ, the incarnation, and the cross. Read Scripture constantly to be reminded of God's love toward us. Pray from the heart and do not just mumble the Lord's Prayer without recognizing that sometimes this same prayer works against us when we ask the Lord to forgive us our sins as we forgive others yet we have not forgiven others. If we are unable to forgive, then we pray for the gift of forgiveness. We pray for the gift of loving everyone equally and without discrimination. We pray for the gift of loving others because we are following Christ and because we are all in God's image. For "God is love, and those who abide in love abide in God, and God abides in them" (1 John 4:16).

Biblical Verses on Love for Further Contemplation:

Read the four Gospels, contemplating God's love for humanity through the incarnation, crucifixion, and resurrection; that is the essence of the Christian message.

Read 1 John 4

Further Sayings for Reflection:

John of Lycopolis said: ". . . For an ascetic is good if he is constantly training himself in the world, if he shows brotherly love and practices hospitality and charity, if he gives alms and is generous to visitors, if he helps the sick and does not give offence to anyone."[30]

Paul of Tamma said: "Be kind my son, because 'those who are kind will dwell on the earth and the innocent will remain on it', because 'love is kind.'"[31]

Abba Antony said: "Our life and our death is with our neighbour. If we gain our brother, we have gained God, but if we scandalize our brother, we have sinned against Christ."[32]

Brother. How is love (*or* charity) acquired by men of understanding?
Old Man. True and pure love is the way of life, and the haven of promises, and the treasure of faith, and the interpreter of the kingdom, and the herald of that which is hidden.[33]

He [Abba Isaiah] also said, "When someone wishes to render evil for evil, he can injure his brother's soul even by a single nod of the head."[34]

He also said, "Evil cannot drive out evil. If anyone hurts you, do good to him and your good will destroy his evil."[35]

Brother. How is love made known?
Old Man. By the fulfillment of works, and by spiritual care, and by the knowledge of faith.
Brother. What are the works?
Old Man. The keeping of the commandments of the Lord with the purity of the inner man, together with the labour of the outer man.[36]

---

30. Russell, *Lives of the Desert Fathers*, 62.

31. Tim Vivian, with Apostolos N. Athanassakis, Maged S. A. Mikhail, and Birger A. Pearson, *Words to Live By: Journeys in Ancient and Modern Egyptian Monasticism*, Cistercian Studies 207 (Kalamazoo, MI: Cistercian, 2005) 176.

32. *ASWard*, 3, Antony the Great #9; *SABudge*, 162, #33; *SSWard*, 177, Charity #2.

33. *SABudge*, 262, #541.

34. *ASWard*, 70, Isaiah #8.

35. *SSWard*, 101, Discretion #53.

36. *SABudge*, 263, #544–45.

Abba Isaiah of Scetis said, "A person in whom the love of God has dwelt can no longer be separated from God by anything worldly, for it is written, '*Who will separate us from the love of Christ? Will hardship, or distress, or persecution, or famine, or nakedness, or peril, or sword?*', and God is powerful to enable us to be found among those whom nothing worldly can separate from the love of Christ, so that we may find mercy with them through the power of our Lord Jesus Christ, for his is the glory, together with the Father who is without beginning and the life-giving Spirit, now and always, and to the ages of ages, Amen."[37]

Abba Isaiah of Scetis said, "I have offered you all <the way> of love, so that whatever you want God to do to you, you may do first, and then you will be set free according to the measure that you have cleansed your heart towards the whole of creation, so as to remember no injury, then you are obliged to keep this way. God requires exactitude and not simply words."[38]

Abba Isaiah of Scetis said, "Woe to us who through egotism do not love God or our neighbor and this is why we have fallen prey to all the passions, dissolute desires, and diabolic pride."[39]

Abba Isaac said, "He who hates the image of God cannot be loved by God."[40]

Abba Macarius said, "If you love each other, God will dwell within you. If there is evil in your hearts, God will not dwell within you.[41]

---

37. *Is. Scetis*, 117.
38. *Is. Scetis*, 140.
39. *Is. Scetis*, 241.
40. *AParadise*, 326.
41. *AParadise*, 44.

10

Keep Watch over the Door of My Lips

The Tongue, Slander, Silence, and Judgment

> Set a guard over my mouth, O LORD;
> keep watch over the door of my lips.
>
> Ps 141:3

JAMES IN HIS EPISTLE discusses the threat of the tongue. The tongue is as treacherous as a fire in a forest: once the fire ignites it takes a long time to control, and even if it is controlled, there is always damage. James also says that the tongue "stains the whole body." The stain is a sign that the body has become impure. The tongue is hard to control or "tame" and is "a restless evil full of deadly poison." What is even worse, the tongue curses "those who are made in the likeness of God." This is a very scary depiction of the power of the tongue. But James also found the tongue capable of some good, for with that same tongue "we bless the Lord and Father" (Jas 3:5–12). The tongue and the ability of speech are what distinguish humanity from the rest of creation. Humanity was granted the privilege of blessing and giving praise to the Lord intentionally, as an act of the will. The Epistle to the Colossians also advises us to control and be careful with our speech, because speech "seasoned with salt" might work wonders in people's heart (Col 4:6). One might not expect the solitary desert fathers and mothers to have paid much attention to this small member of the body, but they did. The solitary monastics advocated silence because of their deep understanding of the power of the tongue. Silence enables a person to examine his or her thoughts and purge the heart of any enmity toward another. Silence also helps a person to be cautious before uttering any word. Words speak what is in the heart and mind; that is the power and at the same time the threat of the tongue.

The desert fathers and mothers wanted to train their tongue to utter praise to God rather than slandering "those who are made in the likeness of God." Abba Hyperechius said, "Do not utter any evil words from your mouth, for the vine does not produce thorns."[1] The tongue that gives praise to God is not to say words unworthy of God and of goodness. The tongue not only slanders and praises, it also expresses the inner thoughts of judgment toward others. The desert fathers and mothers most of the time opted for silence to avoid the pitfalls of the tongue. This chapter will speak about the tongue, slander, gossip, judgment, and silence. These are all matters pertaining to the tongue. In the previous chapter we discussed love. This chapter discusses one practical aspect of love toward the neighbor—controlling judgment and gossip—as an example of how all aspects of spiritual experience are intertwined throughout the whole spiritual journey. A thematic discussion of its various aspects is an orderly way of exploring the depths and complexity of desert spirituality. This discussion will be continued in the following chapter with the theme of humility.

As the psalmist found it imperative to raise a prayer pleading to the Lord to "set a guard over my mouth, O LORD; keep watch over the door of my lips"(Ps 141:3), the early desert fathers and mothers also raised prayers pleading to the Lord to guard their tongue. "Sisois once said with confidence, 'For thirty years I have not prayed to God without sin. When I pray, I say "Lord Jesus Christ, protect me from my tongue." Even now, it causes me to fall every day.'"[2] Apparently Sisois had to struggle with his tongue, that small but uncontrollable member of his body, and realized that if he could control his tongue and be careful with his words he would avoid falling and transgressing against God. He confessed that he transgressed every day.

Abba Arsenius, one of the famous desert fathers, on his deathbed told his disciples, "I have often repented of having spoken, but never of having been silent."[3] The last word of wisdom that Arsenius left his disciples was to be careful about their speech. This just indicates that the desert fathers did not take lightly what they said and understood the power of the word.

1. *SAChaîne*, 3, #13; *SAHartley*, 29, #13.
2. *SSWard*, 26, Self Control #39.
3. *ASWard*, 18, Abba Arsenius #40; *SABudge*, 14, #53.

Similarly, Abba Pambo said, "By the Grace of God, since I left the world, I have not said one word of which I repented afterwards."[4] Pambo seems to be more in command of his tongue than Arsenius, for the latter regretted the words that slipped from his tongue; Pambo did not even let his tongue slip. Abba Or had the ultimate control over his tongue: "They said of Abba Or that he never lied, nor swore, nor hurt anyone, nor spoke without necessity."[5] Abba Macarius the Great once advised his fellow monks to flee. The brothers were puzzled when they heard this advice for they had already fled the city; from where else could they flee? Then Abba Macarius "put his finger upon his lips and said, 'I tell you, you must flee this.'"[6]

The word has great power as it is the guardian of the heart. The mouth is the door to our inner thoughts. "A brother asked Abba Tithoes, 'How should I guard my heart?' The old man said to him, 'How can we guard our hearts when our mouths and our stomachs are open?'"[7] Since the desert fathers and mothers considered the purity of their thoughts and hearts key to their spiritual journey, speech, the tongue, talk, slander, and all activities of the mouth became the center of their concerns. One of the desert elders summarized the connection between the inner thoughts and the tongue as follows: "If the inner man is self-controlled, he is able to guard against the outer (man). If this is not so, let us guard our tongue against every evil by every effort."[8] Thus, many discussions were carried out in the desert to find a way to guard against the lapses and shortcomings of the tongue. On another occasion, Abba Sisois gave the following advice to a brother who asked the same question regarding the guarding of the heart: "How can we guard the heart if our tongue leaves the door of the fortress open?"[9]

A young brother came to Abba Amoun of Nitria asking him, "When I go to my neighbour's cell, or when he comes to mine for some need or other, we are afraid of entering into conversation, for fear of slipping into worldly subjects."[10] A very valid question: when we receive guests, what will we talk about so as not to commit any transgressions of the tongue? We all know how easily and quickly conversations take an unintentional

4. *ASWard*, 197, Abba Pambo #5.
5. *ASWard*, 246, Abba Or #2.
6. *SSWard*, 25, Self Control #27; *SABudge*, 11, #30.
7. *ASWard*, 236, Tithoes #3.
8. *SAChaîne*, 15, #65; *SAHartley*, 55, #65.
9. *SSWard*, 123, Sober Living #27.
10. *ASWard*, 31, Amoun of Nitria #2.

turn to gossip, which seems to be the most attractive and juicy of all conversation. Gossip is so attractive that some media specialize in gossip, especially about celebrities. Gossip is a very lucrative business; these media outlets have been very popular and they do not seem to be going out of business any time soon. Gossip and the pitfalls of the tongue have been a struggle for humanity through all ages. Abba Amoun answered, "The old men who have advanced in virtue, have nothing in them that is worldly; there is nothing worldly in their mouths of which they could speak." The young brother was still worried about what type of conversation he was to have with a visitor: "'When I am obliged to speak to my neighbor, do you prefer me to speak of the Scriptures or of the sayings of the Fathers?' The old man answered, 'If you can't be silent, you had better talk about the sayings of the Fathers than about the Scriptures, it is not so dangerous.'"[11] The surprising answer—not to speak about Scripture—is for young novices, who, when they speak about biblical interpretation, usually end up in heated discussions that might lead to more harm than good. Abba Amoun suggests a topic that is beneficial and does not lead to not only heated debates but also to arrogance in discussing lofty matters, or the ultimate pitfall of the tongue, slander.

The desert fathers and mothers understood the grievous consequences of hurting or slandering another person. Abba Hyperechius said, "It is better to eat meat and drink wine and not to eat the flesh of one's brethren through slander."[12] Slander is like eating your neighbor's flesh; it is compared to murder. It destroys his soul and drags it downwards. The following advice was given to a brother: "When brothers are present, do not open thy heart. At such a time rather pray in secret, for it is then that there is fear of slander."[13] Opening one's heart means not only speaking, but speaking inattentively. If speech is guarded by prayer then prayer guards the thoughts and gives one pause before uttering a word so as not to speak impulsively. One of the desert fathers lamented earlier meetings of the brothers that were supposed to be for the building of the soul: "[N]ow whenever we assemble together, we come to slander, and each one continues to drag his neighbor down to the abyss."[14] The same sentiment was repeated by another of the desert elders:

11. *ASWard*, 31, Amoun of Nitria #2.

12. *ASWard*, 238, Hyperechius #4.

13. *LQ*, 168, Apophthegm 98.8.

14. *SAChaine*, 14, #64; *SAHartley*, 54, #64.

> One of the hermits said, "When first we used to meet each other in the assembly and talk of what was helpful to our souls, we were always withdrawn more from the things of sense and we ascended to the heavenly places. But now when we meet we spend our time in gossip, and so we drag each other down."[15]

This happens not only with the assemblies of the monks in the desert; it happens in most of our gatherings. Most gatherings start well and on a positive note as people are still not familiar with each other. With the growth of familiarity we become more comfortable with our new friends, formalities fade away, and we cease guarding our tongues. We notice that the more familiar we are with a person, the less cautious we are about what we say and the easier it is to slip with our tongue into gossip or slander. Close friendship does not give license to gossip or rumors. Being guarded in our words does not mean we are not honest and fully invested in our friendship. Being guarded means we care about the purity of our thoughts, we care that our prayer is not tarnished with slander against our neighbor. Being guarded means we care about our salvation and being blameless before God. Being guarded means we care about the person we are speaking to, for with slander we are going to drag down our partner in the conversation. One of the desert fathers said, "Do not stay with anyone who is always scornful when they speak."[16] The true friend is the one whose conversation lifts us up spiritually, does not disturb the inner peace of our heart and thoughts, and fills us with inner joy. An unguarded tongue diminishes inner spiritual peace.

Amma Theodora said, "Someone with a tainted reputation insulted a pious person. He answered, 'I am able to respond as befitting your words but the testimony of my God shuts my mouth.'"[17] This person got his courage and his self-restrain from his knowledge of Scripture; the words of Scripture spoke to him more powerfully than the insults targeted at him. Scripture gave him courage and humility not to respond with retribution to insults, slander, gossip, or rumors. This is an example of how reading and memorizing Scripture safeguards a person's thoughts. It also requires a person who knows him- or herself well enough not to care about the

---

15. *SSWard*, 115, Discretion #108.

16. *SSWard*, 123, Sober Living #25.

17. Amma Theodora, under the title "Sayings of Various Saints on Judgment," in a revised edition of Manuscript 5 and Manuscript 6 in the Monastery of St. Macarius in Wadī al-Naṭrūn, complied by the monk Epiphanios of St. Macarius. [My translation.]

opinion of others. Abba Isaiah of Scetis explained this very well when he
said,

> Therefore, dear friends, love your brothers with holy love, and
> hold your tongue, not letting out of your mouth any random
> word of strife that might offend your brother. Our Lord God
> is powerful enough to give each one of you the ability to carry
> out and keep these commandments, so that we may find mercy
> through his grace, together with all the saints who have pleased
> him, for his is the glory, honor, and worship, now and ever, and
> to the ages of ages, Amen.[18]

In the dialogue *Concerning Thoughts* someone asks, "What is the sin
of slander?" To which the answer is, "The sin of slander most assuredly will
not allow a person to come before God." The reference is to Psalm 101:5:
"One who secretly slanders a neighbor I will destroy. A haughty look and
an arrogant heart I will not tolerate."[19] We use the Psalms for prayer. If we
pray Psalm 101 and ask God to destroy all those who slander we should
be careful not to slander anyone lest we be asking for our own destruction. This is similar to asking God in the Lord's Prayer not to forgive our
sins until we forgive others, or to what we read in Matthew 18:35: "So my
heavenly Father will also do to every one of you, if you do not forgive your
brother or sister from your heart." Abba Moses explained it well when
he said, "'If a man's deeds are not in harmony with his prayer, he labours
in vain.' The brother said, 'What is this harmony between practice and
prayer?' The old man said, 'We should no longer do those things against
which we pray . . .'"[20]

One measure of truthfulness is when our heart, thoughts, and speech
conform to each other. Abba Poemen said, "'Teach your heart to follow
what your tongue is saying to others.' He also said, 'Men try to appear
excellent in preaching but they are less excellent in practicing what they
preach.'"[21] Poemen here does not necessarily mean preaching from the
pulpit, but preaching in the sense of giving advice to others without following it. There are some who always seem to have the right answer but
their actions do not conform to their advice or talk. "A hermit said, 'All

18. *Is. Scetis*, 76.

19. *Concerning Thoughts* 13, #12, in Tim Vivian, with Apostolos N. Athanassakis,
Maged S. A. Mikhail, and Birger A. Pearson, *Words to Live By: Journeys in Ancient and
Modern Egyptian Monasticism*, Cistercian Studies 207 (Kalamazoo, MI: Cistercian,
2005).

20. *ASWard*, 141, Moses #4.

21. *SSWard*, 81, Nothing Done for Show #14; similarly, *SABudge*, 184, #144.

chatter is unnecessary. Nowadays everyone talks but what is needed is action. That is what God wants, not useless talking."[22] "A hermit said, 'If a man has words but no works, he is like a tree with leaves but no fruit. Just as a tree laden with fruits is also leafy, the man of good works will also have good words.'"[23] Abba Poemen has summarized it succinctly: "Teach you mouth to say that which you have in your heart."[24] When the mouth and heart conform to each other, it is an indication of truthfulness, honesty, and a pure heart that does not need to alter words so as not to reveal its darkness.

As with the transgressions of the tongue and slander, we also have to be careful about thoughts of judgment. From our experience we know that many of our judgments are flawed because we make them not knowing the full facts or based on one event and we generalize. The following story explains this: There was a group of monks who lived in community and had fewer ascetic practices than the solitaries of Scetis. When the monks living in community arrived at Scetis for a visit they saw the monks eating early and were greatly offended. The leader of the group understood that the monks living in community had judged the monks of Scetis wrongly. When all were in church he proclaimed that everyone was going to follow the fast of the monks of Scetis. The visiting monks fasted the first day and became faint. Then they were asked to fast a second day, as the monks of Scetis did. By the end of the week, on the Sabbath, they were so hungry so that when food was laid before them they ate "hurriedly and voraciously." One of the elderly monks of Scetis held his hands and said, "Eat moderately." The monks learned their lesson.[25] The visitors judged the monks of Scetis with their thoughts based on the way they ate, not knowing that these monks had not eaten for a full week. When they experienced the same rigorous ascetic practice they understood they had wrongly judged them. Though later ascetics advised that fasting should be moderate, still we should not judge others without understanding their spiritual practices.

In another saying a brother was inquiring about how one knows that he has acquired humility. The older monk said that when you see a person sinning you weep bitterly, saying, "This man may sin today, but how many times shall I sin tomorrow?"[26] This saying grasps an important aspect of

---

22. *SSWard*, 108, Discretion #80; also *ASWard*, 104, James #4.

23. *SSWard*, 110, Discretion #87; also *SSWard*, 100, Discretion #49.

24. *ASWard*, 175, Poemen #63.

25. *SABudge*, 20, #87.

26. *SABudge*, 122, #540.

our judgments: we think we are holier than others because our sins are not before our eyes. Just as the person we saw sinning has sinned, so we also have sinned by condemning him while we ourselves are sinners both today and tomorrow. In one of the sayings the monks were worried about visitors coming to visit and condemning the monks for not meeting their expectations. To appease their worries a father listed many figures of the Old and New Testament who exhibited their frailty: "the blessed and perfect men Moses, and Aaron, and David, and Samson, and Hezekiah, and Peter and Paul."[27] If these preeminent biblical figures sinned, how can we judge others for their frailty? We put our parents, teachers, church leaders, politicians, and other figures with authority on pedestals and most of the time they disappoint us. This was actually the question of the monks: What do we do? If major biblical figures could not withstand temptations—Peter himself denied Christ—how can we judge others in our thoughts? Even worse, we sometimes air this judgment to others while neither we nor the great biblical figures are perfect. Non-judgment requires love, compassion, understanding, and above all humility; they sinned today and I sinned today and will sin tomorrow. The whole world judged the thief crucified with Christ. But how many heard the promise given to him?: "Today you will be with me in paradise" (Luke 23:43). We do not know what happens behind closed doors. We dwell on our judgment, but the person we judge might have repented and been forgiven while we are still in our sin of judgment.

Someone asked about the meaning of Titus 1:15: "To the pure all things are pure, but to the corrupt and unbelieving nothing is pure. Their very minds and consciences are corrupted." An elder explained that it is when we see ourselves as less than everyone. The brother objected to this explanation; how could he be worse than "the murderer and the fornicator"? The elder responded that we have seen this man committing murder, but "I am at all times a murderer through hatred and a wicked will."[28] In this saying the elder has equated thoughts of hatred and condemnation of others with actual murder; he has killed his brother in his thoughts. He probably had in mind verses such as Matthew 5:22: "But I say to you that if you are angry with a brother or sister, you will be liable to judgment; and if you insult a brother or sister, you will be liable to the council; and if you say, 'You fool,' you will be liable to the hell of fire."

27. SABudge, 307, #638.
28. SABudge, 247, #455.

Avoiding the transgressions of the tongue is an act of love to your neighbor. Abba Poemen said,

> "Greater love hath no man than this that a man lay down his life for his friends." (John 15:13) In truth if someone hears an evil saying, that is, one which harms him, and in his turn, he wants to repeat it, he must fight in order not to say it. Or if someone is taken advantage of and he bears it, without retaliation at all, then he is giving his life for his neighbor.[29]

Part of love is not speaking against or judging our neighbor. Not judging our neighbor requires humility, for we really speak against others in order to vindicate ourselves. Not doing that requires a lot of humility. In desert spirituality all the virtues are intertwined. Observing the commandment of love will eventually make our speech gracious and seasoned with salt (see Col 4:6). Gracious speech does not include harshness or judgment. Non-judgment stems from a humble heart. Each biblical virtue we practice gives birth to another virtue. It is the fecundity and fruitfulness of the Holy Spirit within us.

One of the brothers asked an elderly monk, "What is humility?," to which he answered that it was to not pay evil for evil. If it is hard to fulfill this advice, he added, "Let us flee and follow after silence."[30] Silence is an antidote to the transgressions of the tongue. It is keeping watch over the door of the lips and also the door of the heart; for when the mind and heart are tranquil and at peace the door of the lips is guarded as a natural outcome. A group of monks from Scetis were traveling on a boat to visit Abba Anthony. It also happened that another elderly monk was traveling toward the same destination. The monks engaged themselves in conversations about the sayings of the fathers, Scriptures, and their handiwork. All seemed to be safe conversations. When they arrived at Abba Anthony's place, Anthony commended the group of monks as "excellent brethren," to which the elderly monk responded, "They are excellent brethren, but they have no door to their house." He said that because "they uttered every word which came to their mouths."[31] In this story the brethren were speaking about very commendable topics, but the elder's opinion was that by constantly speaking they were liable to the danger of unintentionally sliding into other topics. His advice is that the less we talk, the less we utter words we regret. In addition, a mind that is engaged with thoughts about

29. *ASWard*, 184, Poemen #116.
30. *SABudge*, 11, #32.
31. *SABudge*, 5–6, #10; *AParadise*, 199.

God will be less engaged with thoughts about anything else. We all experience times when we are consumed by an event or engaged in a project; everything else seems to fade by comparison because of our focus is on the task at hand. The fathers wanted to be engaged with God as intensely as we become engaged with our personal projects. They made God their greatest task and we can do the same if we choose to.

Silence teaches more than words. One of the monks asked Abba Moses of Scetis for a word of advice. Abba Moses told him to sit in his cell and the cell would teach him everything.[32] Sitting in the cell represents sitting in quietness and not being disturbed by many outward activities. When the outward milieu is tranquil the inner senses are quiet; the quietness of the inner senses will lay bare the struggle of the thoughts. Silence crystallizes the inner movement of our mind and thoughts, and knowing the movement of our thoughts will teach us everything. This is one of the benefits of going on retreats: distracting ourselves from all outward reminders of work and obligations to calm our senses in order to listen to our inner thoughts. To have the full benefit of retreats we have to pray for the humility to listen to our thoughts and the courage to face the changes required of us to better ourselves. Listening to inner thoughts requires courage. Many of us do not have the courage to confront ourselves; we prefer being distracted and immersing ourselves in social engagements or work to avoid this inner confrontation. We should pray for humility to confront our inner thoughts courageously.

Silence is one of the ways to guard the heart because it guards the senses. "Antony said, 'He who sits alone and is quiet has escaped from three wars: hearing, speaking, seeing: but there is one thing against which he must continually fight: that is, his own heart.'"[33] Abba Nilus said, "The arrows of the enemy cannot touch someone who lives quiet. But those who wander about among crowds will often be wounded by them."[34] The outward environment helps the inner quietness of the heart. A quite heart will not seek outward stimulation. It will not seek conversations, controversy, or debates, and if any arise the quiet heart flees the arrows that disturb its tranquility. Fleeing to the desert was a way to guard the stillness of the mind and heart. But the desert fathers and mothers soon discovered that outward tranquility is only one aspect of stillness and quietness. Outward tranquility has to be accompanied by inner work of the heart to preserve

32. *SABudge*, 16, #62.
33. *SSWard*, 8, Quiet #2.
34. *SSWard*, 10, Quiet #11.

inner peace and tranquility. Amma Matrona said, "Many solitaries living in the desert have been lost because they lived like people in the world. It is better to live in a crowd and want to live a solitary life than to live in solitude and be longing all the time for company."[35]

As was customary with the desert fathers, a young monk came to ask the elder, Abba Poemen, about his thoughts. The brother said, "I nearly did not come here today." The old man asked him why. The brother said, "'I said to myself, 'Perhaps he will not let me in because it is Lent.'" Abba Poemen said to him, 'We have not been taught to close the wooden door but the door of our tongues."[36] To guard the door of the tongue is not an indication of an anti-social attitude. Abba Poemen received the guest even during Lent, when monastics preferred to be in total seclusion. When we become more attentive to our conversations our friends will observe and most probably appreciate that we are careful about our conversations. They will trust us more, for if we do not slander or gossip about others they are assured we will act the same toward them. We are not asked to close the wooden door but the door of our tongues.

A controlled tongue is an indication of controlled thoughts that have reached a quiet stage. Controlling the thoughts quiets the tongue and controlling the tongue quiets the thoughts. Controlling both alleviates the person from further slipping into more regretful actions. Thus Abba Hyperechius said, "He who does not control his tongue when he is angry, will not control his passions either."[37] Thoughts are very important in desert spirituality. Thus, if we avoid company that drags us into transgressions of the tongue but we let our thoughts condemning the neighbor wander freely, they will ultimately make their way to our tongue. One should be as careful with inner speech as with spoken speech. Abba Poemen said, "If a man appears silent in speech but is condemning other people in his heart, he is really talking incessantly. Another man may seem to talk all day, but he is keeping silence since he always speaks in a way that is right with his heart."[38] The fathers understood outer silence as an indication of inner silence. What is in our mind (*nous*) determines our silence, for our inner silence and inner peace determine our speech.

---

35. *SSWard*, 11, Quiet #14.

36. *ASWard*, 174, Poemen #58; *SABudge*, 7, #17.

37. *ASWard*, 238, Hyperechius #3.

38. *SSWard*, 101, Discretion #51; also *SABudge*, 10, #27. Abba Poemen has an identical saying in *SABudge*, 66, #298.

James in his epistle rightly wrote, "The tongue is a small member, yet it boasts of great exploits" (Jas 3:5). Though the tongue is culpable of slander, gossip, judgment, rumors, and other transgressions, the tongue is just the tool that expresses the inner workings of the mind and heart, "for out of the abundance of the heart the mouth speaks" (Matt 12:34; Luke 6:45). Transgressions of the tongue have ruined lives and whole communities; they affect us at work, in our schools, and in our churches. The devastating results of bullying are making headlines; it is ruining the lives of children and their families. Bullying is slander, judgment, and transgressions of the tongue; it is expressed not only by words of the mouth but also by cyberwords. Everyone seems to hate it, yet everyone is culpable of committing a transgression of the tongue in one form or the other. The desert fathers and mothers, guided by Scripture and experience, understood that it is not a matter of self-control or manners or etiquette; the root of the problem is in our thoughts. It is a symptom of other frailties, such as lack of love toward the neighbor and lack of humility. The previous chapter discussed love; this chapter is about one expression of the lack of love. All topics that the desert fathers and mothers tackled are interconnected. Lack of humility judges others. While we are in the act of judgment, we are committing a transgression of equal magnitude to the action we are judging. Noticing the speck in our neighbor's eye before noticing the log in our own eye (see Matt 7:3 and Luke 6:41–42) is a sign of a lack of humility. It is also a sign of inattentiveness to our inner thoughts. If we are aware of our inner thoughts and how unholy they are we will not hate, judge, slander, or gossip about others, for we are equally culpable.

Biblical Verses for Further Contemplation:

PSALM 17:3–4—If you try my heart, if you visit me by night, if you test me, you will find no wickedness in me; my mouth does not transgress. As for what others do, by the word of your lips I have avoided the ways of the violent.

JOB 20:12—Though wickedness is sweet in their mouth, though they hide it under their tongues.

PSALM 49:3—My mouth shall speak wisdom; the meditation of my heart shall be understanding.

PSALM 120:2—Deliver me, O LORD, from lying lips, from a deceitful tongue.

PROVERBS 15:28—The mind of the righteous ponders how to answer, but the mouth of the wicked pours out evil.

PROVERBS 17:20—The crooked of mind do not prosper, and the perverse of tongue fall into calamity.

WISDOM 1:11—Beware then of useless grumbling, and keep your tongue from slander; because no secret word is without result, and a lying mouth destroys the soul.

MATTHEW 15:18—But what comes out of the mouth proceeds from the heart, and this is what defiles.

Further Sayings for Reflection:

Amma Syncletica said: "Therefore it is necessary to guard the tongue and the ear, so as not to say anything about anyone, nor to hear anything with great eagerness. For it is written, 'Do not receive a false report' (Exod 23:1) and 'the one who speaks against his neighbor secretly, I banished him' (Ps 101:5). In the psalmist it says, 'that my mouth might not speak the works of people' (Ps 17:3–4). But we speak of things that are not works. Therefore it is necessary not to believe the things said, nor to condemn the ones who say them. But act and speak in accordance with divine Scripture: 'Like a deaf person I did not hear, and like a mute I did not open my mouth' (Ps 38:14)."[39]

Amma Syncletica said: "Therefore backbiting talk is serious and wicked; for it becomes the food and the resting place of some people. But do you not accept vain hearsay, and do not become the receptacle of other people's evils. Prepare your own soul as free from superfluity. For receiving the stinking impurity of words, you will introduce stains into your prayers by means of thoughts, and you will hate without reason those whom you might encounter. For you will dip your ear under the inhumanity of evil talk, you will contemplate everything lowly born. Just as the eye,

---

39. *Sync.*, 293, #67.

immoderately preoccupied by color, has seen an indistinguishable fantasy surrounding things."[40]

Abba Hyperechius said: "It is through whispering that the serpent drove Eve out of Paradise, so he who speaks against his neighbor will be like the serpent, for he corrupts the soul of him who listens to him and he does not save his own soul."[41]

Abba Or said to his disciple Paul, "Be careful never to let an irrelevant word come into this cell."[42]

He [Abba Or] also said, "If you have spoken evil of your brother, and you are stricken with remorse, go and kneel down before him and say: 'I have spoken badly of you; let this be my surety that I will not spread this slander any further.' For detraction is death to the soul."[43]

A monk said: "When a brother wishes to go to a brother, the demon of slander either seizes beforehand where he is or comes with him to the brother himself."[44]

If thou sayest, "Such-and-such a brother is zealous and understanding, but–if it makes any difference–a bit careless," lo, thou hast slandered him. And if thou sayest that he is a liar and perjurer, this is condemnation, which is worse than slander.[45]

And a brother also asked him, "What shall I do? For I am troubled when I am sitting in my cell." The old man said unto him, "Think lightly of no man; think no evil in thy heart; condemn no man and curse no man; then shall God give thee rest, and thy habitation shall be without trouble."[46]

Amma Syncletica said: "Do not be occupied greatly by speaking too much."[47]

40. *Sync.*, 293, #66.
41. *ASWard*, 238, Hyperechius #5.
42. *ASWard*, 246, Or #3.
43. *ASWard*, 248, Or #5.
44. *LQ*, 160, Apophthegm 74.11.
45. *LQ*, 160, Apophthegm 98.10.
46. *SABudge*, 83, #366.
47. *Sync.*, 301, #87.

The old men used to say, "There is nothing worse than a man passing judgment upon his neighbour."[48]

He who conquers his tongue becomes free, he who avoids evil conversations God will preserve him from transgressions, lengthy talks bring recklessness and boredom.[49]

Let our tongues be in constant praise of God and in righteousness so as to be free of lies. Preserve yourself from lies for it destroys the fear of God within you.[50]

Abba Moses said, "The person who does not guard his tongue is like a house without a door or locks anyone can come in."[51]

Abba Moses said, "He who guards his tongue loves virtue; and not guarding your tongue indicates that the inner person is void of righteousness."[52]

Abba Moses said, "Guard your tongue so that the fear of God dwells in your heart."[53]

Abba Macarius said, "Guard yourselves of slander so that your heart is pure. For the ear that hears evil conversation cannot preserve the purity of the heart."[54]

A monk was asked, "Father, I desire to have a pure heart." The Elder responded, "How can you preserve the purity of your heart when your mouth which is the door of your heart is always opened?"[55]

48. *SABudge*, 196, #198.

49. *AParadise*, 146.

50. *AParadise*, 146.

51. *AParadise*, 198.

52. *AParadise*, 198.

53. *AParadise*, 198.

54. *AParadise*, 199.

55. *AParadise*, 374.

11

Clothe Yourselves with Humility

Humility

And all of you must clothe yourselves with humility in your dealings with one
another, for "God opposes the proud, but gives grace to the humble."
Humble yourselves therefore under the mighty hand of God,
so that he may exalt you in due time.

1 PET 5:5–6

As God's chosen ones, holy and beloved, clothe yourselves with compassion,
kindness, humility, meekness, and patience.

COL 3:12

THE SON OF GOD, the creator, humbled himself to the form of a slave
(Phil 2:7). He made himself the example of humility and instructed
us to learn from him. "Learn from me; for I am gentle and humble in
heart, and you will find rest for your souls" (Matt 11:29). The incarnation
was not the only example of his humility; he also "humbled himself and
became obedient to the point of death—even death on a cross" (Phil 2:8).
Philippians 2 presents two aspects of Christ's humility: the incarnation
and his obedience to the point of death. Thus the real example we have
for humility, if we want to follow Christ's example, is to be obedient to
God, obedient to the point of death. When the Son gave himself on the
cross in obedience to God, "God also highly exalted him and gave him

the name that is above every name" (Phil 2:9). Lest we think it is only Christ who is to be exalted, James 4:10 assures us of the same: "Humble yourselves before the Lord, and he will exalt you" (see also 1 Pet 5:6.). The message is clear: if we are to imitate Christ we are also to imitate his humility; we are to be obedient to God. As we follow Christ in his humility we will find rest for our souls and, through God's mercy, be exalted.

Abba John of Thebaid noted that humility is the first commandment of the Sermon on the Mount: "Blessed are the poor in spirit, for theirs is the kingdom of heaven" (Matt 5:3).[1] Abba John Kolobos said that "humility is the door that leadeth into the kingdom."[2] Humility is the natural outcome of the close encounter with God and of the fear of God. Abba John the Short said that "humility and the fear of God are above all virtues."[3] The prophet Isaiah acknowledged his sinfulness and the sinfulness of his people when he encountered the Lord and stood before him. He was totally humbled when he stood face to face with God (see Isa 6). Humility is not something we work at; it is a state of being that emerges when we experience God's love, mercy, and glory. When we are in the constant presence of God through prayer and meditation on Scripture, God reveals himself to us and with each revelation we get to know the depth of God. The more we encounter God, the more we know about God, the more we are confronted with our unworthiness, as Isaiah was, and humility becomes second nature to us. We encounter God through prayer and by contemplating God and his incarnation. When we experience God's glory through prayer and we contemplate the true humility of Christ in the incarnation, we are filled with humility and the great love of God for humanity. Humility is one of the topics discussed most extensively in desert spirituality. It has one of the largest number of sayings devoted to it. The desert fathers and mothers understood that humility suggests a certain level of spirituality and thus were very keen to discuss it and learn from others who were deemed humble. They did not only want to speak about humility; they also wanted to live with humble people because observing and living with humble people teaches humility.

Abba Isaiah of Scetis talked about learning humility through Christ's example in the incarnation: "This is why the Lord Jesus became human, in order that we may be concerned with endeavoring to behave as he did, searching ourselves as best we can in accordance with his example, asking

---

1. *SABudge*, 116, #509; and *SSWard*, 154, On Humility #23; *AParadise*, 371.

2. *SABudge*, 117, #510; also John of Thebaid in *AParadise*, 324.

3. *ASWard*, 90, John the Dwarf #22; *SABudge*, 113, #479; *AParadise*, 371.

whether or not we are like that seed [mustard seed], its condition and humility, its sweetness and bitterness and taste. His mercy will strengthen us according to his will, for his is the glory, of the Father, and the Son, and the Holy Spirit, to the ages of ages. Amen."[4] Abba Isaiah of Scetis urged us to measure ourselves with the incarnate Son as the yardstick:

> Examine yourself, wretched one, who has been baptized into Christ and his death [Rom 6:3]. What sort of death is it that he died? If you follow his footsteps [1 Pet 2:21], show me your way of life. He is sinless and presents himself to you in everything. He has walked in poverty. He did not make a place to rest his head [Matt 8:20]. You, however, do not joyfully endure being a stranger. He endured insults but you cannot bear any injury. He has not returned evil for evil, you cannot resist returning evil. He was not angry when he suffered. You, on the other hand, are irritated when you do suffer. He was not distressed when someone insulted him, but you become agitated, even when someone is not insulting you. He humbled himself, comforting those who sinned against him. You injure with words even those who love you. He joyfully tolerated afflictions but you are disturbed by the least new unpleasantness. He, he was with those who had fallen but you, you are arrogant to those who expiate you. He was handed over for those who had sinned against him, in order to ransom them. You are incapable of giving anything, even for those who love you.
>
> See what he has given you. What do you give him in return? Know him through his works and you through yours.[5]

Abba Isaiah of Scetis has given us a detailed description of how to think about our actions and thoughts in view of Christ's life and example. Such a spiritual exercise is a truly humbling experience and will bear fruit, especially if the contemplation of Christ's life is done on a regular basis. One of the fathers said that we cannot receive humility if we do not search our souls and remember and acknowledge the mistakes we have made.[6] Self-examination creates self-awareness that makes the person attentive to his or her shortcomings and thus not inclined to boasting or pride.

An elder said that humility is to do good to those who have done evil to us, and if we cannot reach that standard then it is better to be silent.[7]

4. *Is. Scetis*, 101.

5. *Is. Scetis*, 167.

6. *SABudge*, 113, #487.

7. *SAChaine*, 30, #137; *SAHartley*, 86, #137.

Christ has set the example of doing good to those who do evil against us. A hermit was asked to define or explain what humility is. He responded, "It is if you forgive a brother who has wronged you before he is sorry."[8] It should be noted that he defined humility by its outcome: the ability to forgive. Accepting forgiveness, having forgiveness accepted, and forgiving are major traits of humble personalities. Abba Poemen was asked, "If a man be angry with me, and I express my contrition, and he will not accept it, what am I to do?" Abba Poemen's answer, interestingly enough, follows Matthew 18:15–18, which addresses the one who is sinned against, not the one who has sinned against another, as in this saying. Poemen advises the monk to take two of his friends and apologize. If the apology is not accepted, then he is to take five friends. If the aggrieved party is not persuaded by these five friends, then "without anger and without excitement pray unto God that He may put into his mind [the desire for peace], and straightway thou shalt have no further care."[9] According to Abba Poemen's advice we have to make every effort to obtain a person's forgiveness. If the person refuses our various attempts at apology, then we make recourse to prayer, for it is only God who can change the person's heart. Otherwise, we should have our mind at peace.

Abba Poemen on another occasion addressed the issue of why a brother does not accept an apology. Why does one, on some occasions, have a hardened heart and not forgive? Abba Poemen said most probably the person receiving the apology feels that the person apologizing has not apologized from the heart but rather without sincerity in order to fulfill the commandment. In this case the person is not apologizing out of his or her own desire and it sounds like he or she feels that the aggrieved brother is the one who sinned against him or her, rather than the other way around.[10] An apology might not be accepted because we are not sincere and even might be blaming the other in our hearts. A sincere, heartfelt apology, on the other hand, usually melts hearts. But if not, we are not to blame and should have no further care. It is interesting that these two answers are in response to the same question: why is it that we sometimes do not gain forgiveness when we apologize? The two different answers are complementary, but it shows that different scenarios require different answers.

8. *SSWard*, 163, Humility #60; and *SABudge*, 248, #463; *SAChaine*, 30, #134; *SA-Hartley*, 85, #134.

9. *SABudge*, 122, #539.

10. *SABudge*, 250, #481.

A story is told about Abba Macarius that he encountered the devil, who was unable to attack or harm him. The devil said, "'What is your power, Macarius, that makes me powerless against you? All that you do, I do, too; you fast, so do I; you keep vigil, and I do not sleep at all; in one thing only do you beat me.' Abba Macarius asked what that was. He said, 'Your humility. Because of that I can do nothing against you.'"[11] This story reveals that the desert dwellers understood that humility overcomes all adversaries, no matter how strong they are. It is no surprise that humility conquers all evil. The Son of God's incarnation and crucifixion were the means by which Christ conquered Satan and saved humanity. It is through the cross, the sign of the humble Son of God, that all the power of death ceased to have its hold on humanity. Since the cross is the sign of Christianity, humility should be the sign of the Christian. One of the desert elders said, "The outer seal of the Christian is the cross, and his inner seal is humility."[12] The desert fathers and mothers who practiced humility understood that humility gets its power from the cross and as the cross is powerful, so is humility. Abba Isaiah of Scetis said, "Love humility, and it will protect you from your sin."[13] Many of our transgressions are caused by pride. Humility is an antidote to pride and consequently sin.

Pride makes us disregard others, not listen to advice, and not follow instructions or orders because we feel we know better than others. Abba Isaac said, "Do not demand that all things follow your wishes for God is more knowledgeable and knows what is best for you."[14] The proud person disobeys everyone, even God. Abba Isaac is advising us to think and not complain against God if things do not go the way we want or expect them. God knows more than we do and he does what is best for us.

As humility is the basis of many virtues, pride is the basis of many vices. Pride makes us disobedient, grouchy, judgmental, and arrogant, among other things. Abba Pachomius said, "If you are belittled by people or taken advantage of, do not complain; for your Lord was called a deceiver, Beelzebul, and possessed and did not complain. Be gentle in heart and remember your Lord and God was as a lamb led to the slaughter and did not open his mouth" (see Isa 53:7).[15] The means to comprehend humil-

11. *ASWard*, 129, Macarius the Great #11; *SABudge*, 107, #451; *SAChaine*, 24, #102; *SAHartley*, 74, #102.

12. *AParadise*, 310.

13. *Is. Scetis*, 96.

14. *AParadise*, 316.

15. *AParadise*, 317.

ity comes by contemplating Christ's life and example. He, who conquered all evil, endured false accusations of being demonically possessed and he never responded or complained. It is so difficult to follow this example if we are not focused on Christ and reading Scripture daily to be reminded of his teachings; and if we do not have an open heart to accept all grace, we cannot follow or even comprehend humility. Humility cannot be achieved except through God for no human power is capable of making us truly humble without the aid of the Holy Spirit. The major theme in these sayings is that our thoughts have to be centered on Christ and his humility, manifested in his incarnation and life, as a means to safeguard our minds against pride. If our minds and thoughts are constantly centered on Christ we will not be consumed by our ego and self-centeredness since our worldview will be centered on the ultimate sacrifice of divine love.

We crave praise for self-validation and we have made it part of our educational policy to constantly praise children and students to build up their self-esteem. The desert fathers and mothers, however, had a contrary view. Amma Syncletica said, "If you put wax in front of a fire it melts; and if you pour vain praises on the soul it goes soft and weak in seeking goodness."[16] The key words in this saying are "pour vain praises." Excessive praise that has no concrete foundation can be destructive since it is not an honest assessment of children or students and does not help the young to know themselves and critique themselves honestly for self-betterment. On the adult level, pouring vain praise is usually for ulterior motives, usually for one's own advancement or profit, rather than for the benefit of the person praised. Amma Syncletica explains, "The soul is destroyed by praise and loses all the results of its labour."[17] In both cases, vain praise contradicts honest assessment and the truthfulness of the heart. It is a betrayal of trust. It deceives the other and prevents the other from knowing the truth. It does not edify the person receiving the insincere compliment.

One of the brothers sought advice because he loved to be praised and found this was "killing" him. The elder praised him for fashioning the earth and the heavens. The brother was embarrassed at such excessive praise, to which the elder answered that if the creator came into this world in great humility, how can anyone of us boast of anything?[18] The elder was advising the brother that when tormented with praise—either by constantly seeking it or taking pleasure in receiving it—one has to counter these thoughts by contemplating God, who deserves praise but who also

16. *SSWard*, 82, Nothing Done for Show #19.

17. *ASWard*, 234, Syncletica #21, in a different rendering of the previous saying.

18. *SABudge*, 110, #467.

showed utmost humility. Are we equal to the creator that we deserve equal praise? When we are praised, we should think of our unworthiness.[19]

Abba Poemen, speaking within his monastic setting, explained that there are two types of pride. One type covets power, takes pride in ethnic roots or wealth, pays excessive attention to clothing styles and body image, takes pride in the gift of eloquence, etc. The other type of pride boasts in the ability to fast, be ascetic, and pray constantly, is aloof from people, claims sainthood and renunciation, etc.[20] The latter type boasts of virtues supposedly acquired; of course, the moment we brag about our spiritual virtues our prayers and ascetic practices are worthless. The former boasting arises from being consumed with one's self, one's wealth, looks, or even ethnicity, which no one had a hand in determining. Pride, as many of our downfalls, usually comes when we are consumed with ourselves. The solution is to go beyond ourselves. In prayer and meditation we go beyond ourselves and God reveals where we stand before him. One of the elders said that if thoughts of pride have made us very arrogant we should examine our thoughts and conscience and ask these questions, among others: Have we kept all the commandments? Did we love our enemy? Have we loved the praise of our enemy? Have we grieved when our enemy was afflicted? He argues that even if we have followed all the ascetic practices any thought of pride negates all the virtues attained.[21]

Abba Pachomius said, "If someone honors you do not be elated but be rather sad. When people honored Paul and Barnabas they tore their clothes (Acts 14:14); when Peter and the rest of the apostles were flogged they rejoiced because they were considered worthy to suffer dishonor for the sake of the Greatest Name (Acts 5:41)."[22] Abba Pachomius is telling the brethren that not accepting honor and praise is a very apostolic trait and there is good reason for us to emulate the apostles. Scripture and many of these sayings agree that pride is the downfall of the person. When pride and being puffed up with praise overtake our senses and dominate our thoughts, then we must balance these thoughts with self-examination, which will reveal that we have not fulfilled all the biblical commandments, nor are we equal to the model that Christ has set before us.

Balancing leadership with humility is usually difficult. One of the elders responsible for guiding some of the novices in the spiritual journey was unable to reconcile giving orders with humility. Abba Poemen advised

19. *SABudge*, 108, #454.
20. *AParadise*, 318.
21. *SABudge*, 117, #515.
22. *AParadise*, 317.

him to lead by example. The elder was perplexed and asserted that the way to convey his wishes was by giving orders. Poemen responded that the best way for instructing the young is by example and not by giving instructions.[23] Though this advice might not work in all cases, the desert fathers and mothers advised that, when possible, teaching and leading by example were the preferred ways of leadership. The rationale is that modeling is the most powerful type of leadership since deeds speaks louder than words. One of the fathers said, "Be not humble in thy words only, but also in thy deeds."[24] If we are in a position that obligates us to give instructions or commands then, said one of the fathers, we should do so with the fear of God and with humility. If we give orders simply to assert our authority then God, who sees the depth of our hearts, will not allow those who are ordered to be obedient. For the work that is done for God's sake is done with humility, but what is done by our authority brings trouble.[25] This saying, like the rest of the sayings, was spoken in the monastic setting. But it applies to our setting also. When a manager is too bossy employees do the work to survive in the work place but not with energy and enthusiasm. On the other hand, when an order is given with humility and love they do their work not only willingly, but to the best of their ability because they are working in a comfortable and non-threatening environment.

Abba Isaac spoke about his discipleship as a young monk. He was a disciple of both Abba Chronius and Abba Theodore of Parme and neither of them ever asked him to do anything. Abba Isaac asked Abba Theodore how it was that he never asked him to do anything. Abba Theodore did not answer. Abba Isaac went to the elders of Kellia and voiced a complaint against Abba Theodore that he was not teaching or instructing him. The elders came to investigate the frustration of the disciple Isaac. Abba Theodore answered that he never gave orders to anyone but expected a disciple to observe and emulate him, that is, he instructed by example. Isaac learned the lesson "and from that time I was always before him in doing that which the old man was going to do; now whatsoever he did, he did in silence, and in this manner he made me to know and taught me to work in silence also."[26] We can learn a lot with Abba Isaac. Powerful instruction is found in the example and also in silence. Silence can be more profound than many words and Abba Isaac benefited greatly from Abba Theodore's

---

23. *SABudge*, 108, #457.

24. *SABudge*, 110, #468.

25. *SABudge*, 114, #492.

26. *SABudge*, 103, #444.

silence. The power of example is beyond words. We have all observed how children emulate what their parents do rather than follow what their parents say. Likewise, with spirituality we are exhorted to imitate the example before us since it is in imitation of Christ (see 1 Cor 11:1; 2 Thess 3:7, 9; Heb 13:7; 1 Cor 4:16; Phil 3:17; Eph 5:1). This exercise made Abba Isaac become more attentive to his spiritual father's behavior, so much so that he did things before Abba Theodore attempted to do them. It created in Abba Isaac sensitivity toward others that he did not have before.

The story about Abba Isaac and Abba Theodore also informs us about the relationship between a father and disciple. If the disciple did not like or understand the behavior of his spiritual father, he had the right to go and complain to the elders. The elders took these complaints very seriously. The story speaks to the humility of the desert fathers and mothers, who did not consider such behavior to demonstrate insubordination, criticism, or ungratefulness toward the father. Like other stories, it speaks about the egalitarian spirit of desert discipleship. The early desert fathers followed a management style that was built on modeling and not on giving orders. According to the fathers, power exercised with ruthless authority is for the satisfaction of the ego. But of humility the fathers said, "I would rather have defeat with humility than conquest with boasting."[27]

Humility requires us to respect everyone we meet. Christian respect is based on a deep theological understanding rather than social etiquette. One of the fathers says that we should not despise the person before us for we do not know if the Spirit of God is in him or in us. Though the person before us might be serving us, he or she might be more pleasing to God than we are.[28] If the constant thought that we are all created in God's image and that the Spirit of God dwells within us permeates our worldview, and is not merely an intellectual knowledge, we will respect each person, for the one who stands before us might be the dwelling place of the Holy Spirit and might be much holier than we. "Abba Isaac said, 'He who honors every person for the sake of God, finds support from every person by God's hidden gesture.'"[29] Abba Macarius prayed for twelve years for the gift of behaving "towards all the brethren without any wicked suspicion."[30] When we do not suspect others we behave cordially toward them. But when suspicion emerges our behavior will be discriminatory. Abba Ma-

27. *SABudge*, 117, #514.

28. *SABudge*, 112, #478.

29. *AParadise*, 329.

30. *SABudge*, 108, #455.

carius considered treating all people equally without discrimination a gift, for which he prayed for twelve years.

The following story speaks about the power of humility: There was an elderly wise monk who "possessed knowledge and great honour" and had a considerable number of disciples in the valley of Egypt. Abba Poemen arrived in Scetis and soon the disciples of the wise monk left him to follow Abba Poemen. The monk "was filled with envy, and he cursed the followers of Abba Poemen because of this." When Abba Poemen heard of this, he was not pleased and immediately gathered his disciples and said to them, "What shall we do for this old man? For the men who have forsaken him have cast us into vexation, and they have left that holy old man and turned their looks upon us, who are nothing. How then can we satisfy this old man?" This saying of Abba Poemen indicates that he empathized with the hurt of the forsaken monk; he did not claim any superiority of teaching but rather considered himself "nothing." He decided to bake fresh bread—a rarity in the desert—cook some food, take a vessel of wine, and pay a visit to the monk with all the brethren who had left him to follow Abba Poemen. The monk refused to receive them and asked his disciple to send them away. Abba Poemen with the rest of the monks remained and insisted that they would not leave before taking the blessing of the monk. When the monk discovered that they did not leave and "saw their humility and patient persistence, he repented and opened the door to them." At the end of the meal the monk said that what he saw from Abba Poemen exceeded what he had heard, and he became a friend of Abba Poemen from that day on.[31] Abba Poemen had a great sense of empathy and understood the impact of being forsaken on the soul of the monk. The remedy for envy and anger was humility and a true sense of unworthiness from the side of Abba Poemen. Humility not only appeased the anger of the monk, it made a friend of him. That is the power of humility and the true inner understanding of being unworthy. Abba Pachomius said that a humble person is one of the best things one can see, for it is through a humble person that one sees God, whom no one has seen.[32] As humility had the power to befriend the hurt monk, so seeing a humble person has the power to inspire us, for it is the closest we can come to encountering God, who humbled himself for our sake.

---

31. *SABudge*, 124, #555.
32. *AParadise*, 309.

One of the elders gave this advice all the time: if you are humble and feel yourself unworthy and as nothing, you will have rest.[33] The desert fathers used terms such as "unworthy" and "as nothing" to describe humility, as opposed to terms such as "better," "more worthy," "holier," "wiser," or "more ascetic" than others, which are indications of pride. Unworthiness comes from the understanding that whatever we achieve is by God's grace. Abba Nestarion said, "The criminal was on the cross and was justified with one word (Luke 23:43); and Judas was one of the apostles and in one night lost everything; therefore, one should not boast about his good deeds, for all those who had too much confidence in themselves have fallen."[34] No one would have expected that a crucified criminal would be the first to be saved by Christ and be promised eternal life. For this reason, the desert fathers and mothers constantly taught non-judgment, for we do not know the state or the final hour of a person; nor should we consider ourselves above others, for in our weakness we can lose everything. It is humility that guards us. Abba Isaac said, "He who knows his weakness has reached humility."[35] He also said, "[R]emember the fall of the strong so that you gain humility."[36]

The fathers and mothers always prayed for wisdom and discernment; for it is complicated to keep the balance between the self-confidence that leads to pride and the feeling of unworthiness that leads to low self-esteem. The Letter to the Philippians 2:3 says to "do nothing from selfish ambition or conceit, but in humility regard others as better than yourselves." Advice on keeping this balance has been expressed in many of the biblical wisdom sayings, such as Proverbs 18:12 11:2. The balance is preserved by prayer, keeping our thoughts on Christ's image and humility, the work of the Spirit within us, and our response to the work of the Spirit. Abba Isaiah of Scetis wrote:

> Nevertheless, a person must pray a great deal before God, with great humility of heart and body, not considering himself as doing any good through any of his works, feeling neither convinced by compliments nor sad on account of blame, but instead allowing the remembrance of his sins to make peace in his heart with his enemies. He should not permit any bitter word from

33. *SA Budge*, 248, #466; #465 is the same saying but attributed to Abba Paphnutius.
34. *A Paradise*, 326.
35. *A Paradise*, 325.
36. *A Paradise*, 325.

his mouth to be spoken against anyone and should not blame anyone, even before good people who love him.[37]

Humility does not judge others. Abba Pachomius said, "Do not scorn any person and do not judge him even if you see him committing sin, because judgment is from a proud heart. The humble believes everyone is better than him. For how can you judge the servant of God? For his sins are against God and God is capable of lifting him up."[38] Abba Pachomius' advice is that we are not to judge anyone who commits wrong, for the wrong is not done against us but against God himself, and it is not we but God who judges. If we think we have the right to judge a person then we are are equating ourselves to God, who has the right to judge humanity. The early desert fathers and mothers were adamant in promoting the principle of not judging any person for any reason. Only God can judge. Even if we witness a person committing a transgression, we do not know how quickly this person might repent; the most notable example is the conversion of the criminal on the cross. For the desert fathers and mothers, judgment is the outcome of pride.

Humility cannot be faked for long. It manifests itself in our body posture, our speech, our choice of friends, and it is very hard to fake our whole environment for long. In addition, we all perceive and understand true humility sooner or later. We often choose a humble person for our closest friend. That is why the desert fathers and mothers said that humble people find rest. Humility is an inner spiritual state that is reflected on the outside. If it is not based on a solid theological basis in relationship to God and others, it is not true humility. It is only through constant inner reflection on the crucified Christ, the model of humility, that we can gain strength and true understanding of ourselves and the true essence of humility. It is humility that made the Son of God become incarnate, and without humility we would not have been saved. Humility is the virtue least pleasing to our human ego; therefore, without a deep understanding of the humble incarnate Son of God and his crucifixion, the supreme example of humility, we cannot grasp humility and its impact on who we are as Christians. Without the renewed life granted by the resurrection, without the power of the renewed image of God within us granted by the crucified Son of God, we cannot understand and reach humility. It is through our attempt to preserve the divine image within us, one manifestation of which is the humble crucified Son, that we attain humility. It is

37. *Is. Scetis*, 100.
38. *AParadise*, 321.

through the power of the resurrection that we can become humble. The renewed image within us is the renewed person, the renewed thinking (*nous*) that will sustain the image of the incarnate Son within our minds. It is the work of the Spirit within us. It is these inner thoughts that safeguard our humility.

Biblical Verses on Humility for Further Contemplation:

MATTHEW 23:12—All who exalt themselves will be humbled, and all who humble themselves will be exalted.

LUKE 14:11—For all who exalt themselves will be humbled, and those who humble themselves will be exalted.

LUKE 18:14—I tell you, this man went down to his home justified rather than the other; for all who exalt themselves will be humbled, but all who humble themselves will be exalted.

1 PETER 5:6—Humble yourselves therefore under the mighty hand of God, so that he may exalt you in due time.

PROVERBS 15:33—The fear of the LORD is instruction in wisdom, and humility goes before honor.

PROVERBS 16:19—It is better to be of a lowly spirit among the poor than to divide the spoil with the proud.

PROVERBS 22:4—The reward for humility and fear of the LORD is riches and honor and life.

ZEPHANIAH 2:3—Seek the LORD, all you humble of the land, who do his commands; seek righteousness, seek humility; perhaps you may be hidden on the day of the LORD's wrath.

EPHESIANS 4:1–2—I therefore, the prisoner in the Lord, beg you to lead a life worthy of the calling to which you have been called, with all humility and gentleness, with patience, bearing with one another in love, making every effort to maintain the unity of the Spirit in the bond of peace.

PSALM 138:6—For though the LORD is high, he regards the lowly; but the haughty he perceives from far away.

ISAIAH 57:15—For thus says the high and lofty one who inhabits eternity, whose name is Holy: I dwell in the high and holy place, and also with those who are contrite and humble in spirit, to revive the spirit of the humble, and to revive the heart of the contrite.

MATTHEW 11:29—Take my yoke upon you, and learn from me; for I am gentle and humble in heart, and you will find rest for your souls.

PROVERBS 3:34—Toward the scorners he is scornful, but to the humble he shows favor.

COLOSSIANS 2:23—These have indeed an appearance of wisdom in promoting self-imposed piety, humility, and severe treatment of the body, but they are of no value in checking self-indulgence.

JAMES 4:6—But he gives all the more grace; therefore it says, "God opposes the proud, but gives grace to the humble."

LUKE 1:48—[F]or he has looked with favor on the lowliness of his servant. Surely, from now on all generations will call me blessed.

LUKE 1:52—He has brought down the powerful from their thrones, and lifted up the lowly.

ROMANS 12:16—Live in harmony with one another; do not be haughty, but associate with the lowly; do not claim to be wiser than you are.

JAMES 1:9—Let the believer who is lowly boast in being raised up.

Further Sayings for Reflection:

She [Amma Syncletica] also said, "Just as one cannot build a ship unless one has some nails, so it is impossible to be saved without humility."[39]

She [Amma Syncletica] also said, "Imitate the publican, and you will not be condemned with the Pharisee. Choose the meekness of Moses and you will find your heart which is a rock changed into a spring of water."[40]

39. *ASWard*, 235, Syncletica #26.
40. *ASWard*, 233, Syncletica #11.

He [John the Short] also said, "Humility and the fear of God are above all virtues."[41]

Abba Moses the Ethiopian said, "Humility precedes all virtues, and pride is the root of all evil."[42]

Abba Elijah said, "There is no benefit to love where there is pride."[43]

Through humility the enemy is entirely destroyed.[44]

An elder said, "God would not dwell within us without humility, toil, and unceasing prayer."[45]

An elder said, "Humility is the tree of life and those who eat from it do not die."[46]

An old man used to say, "He who is held in greater honour or is more praised than he deserveth suffereth great loss; but the man who receiveth neither honour nor praise from men shall be praised above all."[47]

A brother asked Abba Poemen, "How is it possible for a man to avoid speaking evilly to his neighbor?" The old man answered and said unto him, "We and our brethren possess two images. Whensoever then a man condemneth himself, his brother appeareth unto him beautiful and excellent; but whensoever a man appeareth beautiful to himself, his brother will be found to be, in his sight, hateful and abominable."[48]

Again he [Isaiah of Scetis] said concerning humility, "It has no tongue in order to speak against someone for being careless, or someone else for being contemptuous; nor does it have eyes with which to notice another's faults; nor, again, does it have ears to hear that which does not benefit the soul. Neither does it have anything against others, except one's own sins. Instead, it renders one peaceful with all people for the sake of God's commandment, and not merely some friendship. For, if one fasts six days out

41. *ASWard*, 90, John the Dwarf #22.
42. *AParadise*, 309.
43. *AParadise*, 327.
44. *Is. Scetis*, 47.
45. *AParadise*, 311.
46. *AParadise*, 309.
47. *SABudge*, 117, #516.
48. *SABudge*, 120, #529.

of seven and is entirely given to great toils and commandments, all of that person's toils outside this way of humility are in vain."[49]

He also used to say, "Him who hath become despised for our Lord's sake, will our Lord make wise."[50]

Just as the earth cannot be fruitful without seed and irrigation, so, also it is impossible for us to be spiritually fruitful without ascetic discipline and humility.[51]

Therefore, when the intellect hears this boldness, it becomes daring before the enemy and says, "*Who is my enemy? Let him attack me. Who is my accuser? Let him approach me. Behold, the Lord is my helper, who can do me any evil? Behold, all of you will grow old as clothes, and you will be consumed as cotton by moths*" [Isa 50:8–9]. Our God is powerful, and he will be with those who are humble and protected by their humility, which becomes a helmet for them, protecting them from every arrow of the enemy, through the grace of God, for his is the power and the glory and the might to the ages of ages.[52]

There are four virtues that purify the soul: silence, keeping the commandments, <spiritual> constraint, and humility.[53]

Amma Syncletica said, "For if you fast, and if you give alms, or if you teach: if you are wise and intelligent, it will furnish you again with an impregnable fort. Let humility, the most beautiful of all virtues, reinforce and keep your virtues from dispersing. Look at the canticle of the three holy children, how not mentioning at all other virtues, they included the humble ones with the singers, not mentioning the wise or the poor."[54]

Amma Syncletica said, "Therefore humility corrects by means of reproaches, by means of violence, by means of blows; in order that you might hear through the foolish and the stupid, the poor person and the beggar, the weak one and the insignificant, the one who makes no progress in work, the illogical in expression, the dishonorable in appearance, the

---

49. *Is. Scetis*, 88
50. *SABudge*, 121, #532.
51. *Is. Scetis*, 62.
52. *Is. Scetis*, 68.
53. *Is. Scetis*, 81.
54. *Sync.*, 290, #56.

weak in power. These things are the sinews of humility. These things our Lord heard and suffered. For he spoke to the Samaritan himself and to the one who had a demon. He took the form of a slave, he was beaten, he was tortured with blows."[55]

Amma Syncletica said, "Therefore there are some who pretend by means of external forms and humble themselves, while they hunt glory by these means; but they are recognized by their fruits, for they did not bear being insulted even superficially, but immediately they vomited their own poison like serpents."[56]

55. *Sync.*, 290, #58.
56. *Sync.*, 290, #59.

12

Be Perfect

Life of Holiness

"Be perfect, therefore, as your heavenly Father is perfect."

MATTHEW 5:48

"Then someone came to him and said, 'Teacher, what good deed must I do to have eternal life?' Jesus said to him, 'If you wish to be perfect, go, sell your possessions, and give the money to the poor, and you will have treasure in heaven; then come, follow me.'"

MATTHEW 19:16, 21

"BE PERFECT." WE ARE called to be perfect, as perfect as our Father in heaven. To be perfect like our Father means to be in his image and likeness. We were created in God's image and likeness and Matt 5:48 is calling us to preserve this image within us. We lost this image with the fall, but the incarnation, crucifixion, and resurrection have granted us the renewal of this image within us. This is at the core of our salvation. Christ advises the young man that if he wants eternal life, then he has to be perfect (Matt 19:16, 21). Everyone is seeking eternal life. This is the question every Christian should ask: "Teacher, what good deed must I do to have eternal life?" Christ answered, renounce all your worldly possessions and accumulate a treasure in heaven, then follow me. The answer is not as simple as it seems and successive generations of Christians have kept asking this same question. What to do to be saved? What to do to have eternal life? What to do to follow Christ? The desert fathers and mothers had some answers. They read Scripture, prayed and meditated on its words, and put the words of Scripture before their eyes to follow in their every move. They examined their thoughts to conform to Christ's image within us. They renounced everything so as to be free to follow Christ and not be distracted in their attentiveness to God. They taught us that discernment is important in our spiritual journey. They were most attentive to the commandment to love as encapsulating the essence of the Christian message. They were attentive to every detail of their thoughts and left us numerous pithy statements about various aspects of the spiritual life. Each topic they addressed could be a chapter, or even a book of its own. We cannot cover them all in this introductory book. This chapter will address a sample of the many topics not discussed in this book so far, including spiritual goals, the fear of God, hope, patience, and hospitality. The ultimate purpose of all the topics discussed by the desert fathers and mothers is to be perfect as the heavenly father is perfect.

Spiritual Goals

"I press on toward the goal for the prize of the heavenly call of God in Christ Jesus" (Phil 3:14). Abba Anthony advises his listeners to have certain goals for their spiritual journey. He says, "Whoever hammers a lump of iron, first decides what he is going to make of it, a scythe, a sword, or an axe. Even so we ought to make up our minds what kind of virtue we want to forge or we labour in vain."[1] Setting goals is an indication of spiritual attentiveness. The spiritual exercise of examining the thoughts is to ascertain not only what has occurred but also our present inner state, and to decide where to go next. We should not overwhelm ourselves with too many goals but tackle one thing at a time. Thus Abba Dioscorus of Namisias would make one resolution every year. "This was his system in everything. He made himself master of one thing, and then started on another and so on each year."[2] The examination of our inner thoughts illuminates and directs us to what is more urgent to attend to in our spiritual journey. A

1. *ASWard*, 8, Anthony the Great #35.
2. *SSWard*, 21, Self-Control #13.

brother asked a hermit about his trouble with too many temptations; he did not know where to start or what to do. The hermit advised him, "Do not fight against them all at once, but against one of them. All the temptations of monks have a single source. You must consider what kind of root of temptation you have, and fight against that and in this way all the other temptations will also be defeated."[3] Not only monks, but every one of us has one main issue that galvanizes our thoughts and our behavior. With prayer and the work of the Spirit within us God reveals to us the root of our problems and the rest of the issues will follow. Prayer will not only reveal the root of our problem but also grant us the courage to face it.

Some of the hermits gave the following advice: "Whatever you hate for yourself, do not do it to someone else. If you hate being spoken evil of, do not speak evil of another. If you hate being slandered, do not slander another. If you hate him who tries to make you despised, or wrongs you, or takes away what is yours, or anything like that, do not do such things to others. To keep this is enough for salvation."[4] The hermits are elaborating on Matthew 7:12 in practical terms, summarizing it in the simple words the life of holiness. Abba Poemen gives advice about the inner and outer activity of a monk in his cell: The monk is to work with his hands, observe silence, and meditate, internally "keeping a watch on the secret thoughts of the heart." He stops his work when it is time for prayer and resumes his "work later in tranquility."[5] Similarly, an elder gave the following advice for younger monks: "He must not act iniquitously, and he must not look upon evil things with his eyes, and he must not hearken with his ears unto things which are alien to the fear of God, and he must not utter calumnies with his mouth, and he must not seize things with his hands, but must give especially to those who are in need, he must neither be exalted in his mind nor meditate with his wicked thoughts, and he must not fill his belly. All these things he must perform with intelligence, for by them is a monk known."[6] This saying is actually expressing Athanasius' theology in very simple terms. Athanasius said that the presence of evil is the work of the mind. We were granted the power to contemplate God, which we could do through the purity of our souls. But when we became attached to sensible things, that is, the things near our bodies and senses, we were no longer able to contemplate God. This saying is addressing the purity of

3. *SSWard*, 111, Discretion #91.

4. *SSWard*, 6, Progress in Perfection #21.

5. *SSWard*, 103, Discretion #64.

6. *SABudge*, 244, #436.

the soul and the preservation of the senses so as to be able to contemplate God. Our actions should be moral and ethical. We should keep the purity of the senses: he lists the eyes, the ears, the mouth, the hands that seize and do not give, and the belly, which is gluttony. The mind is to be pure from "wicked thoughts." Athanasius' theology could not be expressed in simpler terms. Our modern civilization addresses the senses as never before in the history of humanity. These sayings and Athanasius' theology could not be more pertinent than they are for us today.

Fear of God

"His delight shall be in the fear of the LORD" (Isa 11:3). Isaiah saw the seraphs in the temple giving praise to the Lord of Hosts, and when the temple was filled with smoke and its thresholds shook, he immediately said, "Woe is me! I am lost, for I am a man of unclean lips, and I live among a people of unclean lips; yet my eyes have seen the King, the LORD of hosts!" (Isa 6:5). When Isaiah encountered God's glory he was struck with awe and reverence. He immediately felt his uncleanness, and not only his own but that of the whole people, in comparison to God's purity. Living in holiness gradually reveals to us God's glory and purity and it is at this moment, when we are in awe and reverence of God, and only at this moment that the truth about our soul and our thoughts is revealed to us. Those who experience such a revelation understand their sinfulness in truth. It is not words that they say, but it is a deep inner awareness of the impurity of their thoughts and soul in comparison to God's holiness and purity; it is with this awareness that we truly become humble and live in the fear of God. Of course, we will not all see the seraphs as Isaiah did, though we might. Many, however, have had a very deep inner revelation, where the image of God within us becomes strengthened and the light shines within us and the full glory of God becomes closer to our reach. We become God fearers with a fear that illuminates our soul and mind, a fear that shines within us, a fear that overwhelms us, a fear that makes us love our neighbor and respect the world we live in. Because we become closer to the creator, we become closer to the world and humanity. The fear of the Lord is the root and source of understanding for many aspects of desert spirituality. It is a spirituality in which everything fades when it stands in close proximity to God's glory; all trouble seems minor, hatred toward others or from others seems trivial, obstacles can be overcome easily, our senses become more engaged with things pertaining to God, our thoughts captivated by God's love.

Abba Anthony is very famous for emphasizing the fear of God as a major spiritual prize that guides us through our journey. He said, "Always have the fear of God before your eyes. Remember him who gives death and life."[7] In other words, the fear of God is to be at the center of the essence of our existence. John the Short said, "Humility and the fear of God are above all virtues."[8] Abba Poemen said that the fear of God, prayer, and doing good to our neighbor are most helpful to our spiritual journey.[9] The desert fathers and mothers expressed in many ways that this one virtue bears as fruit many other virtues. Some have specifically emphasized the fear of God over and above other virtues. Abba Isaiah of Scetis said, "All the virtues have only one mother, which is called the fear of God."[10] Abba Poemen used to say that the fear of God teaches spiritual excellence.[11] Abba Isaiah further explained the fecundity of virtues when he said, "Godly fear begets humility. Humility begets foresight, Foresight begets love."[12] He also said, "[I]f a person knowingly fears God, and his senses are subjected to his conscience in a godly manner, God himself will teach him much more than all of the above."[13] The fear of God guards our consciousness and when we subject our senses to the fear of God we subject them to our consciousness. God will teach us and speak to us through our consciousness, so long as we subject it to the fear of God. He also said, "He who has the fear of God has the heavenly wisdom, and he who does not have the fear of God has no goodness within him."[14] He also said, "[T]he person who says, 'I fear God', yet when the time of need arrives–if he is found at a time of vain talk, or anger, or arrogance, or of teaching others about matters he has not reached, or of people-pleasing, or of seeking a reputation among people, and of similar passions–he does not find the fear of God and all of his toils are in vain."[15] Abba Isaiah explains that if we claim to have the fear of God within us but our actions and behavior

7. *ASWard*, 8, Anthony the Great #33.
8. *ASWard*, 90, John the Dwarf #22.
9. *ASWard*, 189, Poemen #160.
10. *Is. Scetis*, 150.
11. *SABudge*, 183, #136.
12. *Is. Scetis*, 126.
13. *Is. Scetis*, 72.
14. *AParadise*, 148.
15. *Is. Scetis*, 88.

contradict that claim, then we are to understand that we have not attained the status of God-fearing believers. For "woe to us, where fear and love of God are not preponderant and this is why we are so far from Christ who loves us."[16]

Hope

"And now, O Lord, what do I wait for? My hope is in you" (Ps 39:7). With the constant examination of our thoughts and the natural disappointments that occur when confronting ourselves, some might anticipate that frustration and depression would follow. This work, however, is the work of Holy Spirit; it is not we who are confronting our inner selves, but it is God who is revealing himself within us. This revelation magnifies our inner sinfulness, but this confrontation and revelation lead us to better ourselves. It is a healthy spiritual exercise that engenders hope. Hope is one of the gifts of the Spirit. Hope gives us a new beginning every day.[17] The prayers of matins in the Coptic Orthodox Church, the inheritors of this monastic tradition, are dedicated to the theme of the resurrection, so that the day starts with the new hope of the resurrection, a new beginning for every day. This is reflected in the attitude of the desert fathers. Abba Pior made every day a new beginning.[18] Abba Silvanus gave to Abba Moses the following advice when asked if we can lay a new foundation every day: Laying a new foundation is not only done every day but every moment.[19] This shows the true essence of the renewal given to humanity with the resurrection, the renewal of creation. It is a renewal that occurs at every moment.

Many of us seek validation from others. We are devastated if we are not liked by everyone, though we all know that no one whosoever was liked by all. Even Christ himself was not liked by all. Yet we seek validation from everyone. We fall into the vicious cycle of seeking validation, developing low self-esteem when we do not find it, and because we are in this state, seeking more validation. The desert fathers and mothers broke this vicious cycle by saying that we should seek validation not from others but only from God. "Abba John said to his brother, 'Even if we are entirely

16. *Is. Scetis*, 241.

17. Please refer to chapter 3, on *The Life of Anthony*, under the heading "A new beginning every day."

18. *ASWard*, 179, Poemen #85.

19. *ASWard*, 224, Silvanus #11; similarly, *SSWard*, 124, Sober Living #29.

despised in the eyes of men, let us rejoice that we are honoured in the sight of God."[20] If we have faith in the words of Scriptures and in God's promises, and we know we are the dwelling place of the Holy Spirit, and Christ was on the cross for our sake, our hearts should be filled with peace and nothing should disturb this joy. When the early church martyrs were being taken to their death, a sure sign that they were despised by their society, their hearts were joyful and this joy caused many who witnessed their martyrdom to convert to Christianity. It was martyrdom that strengthened and spread the faith in the early centuries of Christianity. If early church Christians lived this advice and it proved very fruitful, I think we can also take this advice to heart and experience its fruits. The unwanted remarks of a colleague at work or a classmate in school or a neighbor should fade by comparison with the scorn and hatred that crucified our Lord and that our early church fathers and mothers endured for the faith. No one has the power to take the joy from our hearts unless we permit them to do so. Abba Benjamin on his death bed said, "Be joyful at all times, pray without ceasing and give thanks for all things."[21]

The following saying summarizes how to approach temptations that might lead us to despair:

> Another hermit said, "We suffer temptations because we are careless. If we always remember that God dwells in us, we shall never bring into ourselves anything that is not his. The Lord Christ is in us and with us, and watches our life. Because we have Him within us and contemplate Him, we ought not to be idle; we should make ourselves holy as He is holy. If we stand upon a rock, the power of the wicked one will be broken. Do not be afraid of him, and he can do nothing against you. Pray with courage this psalm, 'They that trust in the Lord are like Mount Zion; they that dwell in Jerusalem shall stand fast for ever' (Ps. 125:1)."[22]

Patience

"May you be made strong with all the strength that comes from his glorious power, and may you be prepared to endure everything with patience, while joyfully giving thanks to the Father . . ." (Col 1:11–12). Joy resulting

---

20. *ASWard*, 95, John the Dwarf #42.

21. *ASWard*, 44, Benjamin #4.

22. *SSWard*, 38, Lust #17.

from hope and thanksgiving emerges also from a life of patience and endurance. No one can go through life without difficulties and temptations. The way we respond to these life difficulties forms our character; we can be thankful or bitter. Patience becomes a key word for enduring life's difficulties. "A hermit said, 'If you fall ill, do not complain. If the Lord God has willed that your body should be weakened, who are you to complain about it? Does he not care for you in all your needs? Surely you would not be alive without him. Be patient in your illness and ask God to give you what is right, that is, that which will enable you to do his will, and be patient, and eat what you have in charity.'"[23] This hermit puts our life in perspective. If we are worried about our illness, we have forgotten that it is God who has given us life; if we are still alive, then he is very aware of our needs. We should not complain but rather examine our lives and ask the question: How can this difficulty work for our benefit? God has given us illness for our salvation; how can we make our illness a source of our betterment? We will not understand the lesson from it if we are so consumed with complaining and are not patient. We all know many people who have been able to conquer their difficulties. We can learn from their wisdom and life experience.

One of the hermits said, "He who bears scorn and injury and loss with patience, can be saved."[24] This hermit points to different difficulties: scorn, which is humiliating words or actions that might include contempt; injury, which includes suffering from injustice or words which can equal physical injury in their pain; and loss, including physical, psychological, and spiritual loss. Patience will enable us to overcome all these difficulties. Another saying: "If you are able to endure when you are despised, this is a deed greater than all the virtues."[25] And who has been more despised than Christ himself, whose endurance, patience, silent suffering, and forgiveness set the example for all ages and for all humanity? Saintly men and women throughout history have followed Christ's example and given us further examples of extraordinary patience and endurance. If they were able to endure all the temptations and suffering they went through in their lives strengthened by Christ's example on the cross, so can we.

Patience and endurance reap benefits. "Abba Ammonas said, 'I have spent fourteen years in Scetis asking God night and day to grant me the

23. *SSWard*, 75, Fortitude #45.

24. *SSWard*, 168, Humility #84. "As an example of suffering and patience, beloved, take the prophets who spoke in the name of the Lord" (Jas 5:10).

25. *SAChaîne*, 33, #150; *SAHartley*, 92, #150.

victory over anger."[26] The experience of Abba Ammonas is very important because it teaches us that spiritual growth requires patience and perseverance. Similarly, we have observed that it took Abba Anthony around twenty years to reach spiritual maturity.[27] The different experiences of the desert fathers and mothers are consistent: attaining spirituality and spiritual maturity is a long journey. An impatient young brother tormented in his thoughts went to Abba Theodore of Parme seeking his advice. Abba Theodore advised him to humble his mind, leave his seclusion, and to go and live with the brothers. The young brother obeyed, but after some time returned to Abba Theodore saying that he did not want to live with the brothers. Abba Theodore asked him, If you are not content to live either in seclusion or with the brothers why then did you become a monk? Abba Theodore recognized the immaturity of this young brother, who was unable to endure any temptation or suffering faced either in seclusion or with the brothers. When the elder learned after inquiry that the young brother had been a monk for only eight years, he told him that he had lived the monastic life for seventy years; did this young monk want to have peace of mind in eight years?![28] The young brother represents all of us. We look at people who have achieved great status in life, whether spiritual, social, or economic, and we want to acquire their status at a young age. We forget the toil of years that success and maturity requires.

The desert fathers and mothers understood human nature; we want things quickly without doing much work. One of the fathers said, "We do not advance because we do not know our capacity, and we have not sufficient patience in the work which we begin, and we wish to possess spiritual excellences without working for them. . . ."[29] A good example of working for spiritual excellence is found in the story of some brothers who came to Abba Anthony to seek his advice. Abba Anthony said that all one needs is found in the Scriptures and there was nothing more he could add to that. The visiting brethren insisted on getting advice, so he said to them, If someone strikes you on one cheek offer him the other (see Luke 6:29). The brothers said they could not follow this commandment. Abba Anthony told them to keep on receiving the strike on the same cheek. They answered that they could not do that either. Then Abba Anthony

26. *ASWard*, 26, Ammonas #3.

27. Please refer to chapter 3, on *The Life of Anthony*, under the heading "Spiritual Maturity."

28. *SABudge*, 48, #217.

29. *SABudge*, 44, #195.

asked them not to reciprocate the blow with another. That was also difficult for them to follow. Then Abba Anthony said to them that if they could not do any of the commandments of Scripture, then immediate prayers were necessary. In spite of Abba Anthony's frustration with them, he set food before them before they left.[30] This is the type of work that the previous saying was referring to. We do not want to do the work and follow any of the Biblical commandments that require humility, sacrifice, patience, renunciation, and many other virtues, but we insist on having all the promises of Scripture. If we are in the spiritual state of the visiting brothers, Abba Anthony gives us his final advice: Pray. This attitude requires seriousness in our spiritual journey. No excuses are accepted. The desert fathers and mothers took Scriptures very seriously.

When we observe children, we understand that life experience will teach them a lot and we are patient with the small steps they take to learn about basic aspects of life. It takes us twenty-one years to watch a baby mature into a young person capable of living on his or her own and functioning in the society as a responsible adult. Our spiritual journey requires equal patience and equal work. It took hard work for the baby to grow into an adult person, an equal amount of work and time is required for our spiritual maturity. It also requires equal attentiveness and consistency. Any negligence sets us back years in spiritual maturity. But attentiveness puts us forward by leaps and bounds. Patience is a safeguard for our spiritual success, and, in fact, for our success in general.

Hospitality

"Do not neglect to show hospitality to strangers, for by doing that some have entertained angels without knowing it" (Heb 13:2). Scripture emphasizes hospitality as a Christian virtue and the early church consequently valued hospitality as something characteristically Christian. Pachomius, the founder of communal monasticism, converted to Christianity after he encountered the hospitality of Christians coming to his military camp to offer food and comfort to the soldiers camping outside their village. Hospitality provided a powerful example of Christian love and had a lasting impact on Pachomius and his monastic system. The stamp of hospitality migrated to the Benedictine rule, which adopted the Pachomian rule. One act of hospitably had a lasting impact on two monastic systems. The Epistles to the Hebrews 13:2 comments on Abraham's hospitality when he

30. *SABudge*, 44, #202.

received the three men at the oaks of Mamre (Gen 18): He meant to receive strangers but received angels. This has set the standard of hospitality in the early church as well as in the desert. Anyone we receive in the name of Christ we receive as our brother or sister, who is the image of God. As God sent angels to Abraham, so we also receive our guests as angels sent to us by God.[31]

As Christians we are to love everyone and showing hospitality is but one of the aspects of demonstrating love to the stranger among us and to the neighbor in need. One of the brothers knew that hermits change their rule for the sake of hospitality so when he was taking leave of one of the hermits he apologized for preventing him from keeping the rule. The hermit answered, "My rule is to welcome you with hospitality, and to send you on your way in peace."[32] The hermits, who cherished solitude, considered hospitality to be more important because it fulfills a biblical injunction. Hospitality should be offered to everyone, not only to those we like or those whom we think we might profit from.

Some of the brothers went to visit Abba Joseph with the intention of asking him about hospitality. Before they asked the question, Abba Joseph welcomed them, quickly went to his inner room and put on rags and came out to them. He then went again to his inner room and changed to better clothes. The brothers were astonished at his behavior and asked him what he meant by his behavior. He asked his guests, "Did the rags change me for the better? . . . Did good clothes change me for the worse?" When the guests answered "no" to both questions Abba Joseph said, "That is how we ought to be when we receive guests. It is written in the Holy Gospel, 'Render unto Caesar the things that are Caesar's, and unto God the things that are God's' (Matt 22:21). When visitors come we should welcome them and celebrate with them. . . ."[33]

The desert fathers and mothers who renounced the world for tranquility immediately renounced tranquility for hospitality. Since hospitality was crucial for the spirituality of the solitaries, it must be of utmost importance for us living in towns and cities. We are to welcome not only guests who come to attend services in our churches, but also those who have no place to sleep, nothing to eat, and no clothes to wear. Economic recessions come in cycles, and when they hit a society they change the lives of many households. It is not sufficient to depend on organizations to fulfill the

31. In the chapter on "Love" there are some examples of hospitality.
32. *SSWard*, 136, Hospitality #7.
33. *SSWard*, 134, Hospitality #1.

needs of those affected by an economic downturn; it is the responsibility of each person in the society to extend hospitality. The hospitality of each person can transform any society.

Perfect in every way

The list of topics covered in the sayings of the desert fathers and mothers is extensive. This chapter presents a sample of the topics that we could not cover in this book as examples for the reader. They represent major spiritual topics. There are also many sayings that stand on their own that are of equal value. Here are a few examples.

Thanksgiving and table etiquette

A brother cooked for a sick hermit some lentil cake. But he got mixed up and instead of adding honey he added an "evil-smelling linseed oil." The hermit tasted it and did not say anything; he ate the mouthful. When pressed to take another mouthful, he did. And so with a third mouthful. The brother cook noticed the hermit was eating the food with difficulty and to encourage him said he would eat with him. When the brother tasted the lentils he immediately understood the struggle of the sick hermit. He asked for the hermit's forgiveness and inquired why the hermit did not say anything. He answered, "Do not worry, my son. If God had willed that I should eat honey you would have been given the honey to mix in the food."[34]

The hermit took it that he was not to indulge himself even when he was sick. On the other hand, this is also a story about table etiquette. A monk should never complain about food offered him no matter how bad it is. The monks led a thankful life and also took into consideration the feelings of the cook who messed things up. This story is very relevant to our everyday life. It asks us to examine our attitude toward food we do not like or food presented to us that is not well cooked or not cooked to our taste. The fathers have given us the example of eating the food so as not to hurt the feelings of the host, no matter how bad the food tastes. Having love for your host is more important than any meal. Not complaining about food is important table etiquette. We can achieve this by putting things in perspective: how can we complain about the taste of food while millions

34. *SSWard*, 29, Self-Control #59.

in the world are dying of starvation? This thought will keep us from ever complaining and develop within us a life of thanksgiving.

Two more points can be made. The desert culture did not encourage indulgence in foods or satisfying the taste buds. The problem is not in eating nice, tasty food, but rather in obsession with food and letting food take over our lives. Thus the spiritual exercise of fasting was very important in the desert. It is one of the topics that the reader is encouraged to pursue in the sayings. Second, the fathers were adamant about not looking at the other's plate so as not to judge or condemn the other in their thoughts, whether they were eating too much or too little.[35] This is an exercise in guarding the senses, the eyes and the mouth (regarding taste), against judging others, and against being overtaken by food and losing self-control. Guarding the senses guards our thoughts.

Etiquette of visits

Here are some rules for visiting: If you visit another's cell or house, do not let your eyes examine every aspect of the house. If your host leaves the room for any reason do not touch, play, or move things around while the host is not present. Do not move about the place without permission.[36] These rules for visiting are also intended for guarding the senses. If we behave out of curiosity the result will be passing judgment on another's way of life, whether in a positive or negative way. In either case, we have no right to judge others. If our thoughts are to conform to God's thought, why are we distracted with the lives of others?

Other pithy statements

"Abba Agathon said, 'Under no circumstances should the monk let his conscience accuse him of anything.'"[37] This should apply not only to monks but to all of us. A clear conscience is our peace. Spiritual attentiveness is expressed in our daily examination of our souls and in prayers that God would forgive any transgressions committed during the day.[38]

---

35. *AParadise*, 146.
36. *AParadise*, 145.
37. *ASWard*, 20, Agathon #2.
38. *AParadise*, 147.

Abba Arsenius said, "If we seek God He will be revealed unto us, and if we lay hold upon Him, He will remain with us."[39]

Abba Isaiah of Scetis summarized the underlying theology that guided desert spiritualty as follows:

> I do not want you to forget, brothers, that in the beginning, when Adam was created, God placed him in Paradise with healthy senses that were established according to nature. When Adam listened to the one who deceived him, all of his senses were twisted toward that which is contrary to nature, and it was then that he fell from his glory. Our Lord, however, on account of his great love, took compassion on the human race. *The Word became flesh*, that is to say completely human, and became in every way like us except without sin, in order that he might, through his holy body, transform that which is contrary to nature to the state that is according to nature. Having taken compassion on Adam, God returned him to Paradise, resurrecting those who followed his steps and the commandments which he gave us so that we might be able to conquer those who removed us from our glory, indicating to us holy worship and pure law, that we may stay in the natural state in which God created us. The person, then, who wishes to attain this natural state removes all his carnal desires, in order that God may establish him in the state according to nature. Desire is the natural state of the intellect because without desire for God there is no love.[40]

---

39. *SABudge*, 197, #203.
40. *Is. Scetis*, 43–44.

EPILOGUE

Love the Lord With All Your Heart, Soul, and Mind

He said to him, "You shall love the Lord your God with all your heart,
and with all your soul, and with all your mind."

MATT 22:37

THE ESSENCE OF DESERT spirituality is to love the Lord with all our
heart, soul, and mind. The way to express this love is to get to know
God. God revealed himself to us through the incarnation and Scripture.
Most of us attend to the outer aspects of living according to Scripture,
but to scrutinize the inner thoughts and the depth of our heart, to check
that every movement of our soul is pleasing to God, to live the inner
life according to Scripture, is hard and requires honesty, integrity, and
courage. Above all it requires the guidance of the Holy Spirit dwelling
within us. This is what the desert fathers and mothers attempted to do;
they cultivated their inner selves to conform to the word of God. They
left us their spiritual experiences in pithy statements, which have come
to be known as the "sayings." It is up to us to delve into these sayings to
learn their wisdom. To understand the depth of this inner experience we
have had to immerse ourselves in the theological, historical, and spiritual
setting that formed these experiences.

Christianity from its very inception had an ascetic dimension. Christ
lived a simple life and never showed himself as wealthy or as aspiring
to accumulate wealth. Nor did his disciples. This simple life of our Lord

has set the tone of the Christian message. Through the early centuries of Christianity many individuals, as well as families, lived a frugal, simple life. Some, however, thought that living a frugal, simple life in the city was not enough; they wanted to mute the noise of the city and to declutter their senses, with the ultimate goal of being closer to God. Many moved to the city outskirts. One by the name of Anthony decided to go beyond the outskirts; he went to the desert to reach the ultimate place where there was no distraction from God. Many men and women followed his example. That was the beginning of what came to be called desert or monastic spirituality.

The spiritual life and spiritual journey of the desert dwellers was based on trial and error. Do we fast for forty days as Christ did when he was in the wilderness or do we fast for a week? The verdict was that it was better to eat a small amount of food everyday rather than abstain for a long time and then binge on food. Do we pray all the time? The verdict of their experience was that work was an important part of their spiritual journey and they had to sustain themselves and not be a financial burden on society. Many other questions were raised and many variant answers were given based on the different circumstances of the inquirers. The results of these experiences are documented in the sayings. The sayings are not a systematic spiritual program but a collection of diverse spiritual experiences and advice, which readers have to sift through to choose what best fits their circumstances and psychological makeup. The fathers compared the sayings to a paradise, or a garden, of different fruits; each reader must pick the fruit that fits his or her spiritual palate and spiritual level.

Within these very diverse spiritual experiences, there is an overarching theological and spiritual premise that guided all the fathers and mothers. Some expressed their theological principles clearly, others only in their spiritual practices. The major figure who articulated this theological premise was St. Athanasius of Alexandria, who was shaped by the theology of his time and place. He articulated the theology of the church of Egypt, the place of his birth and the birth of desert spirituality. The incarnation and the theology of the incarnation were the central focus of Athanasius' theology. His theology focused on the state of humanity before the fall, the cause of the fall and its effect on humanity, the incarnation as a means of renewing humanity after its fall, and the impact of this renewal on our spiritual life in light of the incarnation, crucifixion, and resurrection of the incarnate Son of God. We have been created in God's image with a rational mind capable of contemplating God at all times. The rational soul and *nous* that resides within humanity, when it is in control of the senses, can behold and contemplate God. However, this state was lost when the senses overtook the rational mind, and we were subjected to the curse of death. The only way to be saved from this eternal death was through the incarnation of the Son of God. He took a body like ours, representing the totality of humanity, and made it his own. When he died on the cross we died with him, and when he rose from the dead we rose with him. Death no longer has hold over humanity. It is through the power of the resurrection that we can overcome death and become a renewed humanity. The Word renewed his image within humanity so that through it humanity can once more come to know God and be in his likeness. With the incarnation, crucifixion, and resurrection the Giver of Life has given life and incorruption to humanity, and introduced virtue, immortality, and the desire for heavenly things.

The power of renewal granted by his resurrection enabled humanity to overcome the power of the senses and restored the power of the *nous*, the mind, to perceive the unseen Father, to contemplate God. It is this new state of saved humanity that the desert fathers and mothers aspired to live out. They sought to acknowledge the power of renewal granted by the incarnation and resurrection in their daily lives and live according to Scripture. This state of renewed creation is preserved through purity of the soul so that the *nous* can be unhindered in its constant contemplation of God. Purity of soul and living a life of virtue guide the mind in its spiritual journey to comprehend God as far as is humanly possible. Lest someone might think this is an unachievable human goal, Athanasius wrote *The Life of Anthony* as a concrete example of the power of the resurrection in the life of the Christian.

The spiritual life of Anthony and those who followed his lead held spiritual themes that the desert fathers and mothers found pivotal in the spiritual journey. They understood the theology of the incarnation and the power of the senses to override our thoughts and also the power of the resurrection to renew our thoughts, so their spiritual exercises revolved around the purification of our thoughts in order to be constantly in God's presence. They constantly examined the thoughts of the mind and attempted to keep the mind on the thought of God. Reading Scripture and memorizing it became one of their main spiritual activities; reading and contemplating Scripture is an activity required of every Christian. Scripture became the source of their prayers and contemplation and the means of preserving their thoughts in God. Scripture became the yardstick against which they measured their thoughts and activities. They discovered that possessions and never-ending daily commitments were the main hindrances to their intellectual and spiritual freedom, so they sought quietness and decluttered their lives from all that was not necessary. With the tranquility of their thoughts and their focus on Scripture, their prayer life got them closer to God. At the same time their souls became bare before them. They began confronting their inner thoughts with great courage, and with the guidance of the Holy Spirit they fought each thought that did not conform to God. Their struggles represent the struggles of all humanity: How do we love our neighbor perfectly? What are the things that hinder us from loving our neighbor as Christ loved us? Why do we covet, judge, slander, and betray others? How do we overcome the spiritual malaise that humanity suffers from? They scrutinized their hearts, thoughts, and every movement of their souls. They constantly weighed the thoughts of their hearts on the balance of Scripture, purity, and virtue. They diligently scrutinized their thoughts so as to eliminate any obstacle that hindered their presence before God. Athanasius assured the reader that this spirituality was attainable because of the power of renewal that the incarnation and resurrection had granted humanity. The modern reader should also be assured that the power of renewal of the incarnation and the resurrection is still ours to grasp.

In our modern times, when the never-ending daily demands of work and family are pressing, when modern technology has made the world noisier and all of us are being exposed to a sensory overload, it is good to take a step back and reflect, contemplate, and decide how to regain our inner tranquility and our inner connection with our own self and with God. Our inner peace is attained when we find the inner balance between our daily activities and our inner tranquility. The experience of the desert fathers and mothers is a road map that guides us to regain our inner tranquility. Their experience does not necessitate that we go into the desert; it brings the desert to us, into our homes and our workplaces. All their inner experiences are shared human experiences; they are humane, down to earth, practical, and presented simply. The simplicity of their questions and concerns and their investigation of every minute detail, no matter how trivial, make us hopeful. Many have trodden the path of spiritual struggle before us and have reached great stature, so it is also attainable for us. They teach us to be patient and persistent in our spiritual journey and never lose sight of God as the center of our attention. They warn us of the pitfalls that we will encounter and they chart a way out of them. That these sayings have been passed down from the fourth and fifth centuries to our present time speaks about their enduring character.

Desert spirituality is an examination of thoughts; it is the discernment of the soul; it is the balancing of the heart. Desert spirituality is living Scripture in our daily lives. It is the renewal of humanity and living the fullness of the incarnation, crucifixion, and resurrection. Desert spirituality started in the city and was perfected in the stillness of the desert. Many went to the desert seeking advice, then became so enamored with its spirituality that they remained and never returned to the city. This resulted in a mass exodus to the desert, which St. Athanasius described as a "city in the desert."[1] Other city dwellers went to the desert seeking advice and then returned to their homes and cities to apply the teachings of the desert fathers and mothers in their daily lives. They returned to the city to establish a "desert in the city." This was done in the early centuries of Christianity and many have continued this to the present day. I hope that after reading and practicing desert spirituality the reader will recover the spirituality that once emerged from the city and was perfected in the desert, reclaim it for the city, and create his or her own desert in the city.

1. Tim Vivian, trans., *The Life of Antony: The Coptic Life and the Greek Life*, Cistercian Studies 202 (Kalamazoo, MI: Cistercian, 2003) 93; *v. Anton.* 14.

Glossary

Not much is known about most of the monastics mentioned in the sayings. For people not discussed in depth in the text, this scant information is known:

Abba: Title meaning "Father," given to elder or experienced male monastics.

Amma: Title meaning "Mother," given to elder or experienced female monastics.

Anchorite: Solitary monk who lives independent from other monks. Some live totally on their own and others lived as part of a semi-anchoritic settlement.

Arsenius (360–449): Highly educated tutor assigned to educate Arcadius and Honorius, the two sons of Emperor Theodosius I the Great. He left the imperial palace and became a monk in Scetis and the disciple of John the Little. He was known for his silence. He left Scetis when it was raided in 434 and went to Tura, where he remained until his death.

Brother: Newcomer to the desert still learning the monastic way of life, regardless of age.

Cell: Monastic dwelling for either men or women. It could be one room or two rooms, the latter with an inner room for sleeping to preserve the privacy of the monastic and an outer room used mostly for work, eating, and receiving guests. The cell is usually simple and holds the necessities of the monastic.

Cenobitic: From the Greek for "common life," it refers to the type of monastic philosophy in which monastics live in community and have everything in common. This is different than the desert anchorites, those monastics living in a solitary life independent from the other monks.

Elder: Title given to experienced monks capable of giving advice to younger monastics or newcomers to the desert. Not all old monks are elders. On a few occasions, a young monk became an elder because of his wisdom and piety.

Eremitical: From the Greek for "desert," it refers to the style of monasticism in which a person (a hermit, from the same Greek word) lives a solitary life of prayer.

John the Short (or the Little, or the Dwarf; 339–409): He went to Scetis at the age of eighteen and remained as a disciple of Abba Ammoes for twelve years.

Inner Desert: Some monastics lived in the desert in locations close to main caravan roads. With fame and frequent visits, they had to leave to the inner desert, far from any trodden road, for seclusion, as in the case of Anthony.

Kellia or Cellia (the Cells): Location of a monastic settlement east of the Nile Delta

Moses the Black (or the Ethiopian; d. 434): Freed slave who earned his living through theft, especially in Nitria. He repented, became a monk, and eventually was ordained a priest. He became one of the most famous and respected monks of Scetis. He was killed by barbarian invaders.

Nitria: Location of a monastic settlement north of Scetis.

Nous: Greek word that generally means *mind* as in *perceiving* and *thinking.* It can also mean *thought, reason,* or *intellect.*

Pambo (303–373): Joined Amoun in Nitria and was ordained a priest in 340. He became famous for his wisdom, and many of the visitors to the desert, including Melania and Jerome, met with him.

Poemen (or the Shepherd): Has the largest number of sayings in the collection of sayings. He remained in Scetis with his six brothers and left with the devastation of Scetis caused by the barbarian raids in 407. He was known in Scetis and many came to learn from his wisdom. Most probably his sayings were the nucleus of the collection of sayings available to us today.

Sarah: One of the desert mothers and a solitary monastic from whom many sought advice.

Semi-anchoritic: Refers to monastics living in their separate cells but connected to a larger community of semi-anchoritic monastics who gather on Saturdays and Sundays at a central church to attend the liturgy and share an agape meal, exchange advice, and collect what they need for the following week. The sayings were shaped and shared in such semi-anchoritic communities.

Scetis: From the Coptic *'Ši-hēt'* (pronounced shi-het), meaning "the balance of the heart." *Hēt* translates as either "heart" or "mind"/ *nous*. Scetis/*'Ši-hēt'* became the name of the northwestern desert of Egypt and the monastic settlement located there. Most of the sayings take place in Scetis. Presently, the Scetis desert is called Wadī al-Naṭrūn and hosts four active monasteries: the Monastery of St. Macarius, the Monastery of St. Bishoy, the Monastery of the Virgin Mary (known as *al-Suryān*), and the Monastery of the Virgin Mary (known as *al-Barāmūs*).

Sisoes: Trained and lived as an ascetic in Scetis. He left Scetis and moved to Anthony's mountain after the death of Anthony.

Theodora: One of the desert mothers and a solitary monastic from whom many sought advice.

"A Word": A newcomer to the desert seeks advice by making this request: "Give me a word to live by" or simply "Give me a word."

Another variant is "How can I be saved?" The latter follows a similar biblical formula of Luke 18:18: "Good Teacher, what must I do to inherit eternal life?" At the advice Christ gave to the ruler the disciples wondered, "Then who can be saved?" (Luke 18:16). It is with this biblical understanding that the newcomer asks "How can I be saved?"

Work: Refers to either manual work or spiritual work, or both combined. Manual work is important for Egyptian monastics, who must support themselves financially and give alms. Spiritual work refers to the "work of the mind," which would include reading Scripture, prayer, contemplation, fasting, charity, hospitality, and humility, among other spiritual activities. In most instances, references to "work" include both aspects because all manual work is accompanied by spiritual work such as prayer, contemplation, or reciting and meditating on Scripture.

Suggested Titles for Further Reading

Translations of Collections of Sayings and Lives

Ammonas. *The Letters of Ammonas, Successor of Saint Antony*. Translated by Derwas J. Chitty, revised by Sebastian P. Brock. Fairacres Publication 72. Oxford: SLG, 1979.

Anthony, Saint. *The Letters of St. Antony the Great*. Translated by Derwas J. Chitty. Fairacres Publication 50. Oxford: SLG, 1975.

Athanasius, Saint. *The Life of Antony: The Coptic Life and the Greek Life*. Translated by Tim Vivian and Apostolos N. Athanassakis, with Rowan A. Greer. Cistercian Studies 202. Kalamazoo, MI: Cistercian, 2003.

——. *The Monastic Letters of Saint Athanasius the Great*. Translated by Leslie W. Barnard. Fairacres Publication 120. Oxford: SLG, 1994.

Barsanuphius, Saint, and John. *Letters*. Translated by John Chryssavgis. 2 vols. Fathers of the Church 113–14. Washington, DC: Catholic University of America Press, 2006–7.

Besa, Abbot of Athripe. *The Life of Shenoute*. Translated by David N. Bell. Cistercian Studies 73. Kalamazoo, MI.: Cistercian, 1983.

Budge, E. A. Wallis, translator. *The Paradise of the Fathers: Being Histories of the Anchorites, Recluses Monks, Coenobites and Ascetic Fathers of the Deserts of Egypt between A.D. CCL and A.D. CCCC Circiter*. Seattle: St. Nectarios, 1984.

Isaiah, Saint, of Scete. *Abba Isaiah of Scetis Ascetic Discourses*. Translated by John Chryssavgis and Pachomios Penkett. Cistercian Studies 150. Kalamazoo, MI: Cistercian, 2002.

Pseudo-Athanasius. *The Life & Regimen of the Blessed & Holy Teacher Syncletica*. Vol. 1. Translated by Elizabeth Bryson Bongie. Peregrina Translations 21. Toronto: Peregrina, 1996.

Rubenson. Samuel. *The Letters of St. Antony: Monasticism and the Making of a Saint*. Studies in Antiquity and Christianity. Minneapolis: Fortress, 1995.

Russell, Norman, translator. *The Lives of the Desert Fathers: The Historia Monachorum in Aegypto*. Cistercian Studies 34. Kalamazoo, MI: Cistercian, 1981.

Stewart, Columba, translator. *The World of the Desert Fathers: Stories and Sayings from the Anonymous Series of the Apophthegmata Patrum*. Fairacres Publication 95. Oxford: SLG, 1986.

Swan, Laura. *The Forgotten Desert Mothers: Sayings, Lives, and Stories of Early Christian Women*. New York: Paulist, 2001.

Veilleux, Armand, translator. *Pachomian Koinonia*. 3 vols. Cistercian Studies 45–47. Kalamazoo, MI: Cistercian, 1980–82.

Vivian, Tim, translator. *Histories of the Monks of Upper Egypt; and, The Life of Onnophrius*. Cistercian Studies 140. Kalamazoo, MI: Cistercian, 1993.

———, translator. *Journeying into God: Seven Early Monastic Lives*. Minneapolis: Fortress, 1996.

———, translator. *Saint Macarius, the Spiritbearer: Coptic Texts Relating to Saint Macarius the Great*. St. Vladimir's Popular Patristics. Crestwood, NY: St. Vladimir's Seminary Press, 2004.

———, editor. *Witness to Holiness: Abba Daniel of Scetis*. Translated by Sebastian P. Brock et al. Cistercian Studies 219. Kalamazoo, MI: Cistercian, 2008.

Vivian, Tim, with Apostolos N. Athanassakis, Maged S. A. Mikhail, and Birger A. Pearson. *Words to Live By: Journeys in Ancient and Modern Egyptian Monasticism*. Cistercian Studies 207. Kalamazoo, MI: Cistercian, 2005.

Vivian, Tim, translator, with Rowan A. Greer. *Four Desert Fathers: Pambo, Evagrius, Macarius of Egypt, and Macarius of Alexandria: Coptic Texts Relating to the Lausiac History of Palladius*. St. Vladimir's Popular Patristics. Crestwood, NY: St. Vladimir's Seminary Press, 2004.

Ward, Benedicta, translator. *The Desert Fathers: Sayings of the Early Christian Monks*. New York: Penguin, 2003.

———. *Harlots of the Desert: A Study of Repentance in Early Monastic Sources*. Cistercian Studies 106. Kalamazoo, MI: Cistercian, 1987.

———, translator. *The Sayings of the Desert Fathers: The Alphabetical Collection*. Rev. ed. Cistercian Studies 59. Kalamazoo, MI: Cistercian, 1984.

———, translator. *The Wisdom of the Desert Fathers: Systematic Sayings from the Anonymous Series of the Apophthegmata Patrum*. Fairacres Publication 48. Oxford: SLG, 1986.

Zacharias of Sakha. *The Holy Workshop of Virtue: The Life of John the Little*. Translated by Rowan A. Greer, Maged S. A. Mikhail, and Tim Vivian, edited by Maged S. A. Mikhail and Tim Vivian. Cistercian Studies 234. Collegeville, MN: Liturgical, 2010.

Writings of Visitors Documenting Their Observations and Experience in the Egyptian Desert

Cassian, John. *John Cassian: The Conferences*. Translated by Boniface Ramsey. Ancient Christian Writers 57. New York: Paulist, 1997.

———. *John Cassian, The Institutes*. Translated by Boniface Ramsey. Ancient Christian Writers 58. New York: Newman, 2000.

Evagrius, Ponticus. *Evagrius Ponticus: Ad Monachos* (To the monks). Tranlated by Jeremy Driscoll. Ancient Christian Writers 59. New York: Newman, 2003.

———. *Evagrius of Pontus: The Greek Ascetic Corpus*. Translated by Robert E. Sinkewicz. Oxford Early Christian Studies. New York: Oxford University Press, 2003.

———. *The Praktikos: Chapters on Prayer*. Translated by John Eudes Bamberger. Cistercian Studies 4. Spencer, MA: Cistercian, 1970.

General Introductions to Early Monasticism

Chitty, Derwas J. *The Desert a City: An Introduction to the Study of Egyptian and Palestinian Monasticism under the Christian Empire.* Crestwood, NY: St. Vladimir's Seminary Press, 1995.
Harmless, William. *Desert Christians: An Introduction to the Literature of Early Monasticism.* New York: Oxford University Press, 2004.
Regnault, Lucien. *The Day-to-Day Life of the Desert Fathers in Fourth-Century Egypt.* Petersham, MA: St. Bede's Publications, 1999.

Theological Texts

Athanasius, Saint. *Contra Gentes; and, De Incarnatione.* Translated and edited by Robert W. Thomson. Oxford Early Christian Texts. Oxford: Clarendon, 1971.
———. *On the Incarnation: The Treatise De Incarnatione Verbi Dei.* Translated and edited by a religious of CSMV. Rev. ed. Popular Patristics 3. Crestwood, NY: St. Vladimir's Seminary Press, 1998.

Biblical Index

~

DEUTERO-
CANONICAL
[FROM THE
SEPTUAGINT]

Index of Quoted Desert Fathers and Mothers

Lightning Source UK Ltd.
Milton Keynes UK
UKHW011314060120
356462UK00006B/1803/P